CUBA
LOST AND FOUND

LOST AND FOUND

Edward J. Neyra

CLERISY PRESS

Copyright © 2010 by Edward J. Neyra

All rights reserved. No portion of this book may be reproduced in any fashion, print, facsimile, or electronic, or by any method yet to be developed, without express permission of the copyright holder.

Published by Clerisy Press
Printed in the United States of America
Distributed by Publishers Group West
First edition, first printing

For further information, contact the publisher at:
Clerisy Press
PO Box 8874
Cincinnati, OH 45208-08074
www.clerisypress.com

Library of Congress Cataloging-in-Publication Data

   Neyra, Edward J.
      Cuba, lost and found / by Edward J. Neyra.
      p. cm.
      ISBN-13: 978-1-57860-390-9
      ISBN-10: 1-57860-390-0
         1. Neyra, Edward J. 2. Neyra, Edward J.—Childhood and youth. 3. Cuban Americans—Biography. 4. Immigrants—United States—Biography. 5. Operation Peter Pan. 6. Cincinnati (Ohio)—Biography. 7. Cuba—Biography. 8. Cuba—History—Revolution, 1959. I. Title.

E184.C97N49 2009
972.91—dc22

                              2009031060

Edited by Richard Hunt and Teresa Lewis
Cover designed by Jim Fenster, Miller–Myers Design Group
Cover painting by Lynn B. Neyra
Text designed by Annie Long
All other photos provided courtesy of Edward J. Neyra

Dedication

To my dear mother, for her unconditional love and enormous courage

Maria Caridad Neyra Pérez

Preface

I began to write this book to document my journey as a Cuban immigrant and build a bridge between my parents' world of the past and my children's world of the future. I felt a responsibility to take this thin thread that still ran through my life and recreate the fabric of my Cuban heritage for my American sons.

But along the way what seemed to be a simple, straightforward task became something far richer and much more intriguing. I thought I was tying together a few loose strings, but what I discovered was a colorful, ancient tapestry, and my own doubts and demons were woven within its shadowy folds.

I have constructed this story to the best of my own recollection with extensive research and the help of family and friends. I am very aware of the importance of accuracy and the inherent responsibility when writing about other people's lives as well as my own, so some names have been changed to protect the privacy of those individuals. Also, please keep in mind that time dilutes memories, even if the emotional imprint of the event seems indelible.

It is imperative that as you read this book, you are aware that the facts, figures and conditions presented regarding Cuba are based on my own observations from the time period in which I visited the island, beginning in the mid-nineties. As we all know, the economic conditions and political policies within both Cuba and the United States, as well as the relationship between the two countries, have changed over time and will continue to do so.

EDWARD J. NEYRA

*Celebrating Independence Day
in Cincinnati, Ohio, July 1962*

CUBA LOST AND FOUND

Often I think of the beautiful town
That is seated by the sea;
Often in thought go up and down
The pleasant streets of that dear old town,
And my youth comes back to me.
And a verse of a Lapland song
Is haunting my memory still:
"A boy's will is the wind's will,
And the thoughts of youth are long, long thoughts."

—from *"My Lost Youth"*
by Henry Wadsworth Longfellow

EDWARD J. NEYRA

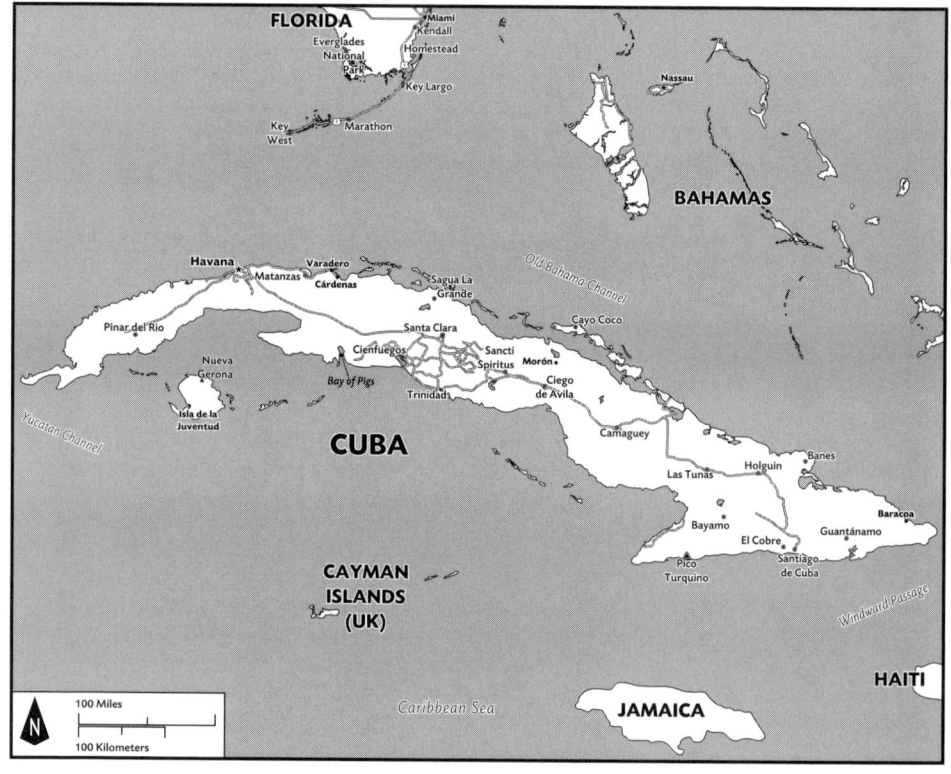

Caught in the Crossfire

*The peril of living in the midst of a revolution was swiftly delivered to my doorstep one tumultuous spring day in 1957 when I was just seven years old. A student activist from my hometown of Cárdenas, José Antonio Echevarría, had been shot and killed in Havana during a failed coup attempt against dictator Fulgencio Batista. Echevarría's body had been brought home for burial and as his funeral procession passed by, I had an ideal view from our home on *Calle Calzada*, the main artery that connected the center of town to the rural cemetery. Never before had so many people marched past our front door, and the lines went on for blocks. It seemed as if the entire city was dressed in black, following his casket on foot. There had been an overwhelming outcry after the outspoken student's slaughter, and the processional had become a political statement protesting Batista's cruel dictatorship.

Suddenly, right over our roof, rapid gunfire from a low-flying helicopter buzzed the processional, shattering the respectful silence. The solid mass of mourners scattered as most dove for cover. Some scrambled into San Antonio church on the corner. Others jammed themselves into a small grocery store across the street or into any home with an open door. But a devoted core defiantly continued to follow the slow-moving hearse.

In the whirlwind of confusion I lost my grip on our front door and found myself locked out and swept into the turbulent current of the fleeing crowd. I kept ducking and searching for shelter, while the rapid fire of the machine guns spattered overhead. The mechanical roar of the flying predator intensified the terror caused by the angry and incessant bullets. Suddenly, I saw salvation.

Teresa Cruz, the midwife at my birth, stood in the open doorway of her house across the street. I can still see her clearly outlined there—wearing her white nurse's uniform, appearing like a guardian angel. She was guiding people into her home, so I bolted through the crowd and into her living room.

It all happened so fast, but it seemed to unfold in slow motion. Amid the noise and confusion my mother had discovered I was missing. I could barely hear her hysterical cry, "Eduardito! Eduardito! Eduardito!"

"Mami, I am here, at Teresa's house!" I shouted in reply.

She frantically darted back and forth on the sidewalk, but she could not hear me. Finally, Mami heard Teresa yell her nickname, "Cuca! Cuca! He is here with me! Go back home!"

Instead, Mami lunged across the street, ignoring the deadly flying bullets, her face covered in tears. She burst through Teresa's door, relieved and overjoyed. We embraced, and she held me close while we waited for the chaos to wane, as if pausing under a shelter during a tropical cloudburst.

These political thunderstorms were nothing new to our island paradise. "Cuba" comes from the word *cubanacan*, which meant "the center place" to the indigenous Taíno Indians, and for centuries, the island claimed center stage in the Caribbean. Due to its size and strategic location, the "Pearl of the Antilles" was coveted as an irresistible jewel to many world powers, from the Spanish conquistadors to the Communists of the Soviet Union. For over five hundred years, Cuba has found herself repeatedly embroiled in the center of world conflict and torn internally by struggles between corrupt leaders who enriched themselves at the expense of the country's political, economic and social stability.

When I was a young child, a new wave of rebellion was brewing when Fidel Castro and his trusted band of *Fidelistas* attacked Batista's army at the Moncada barracks in Santiago de Cuba on July 26, 1953. Although the assault was crushed, the date would later be used as the rallying cry of Castro's revolutionary movement. Fidel was imprisoned, but then released in a general amnesty two years later. He fled to Mexico, joining his brother Raúl and Che Guevara to reorganize and train a new gang of revolutionaries.

Full of fury, Fidel Castro returned in December 1956 to once more foment rebel activity throughout Cuba. As Castro's July 26th Movement gathered strength across the island, Batista ordered his army to crack down and suppress social unrest. Suspects were incarcerated, interrogated, tortured and often killed. Army barracks and police stations were on high alert, barricaded with stacked sandbags to protect them from a rebel ambush while armed soldiers stood guard around the clock. We heard daily reports and rumors of intermittent shootings, bombings and kidnappings throughout the island.

As a young boy growing up in Cárdenas, I would peer through nearly closed shutters to catch a glimpse of Castro's rebels sneaking around late at night to terrorize our town. The shadowy figures crept from their secret camps in the nearby thickly wooded *montes* and lurked in darkened doorways to avoid detection from Batista's armed jeeps patrolling the streets. We were caught in the crossfire of a battle between a brutal dictator and a ruthless revolutionary.

Evening conversations at home were held in low tones, keeping one eye on the front door, alert to who might be listening. Family and trusted neighbors would huddle in a circle and share the latest gossip on the street—what kind of military surveillance they had detected, who was the latest victim of Batista's crackdown and what town had been terrorized by the *Fidelistas* that day.

I loved being a part of these adult conversations, sitting quietly on my mother's lap, listening intently. I was entrusted to not repeat a single word I heard, and I never did. There was something oddly exciting in spite of the danger, and perhaps my addiction to adrenaline was triggered during these turbulent times.

Castro's relentless terrorist tactics destabilized the Cuban economy and inflamed social disorder, putting a choke hold on Batista's regime. To further hasten his demise, Batista lost the support of the United States government, which cut off arms and ammunition shipments. The many years of bloody conflict between the two tyrants finally ended before dawn on January 1, 1959. Fulgencio Batista fled Cuba in the middle of the night with hundreds of millions in stolen dollars, leaving his nemesis Fidel Castro as the new ruler of our politically turbulent paradise. The jubilant New Year's celebrations in the streets quickly turned into riots to hail the victorious Revolution. Cubans were full of wild optimism inspired by a young, charismatic leader who had cunningly promised them social reform and free elections.

But Cubans' hopes for democracy were quickly shattered. The elections were never held, and Castro systematically eliminated political parties, labor unions and business associations. He seized control of newspapers and television and radio stations. He kicked out the clergy, closed churches and abolished private schools as well as professional sports. He confiscated businesses and private property. Castro's desire for complete control had no boundaries, and we were once again under the iron grip of yet another dictator. A defiant dictator who, once he secured absolute power, revealed the true colors of his ideology: Communist red.

The growing anti-Castro underground then intercepted a proposed government plan even more alarming: children would be taken from their parents and indoctrinated in Communist camps, conscripted into the army or sent to Russia. Rumors ran rampant throughout the island. Castro was hell-bent on brainwashing young minds, and concerned parents frantically searched for ways to protect their children and get them out of the country.

A clandestine program had been organized by valiant volunteers to transport about two hundred children of counterrevolutionary parents to safety in the United States until Castro could be toppled. Operatives were strategically positioned in Havana, Miami and Washington, D.C. The program soon expanded exponentially to include thousands of additional children and was dubbed *Operación Pedro Pan*, named after the mythical orphan boy who could fly.

My parents, like many others throughout Cuba, faced an agonizing dilemma: should they do nothing and helplessly watch us be raised as wards of the state? Or should they risk relying on this underground network to help us flee the country?

Te Quiero, Adiós

La Pecera, *the fishbowl, was a large, solid glass enclosure at the departure gate of José Martí International Airport in Havana and is indelibly etched in my mind. Aside from the armed guards and immigration officials, only those leaving Cuba were allowed inside this expansive holding pen. Once escorted into *La Pecera*, you were totally on display. There was no way to go back, no way to speak with loved ones again.

I was determined not to cry. I did not want to give the *milicianos* the satisfaction, nor upset my mother even more. My father had conditioned me, in the proud tradition of the Neyra family, *los Neyras no lloran*, Neyras don't cry, but my heart was pounding and my stomach was tied in knots. I was an eleven-year-old boy trying hard to be a man.

My older sister Melba and cousin Lalita, who were also leaving with me, already had endured the extensive document inspection to pass the first level of security clearance and were waiting for me in *La Pecera*. But

I had been pulled aside by a zealous *miliciano* and detained over a perceived problem with my departure papers.

Once the contrived controversy had been resolved, I too was corralled into *La Pecera*. From behind the dividing glass wall, I could not bear to look directly at any of my family or friends. We already had hugged and said our good-byes. Occasionally, I would steal a sideways glance and catch a glimpse of their forced smiles and flowing tears. But making eye contact would only be confronting the grim reality of all I was leaving behind, and the glass divider was a bitter reminder that we were already in two separate worlds.

Inside *La Pecera*, our final hours in the motherland dragged on interminably. The tension was unbearable. There were intimidating guards with guns in every direction I looked, as we anxiously awaited our final luggage and body search. My fear triggered every imaginable insecurity. How could I leave my mother and father? Would I ever see them again? What would *el Norte* be like? How could I defend myself; I didn't even speak English! Why hadn't I studied? I was terrified I would forget my Spanish before I could learn English. Would I be left unable to speak at all?

I clung to the words I hoped never to forget, a poem that all Cuban schoolchildren had to memorize, *Cultivo Una Rosa Blanca*, written in 1891 by José Martí, our national hero who died in battle to liberate Cuba from Spain:

Cultivo una rosa blanca	I cultivate a white rose
En junio como en enero	In June as in January
Para el amigo sincero	For the sincere friend
Que me da su mano franca	Who shakes my hand in honesty.

Y para el cruel que me arranca	And for the cruel person
El corazón con que vivo	Who would want to break my heart,
Cardo ni ortiga cultivo	I cultivate neither thorns nor thistles,
Cultivo una rosa blanca	I cultivate a white rose.

As the meaning of these words echoed in my heart, I wondered what our patriotic poet would think of all this turmoil. Here I was, at the airport named in his honor, wondering why our country could not abide by the wisdom of his words. José Martí espoused freedom, forgiveness and brotherhood—but all I could see was oppression, intimidation and families being torn apart.

The time had come to get in line and walk out to the tarmac where our KLM prop plane awaited us. I thought of my mother's back rubs, my grandmother's cooking and the toy car collection I had to leave behind. I was already missing the crystal-clear turquoise water; the sensation of the soft, sugar-white sand between my toes; and the salty ocean breeze stirring the gentle rhythm of the Caribbean waves. I thought of all the warm summer nights I had snuck out of my room to dip my feet into the surf. Why couldn't there have been a thousand more?

While waiting in line to walk to the plane, I signaled the child behind me to go ahead, allowing me one last look at my mother's face. And then, I let another one pass. And another. Finally, my compulsive courtesy ran out of benefactors, and I summoned the courage to walk back to the impenetrable glass wall that divided us. As I approached Mami, she forced a smile and briefly closed her eyes. Then she mouthed the words, "*Te quiero*. I love you," as she placed the palm of her hand flat against the glass. I matched her hand's position with my own on the other side, so for a moment it seemed almost like a smaller reflection. Then I looked into her eyes one last time and said, "*Te quiero. Adiós.*"

Los Neyras No Lloran

I was one of the very last to board the plane. There were children of all ages on the flight, some so young they needed to be carried up the steps. Many were just like me—believing they were leaving Cuba temporarily to go to school in the United States. Families had endured cycles like this throughout Cuba's turbulent history—sending their children abroad to be educated and then bringing them back home after the political climate had cooled.

Once on board, I sensed a transformation taking place, a feeling of responsibility that had not existed even an hour earlier. Awash in the realization that I needed to grow up fast and take care of myself without my parents' guidance, I wondered who would protect me.

It was my very first airplane flight, but I wasn't excited. The mechanical marvel of this massive machine going airborne would have ordinarily enthralled me, but it was by far secondary to my other concerns. I was too overwhelmed by having just left my parents, my friends and the life I knew behind.

As I struggled with my emotions, I felt a great sense of obligation to keep them in check. After all, this departure had been planned for many months; I had promised my father I would not cry, and I had no intention of violating this vow. My last tear had been wiped away at *La Pecera* when I had said good-bye to my mother.

I was inordinately proud of the self-control I displayed in withholding my own feelings. Instinctively, I discovered the perfect defense mechanism during this hour-long flight. I compulsively talked to anyone who would engage in conversation to distract them from their tears. It was an intoxicating sense of empowerment.

Many of the adults were also trying to console the crying children, but they themselves were breaking down. The fuselage became more like a funeral in flight, with so many refugees of all ages sobbing. The cabin crew kept offering candy, Chiclets and soft drinks in an attempt to calm the hysterical children, but few were willing to eat or drink anything. They just continued to wail.

As the plane approached Miami, the desolate passengers finally settled into a somber silence. I flashed back to the departure and the events of the day, and to so many conflicting feelings. I tried to resurrect the image of the beach I had left behind and retrieve emotional souvenirs I thought I had successfully stored—but I was just too tired. Sinking back into my seat, exhausted and depleted of adrenaline, a wave of sadness washed over me. The abrupt bump of the landing gear jerked me out of my trance. As we taxied from the runway, I turned to stare out of the window. Only one thing was certain now: I would never allow myself to feel this vulnerable again. Not ever.

Operación Pedro Pan

In a span of twenty-one months, Operación Pedro Pan *transported over fourteen thousand children out of Communist Cuba without their parents in the largest child rescue ever recorded in the Western hemisphere.* It all had begun in November 1960, when Pedro Menéndez, a fifteen-year-old Cuban boy, was brought to the office of Father Bryan O. Walsh, the young director of Miami's Catholic Welfare Bureau. Pedro had been sent to the United States alone, to be cared for by relatives—but the family was destitute, barely able to feed themselves. Pedro lost twenty pounds in just thirty days.

Father Walsh realized there were countless more Pedros to come. He sought help from the federal government and President Dwight Eisenhower approved funds crucial for the care of unaccompanied Cuban children, accepting them as welfare cases.

Operación Pedro Pan, personified by young Pedro Menéndez, was organized by Father Walsh in Miami and in Cuba by James Baker, the headmaster of the Ruston Academy, a private American school in Havana, with cooperation from the U.S. government. Baker had informed Walsh about the revolutionary "reforms" and Cuban parents' fear for their children's welfare. The two men forged an agreement that if Baker could get the children out of Cuba with student visas issued by the U.S. embassy in Havana, the Catholic Church would look after them once they arrived in Miami.

On December 26, 1960, Baker sent the first two *Pedro Pan* children, Sixto Aquino and his sister Vivian, who were met at the Miami airport by the benevolent Father Walsh. Unfortunately, within a week the United States broke off relations with Cuba. The embassy closed and James Baker was forced to return to the United States after only twenty-five children had fled. But before leaving Cuba, Baker mobilized a small group of trusted friends to continue his plan under the supervision of Penny Powers, an English teacher and nurse at Ruston. Powers was no stranger to such secret operations. Decades earlier, she had been instrumental in helping Jewish children escape Nazi-occupied Europe to safe haven in her native Britain.

The closing of the U.S. embassy in Cuba did not discourage the determined young priest in Miami, either. Father Walsh petitioned the State Department for assistance and received the unprecedented and extraordinary authority to issue so-called "visa waivers," which were permits to grant entry into the United States for children between the ages of six and sixteen. There was only one condition—a recognized and established organization must assume ultimate responsibility for the children's welfare.

Visa waivers signed by Walsh were smuggled into Cuba in diplomatic pouches. The forms were distributed countrywide to schools and churches by the underground network. Children were then allowed to buy their twenty-five-dollar plane tickets to freedom.

After the Bay of Pigs invasion in April 1961, *Operación Pedro Pan* grew dramatically. There were so many applicants that when the underground ran out of authorized forms, photocopies were mass produced. Allegedly it was still kept secret from the Cuban government, but it was hard to imagine that Castro was not aware of this mass exodus of children as well as the "brain drain" of the professional class. Perhaps he allowed the stampede and viewed it as a cleansing of his future opposition.

As planeloads of Cuban children flooded into Miami every week, the greatest problem facing Father Walsh quickly became a lack of facilities to house the newcomers. Although housing was hastily assembled at Camp Matecumbe, the Opa-locka Airport Marine barracks and several other locations, all the facilities quickly became overcrowded. This massive effort to care for thousands of children took on a life of its own, although for the most part, it was unknown outside of Miami.

However, all that changed when the *Plain Dealer* in Cleveland, against the wishes of Father Walsh, featured an article about the plight of these Cuban children. Walsh feared that the publicity would put the efforts in Cuba at risk. Instead, the news brought assistance from Catholic charities throughout the United States. Orphanages and foster homes eventually provided care in over a hundred cities across the country.

But *Operación Pedro Pan* screeched to a halt during the Cuban Missile Crisis in October 1962 when all flights to the United States were abruptly canceled. By then the program had become so extensive that over fourteen thousand of us already had escaped Cuba. Sadly, fifty thousand other children with visa waivers in hand were left behind.

Miami Layover

Melba, Lalita and I were extremely fortunate. Not only had we gotten out of Cuba just in time, but we also had distant relatives living in Miami waiting for us at the airport who were actively involved in *Operación Pedro Pan*. Mary Fernández, a nurse by training, had moved to the United States in the early 1950s with her husband, Mario, a pediatrician. Mary and Mario agreed to temporarily look after us, along with five other cousins who already had arrived: Uncle Gilberto's two sons, Gilbertico and Jorge, and Uncle Toto's children, Julio, Elenita and Mayra. We would stay with them for a week until we joined our new guardians in Ohio.

There were eight children sharing Mary's home. To maximize the space and keep some semblance of organization, we kept our luggage lined up in a neat row in the garage. The four boys slept on the floor of the sunroom and recounted as bedtime stories the fun days spent at Varadero Beach—

memories that were now bittersweet reminders of our stolen childhood.

Mary tried her best to make our week in Miami as pleasant as possible. We enjoyed long walks exploring the city and sometimes stopped by Robert's Drug Store on Flagler Street and Sixth Avenue for a soda. Sitting at the counter with a foaming fountain drink was for me the quintessential American experience.

But our brief stay was life in limbo, for we knew we would soon be moving on. Although there was some comfort in being in Miami with my cousins and in speaking my native Spanish, I was still full of conflicting emotions.

I missed my parents and was nervous about moving to the frigid north. My cousins teased me as to how cold it would

The six-shooters and leather holster were a Christmas gift given to me by Herbert Newman and Quincy Bass on one of their regular holiday visits to the island.

be, and I wistfully wished I could stay with them in Miami. I shivered just remembering those occasional arctic blasts from *los Nortes*, which had made the ocean roar like a lion.

Of all the children, my cousin Lalita had the most difficulty adjusting. She was desolate at having left on the plane her pink diary, a parting gift from her father. Mary called Tía Gladys, Lalita's mother, in Cuba and suggested that perhaps Lalita might be happier staying with her and Mario in Miami. However, Tía Gladys insisted that we stick to the plan that she had arranged and instructed Mary that under no circumstances were the three of us ever to be separated.

On our last full day at Mary's house, we celebrated my twelfth birthday with ice cream and cake. Although my cousins sang "Happy Birthday," it was far from happy. I had been gone less than one week but already had missed *El Día de los Reyes Magos*, the Cuban version of Santa Claus, and experienced the emptiness of a birthday celebration without my parents.

The next day, on January 10, 1962, Mary drove Melba, Lalita and me to the Miami airport to join our guardians, Herbert Newman and Quincy Bass. They were American friends who had visited us regularly in Cuba for many years and who would now take us to their home in Cincinnati, Ohio, a world away from where I was born.

Quincy Bass, Kendrick Bell, Eleanor Bell and Herbert Newman enjoying one of many summer sojourns to the Imperial Hotel at Varadero Beach.

Mi Vida Cubana

My hometown of Cárdenas was a coastal city about eighty miles east of Havana that had grown from a small fishing village into a sophisticated colonial town during the 19th century, the era of big sugarcane plantations. The large bay and flat, fertile fields created an ideal sugar-growing center, and the expanding railroad system furthered its development. At one time, the city rivaled Havana as the possible capital for the country. But the 1895-1898 War of Independence from Spain took its toll, as nearly all its sugar mills were burned to the ground. By the early 1900s, Cárdenas' glory years had faded into the past, and Havana dominated the country's commerce, politics and prestige.

My mother already had her hands full by the time I was born in January 1950. My sister Melba was nearly four years old. My brother, Alfredito, was only two and very ill, having contracted hepatitis in the hospital at birth. Because of that terrible experience, my mother decided to deliver me at Tía Elena's house, with the help of Teresa Cruz, the midwife who lived across the street. Mami was so preoccupied with Alfredito at the hospital in Havana that she spent very little time with me during the first six months of my life, and she was devastated when Alfredito passed away that June. Fortunately, I had a doting grandmother and several aunts to care for me.

Mami, whose given name was Maria Caridad was affectionately called Cuca and she and her sisters—Gladys, Gisela and Elena—had an unbreakable bond. Often it seemed as if I had four mothers—four to please but also four to spoil me. They had been raised through tough times, including the Great Depression. Their trust and reliance on each other was inspiring to me. I admired their loyalty and how they looked after each other's children.

Although my grandmother, Abuela Caridad, was diminutive, she was a demanding disciplinarian who was particularly tough on her daughters. She did not hesitate to use physical punishment, sometimes bordering on abuse.

The inseparable sisters: Elena, Gladys, my mother and Gisela

One day, she stepped out of the kitchen for just a minute, leaving my aunt, Tía Gladys, to keep the cat away from the food. Tía Gladys got distracted, and when Abuela returned, she spotted the cat gnawing on the meat that was set aside for their dinner. In a blink, she picked up a cooking ladle and clobbered Tía Gladys on the head. But no one bore the brunt of Abuela's wrath more than Tía Elena, the eldest, who was often assigned to watch over her younger siblings. If they misbehaved, Tía Elena got a whipping too.

Like many women of her generation, Abuela believed that her daughters did not need higher education, which was why Tía Elena, Tía Gisela and my mother never got past the lower grades. Only Tía Gladys, younger and more assertive, insisted on staying in school to finish the eighth grade.

Sometimes my grandmother's passion got the best of her. Once during a big family dinner, she got into a political argument with her son, Alberto, and she pounded her hand on the table to make a point while holding a glass of water. The glass shattered in her hand, and the deep cut required many stitches.

My grandmother married for the first time at fourteen a man more than twice her age. Her much older husband, Raimundo Lincheta, owned a shipping business that shuttled merchandise between the Caribbean islands. A heavy drinker and a notorious gambler, he hanged himself after losing his company in a card game, leaving my grandmother a sixteen-year-old widow with two small children.

Abuela's second husband, Benigno Pérez Valdez, my grandfather, was known by the nickname Matanzero since he hailed from the city of Matanzas. He met Abuela when he was seeking a job from her mother, Teresa Pastoriza, a widow who ran the family's carriage business after my great-grandfather died. My great-grandmother Teresa hired Matanzero, and soon after he married Abuela. They went on to have ten children of their own, but three of them died at birth, and their youngest son, Luis, drowned as a teenager at Varadero Beach. After his death, my grandmother dressed in black for the rest of her life and refused to even look at the ocean ever again.

Abuelo Matanzero was crude and uneducated but loving and sweet. He was a simple man, not much for fancy dressing or any kind of pretense. He had been abandoned by his mother and raised by his father who, as a baby, had been left in a basket with no name or note at the front door of an orphanage. His last name, Valdez, was often given to orphan children.

Abuelo Matanzero and Abuela Caridad

Perhaps that was why he was so easygoing, so compliant. When Abuela would confront him in a loud voice, he never responded in kind. But one thing he was loud about was passing gas. Sometimes I could even hear him from the next room. My grandmother would complain, but to no avail. This was one thing Abuela had no control over.

Over the years my great-grandmother's carriage business had evolved into a taxi service, and my grandfather, Abuelo Matanzero, carted me with him everywhere he went. He taught me how to drive when I was only eight years old and even let me steer the car down side streets perched on his lap. Abuelo drove us to school in his 1947 black Chevrolet sedan, and on the way we picked up other neighboring students, one being my first crush, Isabelita. Abuelo feigned surprise when I suddenly went from wanting to ride in the front with him to preferring to sit in the back with the girls.

Isabelita was the baker's daughter. She had extremely fair skin, almost albino, and her hair was a golden shade of amber. I wrote her romantic little notes and stuffed them in her bookbag while we rode to school. Late at night in my bed, hidden under the protective netting of my *mosquitero*, I would make the envelopes by sewing paper together with my mother's needle and thread. I was petrified that one of the girls would catch me—especially my cousin Lalita, who used to tease me and claim that Isabelita's skin was so white because her father dipped her in baking flour.

It was not uncommon in the Latin culture for a family to live with maternal grandparents as we did, and I was their favorite grandchild. Abuela had a blind spot for all of my mischievous antics. She always stood up for me and even pleaded my case when my mother tried to discipline me. When I was about five, my parents had made plans to attend a masquerade party. I repeatedly banged my head against the window bars, hoping a tirade would keep Mami from leaving me. But she did not cave in. Once they were out of sight, I calmed down and soaked up Abuela's sympathy. She gave me hot chocolate, rubbed my back and allowed me to stay up late—a secret we never revealed.

Abuela had a reputation as a good cook, but some of her recipes were rather rustic; her family had come from the countryside near Pontevedra in Galicia, an impoverished region in Spain, where empathy was secondary to survival. She made a delicious rabbit stew using homegrown rabbits—unappetizing to me due to my emotional attachment to the entrée. She would also serve fried red snapper whole, eating the eyes and even swallowing the crunchy fin and tail. No wonder I so often lost my appetite.

No dish was more difficult for me to digest than her *plato de pollo*, since I was an accomplice in its preparation. Abuela would go outside and select the unlucky chicken. "*Mira, ése, ¡el más grande!* Look, that one! The biggest!" she would point. I would prop up one end of an old wooden crate with a sturdy stick tied to a long string, and then place corn kernels underneath and wait for the fowl to take the bait. When I pulled the string, the crate would fall, trapping the squawking chicken.

While I was busy with entrapment, Abuela would begin boiling water in a large metal can over a coal fire in the middle of the yard. After I had successfully secured our dinner, I would lean over the boiling pot, mesmerized by the bubbles releasing steam.

Then came the most gruesome part—Abuela would grab the prisoner from under the crate and, with a firm grip on its neck, spin it. After a few twirls, the cackling, frantic, wing-flapping bird slumped lifeless. She would then dip it into the boiling water for a few minutes, pull it out and begin to pluck its feathers. If all the feathers did not come loose, she would dip it once again. No matter how hard she tried to get me to do the full routine, I would never go beyond setting the trap. Often I could not eat my dinner after helping her and just drank a large glass of warm milk spiked with sugar.

My Favorite Playmate

*O*ne day on the way home from school, Abuelo let me steer the car all the way down our street. He was radiant and told me he had a surprise waiting for me at home. I tried to pry the secret from him, but the more I begged, the more he savored the suspense. When we finally arrived at home, he led me straight to the backyard and introduced me to my new friend, a tiny black and white goat.

"*¡Es tuyo!* It's yours!" Abuelo Matanzero proclaimed.

I was delighted. I had never seen one so cute. "*¿Cómo se llama?*"

Abuelo stood back with a grin. "Give him whatever name you like."

The week before I had tried to bathe my kitten and had accidentally drowned him. Abuelo knew that I had been very upset about it and probably had thought that a new companion would help me get over it.

I decided to call him Perico. The little kid was very frisky and loved for me to pat him on the head and rub his chin. He became my shadow, following me when I carried food to the hog pen at the rear of the yard. He would always make his bleating goat call as I lugged the heavy buckets full of hog slop, a disgusting mixture of leftovers, scraps, rotten fruit and vegetables—anything no longer fit for human consumption. Abuela would dump it all together and instruct me to add water and stir with a broomstick. I was not always able to tolerate the smell and would sometimes have to wait until my dinner settled before I could feed the stinky creatures.

The hogs would fight and squeal to be first and to eat the most. But I often thought, "If I were you, I would not be so eager," as the fattest one was destined to be slaughtered for the annual *Noche Buena* feast. I tried not to look at them very closely. It was unpleasant to cut up the pork on your plate with such a vivid memory of them gobbling the slop.

Perico would also follow me everywhere around the yard. I would climb into an old car that one of my uncles had abandoned under the shade of a huge *ceiba* tree. While proudly perched on an empty orange crate propped where the driver's seat used to be, I would explain to Perico, "I am going to fix this old jalopy, and it is going to be my car." Even a goat probably knew that this stripped and rusted shell mounted on blocks with no engine, wheels, doors, fenders nor seats was beyond repair. But as I gripped the bent steering wheel, I would dream about someday making it my own hot rod.

After six months, Perico had grown and occasionally seemed to be in a bad mood. One day he bucked me from behind and knocked me down. I went into the house and told my mother what had happened. She thought that the goat was getting too big and aggressive. Sure enough, the very next day, Perico knocked me to the ground again. Mami was on the lookout from the kitchen window and had witnessed the whole thing. That night I overheard Mami and Abuelo talk about having to do something about Perico. A few days later when I returned from school, Perico was gone.

"*¿Dónde está Perico?*" I asked.

"Perico jumped the fence and escaped," Mami told me. About a week later, she sat me down and explained that the goat had become too dangerous, so Abuelo had taken him to the market. "I'm sorry," she said. It was hard to accept the loss, but I always trusted my mother's judgment.

Unfortunately, Perico was soon the least of my losses. One evening, while Abuelo was playing with me, his face suddenly became contorted and he began making rasping noises. He often played pranks on me, but this time his antics scared me, and I frantically cried for help. When my mother and grandmother ran into the room, they realized he was having a stroke. In anguish, the family blamed the stress of the Revolution for triggering his collapse.

Even though his speech was impaired, he survived. But only months later we discovered that he also had colon cancer, which had spread to his liver, and he died on May 18, 1959. My favorite playmate was suddenly gone forever, and for the first time I experienced an indescribable emptiness. At age nine, death seemed so hard to understand and its finality so difficult to accept.

La Familia

My father was named José Alfredo, but everybody, even my mother, called him "Neyra." He was the youngest of four siblings, with an older brother, José Antonio, known as José, and two older sisters, Margo and Nina. Papi attended *Los Maristas*, a private Catholic school, until age thirteen—then dropped out during the Great Depression for financial reasons, which he was too proud to discuss. The Neyra family apparently had fallen from great wealth and political influence. In spite of this, my father's family was still very involved in the town's social hierarchy. Yet, to their credit, they loved and treated my mother very respectfully despite her family's lower social status.

Papi was hired at eighteen to work at *El Cárdenense*, a manufacturing company owned by a family friend that processed phosphorus to make matches. It was there that he met my mother and began their four-year courtship. They frequently attended weekend dances at the social club *El Coliseo*, where my beautiful mother was always under the watchful eye of a chaperone, an older brother or sister vigilantly upholding that Latin tradition.

They were married on December 20, 1944, and in less than two years, their first child, my sister Melba, was born in May of 1946. Soon after, my father was promoted to a national salesman for *El Cárdenense*, which had moved operations to Havana. He traveled extensively across the island, which took him away from home for a considerable amount of time.

When he was home, Papi was compulsive about cleanliness and organization. Although he rarely did any housework, when he washed the dishes, he would insist on very hot water and a lot of soap, like an imperious domestic surgeon. He would scrub the shine off the porcelain and wear out the bottoms of the kettles. Papi seldom did yard work, but when the rare urge overtook him to clean the patio area, no nook or cranny was safe from his persistent spray as he hosed down the tile terrace.

Papi did not joke around. He was also elusive, reticent and self-absorbed and was very guarded about divulging any details concerning his personal life. But Papi was passionate politically—discussing politics changed the color of his complexion and made the arteries bulge on his neck. As he grew older, Papi's desire to enter politics trumped his obligation to his family, and he spent most of his time pursuing a political career.

There was one rare occasion that I can vividly remember spending time with Papi when we were building *un papalote*, a kite. But this was not an ordinary one. He wanted to build *un coronel*, a colonel, the name for a big kite. Papi was that way. He wanted to build "*el más grande de Cárdenas.*" He insisted that the design be precise, and he took measurements over and over. "*Esto va volar perfecto.* This is going to fly perfectly," he said.

We built the frame with *guin*, a slender, tapered cane shoot with a

My parents on their wedding day at San Antonio Church in Cárdenas, December 20, 1944

slick and rigid outer layer and used big sheets of red, white and blue paper to build the sail, with a large white star at its center. My patriotic *papalote* resembled the Cuban flag. We also cut paper into frayed strips and glued it to the leading edges, which made an awesome roaring sound. The tail to balance the colonel was rather long, maybe fifteen feet, and equipped with a sharp razor blade at the very end.

All of the kids had their kites armed for neighborhood duels. Some had several razor blades, and all of us practiced tactical maneuvers, but no one ever succeeded in downing a kite. Still, we lived in the excitement of possible victory—or the fear of defeat.

Flying my kite posed some challenges. The other kids were envious of the large colonel and tried to synchronize their attacks against me. The kite was also bigger than me; as a young boy I was very slim and it would nearly lift me off the ground in a strong gust of wind. Fortunately, Abuelo Matanzero always had gone with me to fly it, and was ready with a firm grip on a rope tethered to my belt. This was one of the many activities I missed with Abuelo, since I could not remember Papi ever flying it with me, not even the first time.

On the rare weekend Papi was in town, he would take me with him to visit my grandmother, Amélia, who lived with my aunt Nina and her family in the distinguished home that had originally belonged to my grandparents. Abuela Amélia was paralyzed from a long battle with Parkinson's disease. I was afraid to approach her for a kiss, since spastic tremors possessed her entire body and her shaky, slurred speech scared me. I would bring her caramels, her favorite candy, but Tía Nina had to feed them to her.

When we would visit, Abuelo Neyra was never around. There always seemed to be a sense of secrecy, something the grownups were hiding. Unlike my experience with my maternal grandparents, with the simplicity of their lives and the openness about their shortcomings, my father and his family still clung to the pride and discreet decorum of a privileged upbringing.

I never enjoyed these little jaunts very much, and I felt as if Papi took me along only as a badge of pride. On the way to Tía Nina's, we were stopped many times. Everyone in town knew my father—and they were always asking him for some sort of political favor. He would listen to their entreaties and buy them a drink—and earn himself a supporter. Every outing seemed like a political campaign, and I hated the constant interruptions. Although Papi

My grandparents, Abuela Amélia and Abuelo José Neyra

My great-grandparents, Amélia Sotolongo Limendoux and Alejandrjo Abascal Sotolongo

was very affectionate, I never had much time alone with him; he was too busy winning votes. But he certainly was not winning mine.

Not everyone was a fan of my father. I once spotted an unusual scar on his left calf. I asked him what had caused it. "A bullet," he shrugged. An attempt had been made on his life as he was climbing into the back seat of a car in Havana. But Papi would not elaborate.

My great-grandfather, José de Jesús Neyra

It was not long before Papi's picture was plastered on telephone poles all across town, and the Neyra name was broadcast over loudspeakers mounted on cars campaigning throughout the city. He quickly climbed the ladder of Batista's local government and became the youngest councilman in Cárdenas.

He aspired to follow in the footsteps of previous Neyra generations of public servants—but the political climate had changed dramatically. My father spent most of his time pursuing a political career that was destroyed by the corruption of the old regime and the restrictive reforms of the new one.

Although he often spoke of his family history with great pride and was very close to his siblings, Papi was not very involved with raising Melba and me, and he certainly was not an attentive husband. He never concerned

Papi's political campaign poster

himself with "trivialities" like letting Mami know if he would be late for dinner or when he would be returning from a trip. He took advantage of my mother's sweet nature by simply disconnecting from all of us, which tainted my feelings toward him for many years. He seemed to run his life without regard to our needs.

Mami, on the other hand, was a devoted mother. She was always there for Melba and me with unconditional love. She was a quiet peacemaker who only spoke when there was something kind to say. I don't think I ever saw my mother do anything that was rude or even inconsiderate. Although a person without vices, she understood and accepted everyone else's. Filled with love and grounded in faith, Mami always finished her remarks and wishes with, "*Si Dios quiere.* If the Lord is willing." She had an uncompromising inner strength, and when she drew the line, it was cut in stone.

Mami went beyond selfless caring when it came to my upbringing. Occasionally, I would have a severe nosebleed during the night or I would wet my bed. Mami was never angry or made me feel ashamed. Each morning, she wiped my face with a warm cloth and even put on my socks and shoes while I was still in bed in order for me to get a few more minutes of sleep before school.

By the time I was six, I had outgrown drinking warm milk from a bottle, but occasionally Mami would fill a large soft drink-sized container and cap it with a rubber nipple so that I could drink it in bed. I had a pet rubber nipple that had a comforting smell that I used only for rubbing against my nose. Her caretaking efforts were a little over the top, even within a male-revering Latin culture, but perhaps she was compensating for my father's chronic absence or the loss of my brother, Alfredito.

This may also be why my mother was so protective, always keeping an eye on me when I went outside to play. We shot marbles in the middle of the rough, unpaved side street, and there was always an argument when it came time to measure the distance to the starting line or decide whose marble was closer to the loaded circle. These games often ended in fistfights.

Sometimes we played *Salta la Mula*, Jump the Mule, which became a free-for-all. We would choose sides and take turns jumping over the person who was "It." With each round, the barrier grew higher. "It" started on his knees and continued until he was fully standing. You also had to keep an eye out for someone tripping you in midair. It was like limbo in reverse—how high can you go? The tallest and oldest had a definite advantage. Since I was neither, I often went home with cuts, scrapes and knots on my head.

Mami preferred that I stay inside our yard. Sometimes I would play with my cowboys and Indians. I also loved to pretend I was on a construction site, building garages for my toy cars with wood and a primitive blend of cement and sand I mixed in an old kitchen bowl, adding water from the hose. I would often rollerskate on the large patio or chase an old bike tire with a stick for hours, trying to master turning the tire without it falling or going past our sidewalk. I never sat still.

Once it grew dark, Mami kept a constant eye on me. It was a bit embarrassing, because the other kids stayed out playing longer. I usually complained, hoping for a delay, but once I heard that "¡*Pssst!* ¡*Ven acá!* Come here!" I knew Mami meant business.

But she did allow me to play my favorite game, "Auto Monopoly," past dark with a friend if we stayed on the front stoop. Any car that came from the right was mine; any car that came from the left was his. We kept track of our inventory on paper, and the one with the most valuable and newest cars won. I had a keen eye for American models. I could identify the make and the year even at night just from the spacing of the headlights and the reflection on their distinctive grilles. Once in a while I would spot a Cadillac or Buick in the distance and suddenly suggest swapping directions with my opponent. But unfortunately, it did not take long for my playmate to catch on.

A favorite treat was waiting for *el manisero*, the peanut man. Long after sundown the vendor would make his nightly rounds—walking, singing, yelling "¡*Maní!*" He was dressed in white, sporting a chef's hat, carrying a square metal box full of warm and crunchy peanuts. He deftly scooped them into a *cucurucho*, a rolled paper cone. A delicious memory for only a nickel.

The streets of Cárdenas were full of vendors. Depending on the time of the year, they might be selling mangos, my favorite fruit, or *rasco rasco*, an Icee, or *guarapo*, a sugarcane drink. If you waited long enough, one of these entrepreneurial vendors would come by, singing his rhythmic sales tune. Some were creative and entertaining, others just annoying. But no vendor was more irritating to me than *el carbonero*.

"*¡Carbón, carbón, el carboneroooo!* Coal, coal, the coalman!" This grating holler was his advertisement as he dodged potholes while navigating the unpaved side streets. *El carbonero* constantly berated his old, tired mule pulling the two-wheeled cart loaded with the ancient fuel he had for sale, with a loud giddy-yap, making a clicking sound between his teeth.

I then heard him try to persuade his mule by calling her name and rapidly snapping the reins. He repeatedly implored her name and I could not believe my ears! I was so enraged that I picked up a rock and beaned the unsuspecting mule. It tried to bolt, and the coalman had to pull hard on the leather straps to control the startled animal. He looked around to see who had thrown the rock and caught a glimpse of me running through my backyard as I screamed for my mother.

The coalman was mad and yelling, as he tried to tame his agitated mule, so he could chase after me. He was pounding on our front door while Mami was asking me, "*¿Qué pasa, mi hijo?*"

I was livid, "The coal vendor named his mule after you—and I will not permit that!"

The coalman complained to my mother that I had struck his mule with a rock for no reason. My mother patiently explained that her nickname was also Cuca, the same as the mule's, and that I was very upset at the perceived insult. The aggravated coalman insisted that was no reason for what I had done. I shot back, "I do have a good reason, and I want you to change the name of your ugly mule!"

He just shook his head in frustration, "*Señora*, your son is very spoiled!"

But I couldn't always get Mami to see things my way. By the time I was ten years old, Tía Nina talked my mother into signing me up for dancing lessons at *El Coliseo* on Friday nights. Even at that young age, my father's sister was already lining me up to meet Cárdenas society girls. Although I liked the girls and the music, I used to hate going to those dances. The instructors paired everyone up with a partner and would then begin the lesson. I never liked following directions, and I resented Tía Nina's efforts to orchestrate an early match for me.

The one thing I did enjoy at the social club was drinking Coca-Cola. I used to pretend that I spoke English because I could order it at the bar. Mostly I ignored the dance classes and stood on the second-floor balcony, riveted by the three-toned paint jobs and heavy chrome on the American cars driving by below.

After complaining for weeks to Mami about having to attend, she finally relented, but not because of my protests. Mami felt that the turbulent political climate and increasing social unrest had made it too risky for me to be in any public places after dark.

The Imperial Hotel at Varadero Beach

Tío Ramón and Tía Gladys on the terrace of the Imperial Hotel, overlooking Varadero Beach

Varadero Beach

I looked up to my sister Melba. Even though she was four years older, we spent a lot of time together, and we always got along. She was a model student, earning straight A's while selflessly tutoring other students who were struggling with their schoolwork. Kind, pretty and popular, Melba was also the leading *batutera*, baton-twirler, in the marching band. While she was known school-wide for both her academic excellence and her social skills, my grades were questionable and my behavior even worse.

Lalita was Tía Gladys' and Tío Ramón's only child, which might have been why Gladys wanted the three of us to always be together. Although Lalita was our cousin, she was more like a sister to Melba and me. She lived with us during the week in Cárdenas, where we attended school together. But on the weekends and during the summers, Lalita, Melba and I would all stay at her parents' oceanfront resort in Varadero Beach.

This living arrangement put Lalita at a disadvantage whenever Tía

Gladys tried to inspire her and played the comparison game by reminding Lalita of Melba's scholastic achievements. Ironically, Lalita was a fairly good student herself, but Tía Gladys always demanded that extra effort. Tía Gladys' driving determination was sometimes an obstacle with Lalita, but that same dimension of her character was vital to the success of Tío Ramón's hotel business.

Tío Ramón had emigrated alone from Spain at age thirteen. A hard-working entrepreneur, Tío Ramón started working at a local bar called *El Bate Marino*. He then ran his own hotel, *El Europa*, which is where he met Tía Gladys, who managed the ice cream stand in the lobby.

But the owner of the property, *Doña* Maria Carmen, would not renew Tío Ramón's lease for *El Europa* because of his excessive drinking. His neglect of business details and employee theft were taking a toll on the hotel's profitability. Tía Gladys issued Tío Ramón an ultimatum: Give up alcohol, or our marriage is over.

Tío Ramón sought professional help and was institutionalized to treat his dependency on alcohol. It was then that Tía Gladys made *la promesa*, the promise. She vowed that if Ramón stopped drinking, she would sponsor an annual, fun-filled event for the children of the local orphanage on Lalita's birthday every July.

Tío Ramón fulfilled his commitment. With his vision and hard work, he converted an oceanfront mansion into a charming hotel: the Imperial at Varadero Beach. Varadero had been Cuba's principal resort town for over a century. With twelve miles of soft, white sand and crystal-clear warm waters, it was a popular spot for tourists from all over the world. But to us,

Varadero was more than just a vacation spot; it was a place where we forged friendships with Americans who would later play pivotal roles in our lives.

Very serious and driven, Tío Ramón maintained a schedule that began long before sunrise, going to the market and back before most of us were even awake. If I got up early, I could catch him creating the daily menu that featured the fresh fish and produce he had just purchased. He would be hunched over, pecking away at the typewriter with his reading glasses perched on the end of his nose in his small third-floor office. During the month of September when resorts were closed for the hurricane season, he would roll up his sleeves, put on a respirator mask and spray paint white the patio furniture at the hotel.

With Tía Gladys' help, and the support of her sisters, the Imperial Hotel became a big success. There was nothing that Tía Gisela and my mother were not willing to do to help their sister Gladys. They would clean the rooms, mop the floors and do the laundry. Even I would pitch in, helping Tía Gladys dice fresh cantaloupe for her famous fruit cocktail dessert. Once in a while, I would tease her by dipping a finger into the warm custard before her delicious flan was set. "*¡Cabroncito!* Little stinker!" she would yell affectionately.

Tía Gladys and Tío Ramón were appreciative of this support and very generous with our entire family. I knew that Tío Ramón really loved me and thought of me as a son. In fact, he and Tía Gladys were my godparents. But I was a little afraid of him because he did not laugh much and had a dry sense of humor.

Tío Ramón was also a prankster. One time when we were in the ocean together, he started to play around and held me under water. Once he released me, I rushed to shore and vowed never to go swimming with him again. On another occasion, when I was having a little trouble getting out of bed to go to the bakery and pick up the hotel's order for the day, he awakened me with a splash of cold water and a hearty laugh.

But Tío Ramón also stood up for me since my father was never with us in Varadero. An adult guest at the hotel, Otilio, had been bullying me incessantly. I was only ten years old, and he was able to hold me in a headlock or twist my arms behind my back trying to get me to beg for mercy. But I refused. I endured the pain and just yelled. He still would not let me go. Finally, I told him that I was going to find his son and retaliate. Otilio just laughed and twisted my arms even more. Almost in tears, I once again warned him. Just then someone came by, so he released me.

I went running throughout the grounds and finally found his son upstairs in the lounge area watching television. I approached my unsuspecting target at full speed with a shoe in my hand. After a few punches and shoe-whacks, I assured him these attacks would continue until his father stopped hurting me. Off the boy went, yelling and crying, looking for his parents. I felt bad, for he was innocent, but I had to do something drastic to stop Otilio's abuse.

It was now the middle of the afternoon, *siesta* time. The hotel cooking staff usually took this opportunity to play dominos in the cool ocean breeze, and Tía Gladys often joined them. I knew all of the employees well because I would hang around in the kitchen and sometimes help them peel barrels of shrimp and cut potatoes or carrots. They used to tease me by holding me down on the huge kitchen table, pretending they were going to operate—or worse, castrate me. I would scream with laughter, and they would eventually let me go. But now I was in real danger—Otilio was searching for me with a switchblade in his hand.

When Otilio showed up at the game table, he scared Tía Gladys half to death… it was one of the few times I ever saw her rattled. Thankfully, Benito, the head cook, still had his large chef's knife in the sheath hanging at his waist. Without hesitation, Benito pulled it out and confronted Otilio, warning him that his intentions would only get him hurt. Tía Gladys stepped between the two men, begging Benito not to do anything he would live to regret. After some verbal sparring, Otilio finally backed down and walked away. Tía Gladys rushed to awaken Tío Ramón from his daily nap. I took off running and hid behind a large clay pot in the courtyard. From my hiding spot I heard Tío Ramón tell Otilio and his family to pack their belongings, leave immediately and never come back.

Tío Ramón also came to my defense on one hot July day. I was wading alone in the ocean when suddenly, I heard people frantically yelling from the third-floor balcony of the hotel. At first I did not pay much attention, having no idea the shouts were directed at me. Then, the guests who were eating lunch on the hotel patio joined the screaming. Finally, I realized they were warning me about a shark circling nearby.

"¡*Eduardo, mira para atrás de ti!* Eduardo, look behind you!" I can still hear those frenzied words. Taking heed of their warning, I saw the fin sticking up above the water's surface like a periscope. Terrified, I rushed toward the shore. The water was just above my waist, so I was unsure whether it was faster to swim or run, but with the vision of my trailing legs being gobbled, I decided to run. I reached the sandbar, where the water was only inches deep, but there was still a section of deeper water I had to cross to get to the shore. The shark found an inlet around the sandbar and continued to pursue me.

By now word had spread throughout the hotel, where a crowd had gathered. Tío Ramón stood on the edge of the surf with a rifle, and as soon as he had a clear shot, he fired. The beast escaped the bullets, moving so fast that only his shadow could be seen through the clear, shallow water, and I breathlessly staggered onto the safety of the beach.

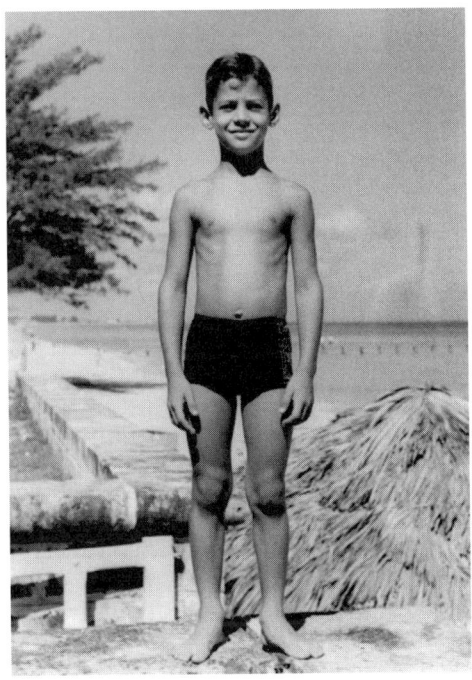

Standing on the seawall of the Imperial Hotel at Varadero Beach

La Revolución

Although we were fortunate to live in the tropical splendor of Varadero Beach, social unrest became prevalent throughout the island. Castro had returned to Cuba from Mexico on December 2, 1956, with eighty-one men aboard the *Granma*. After barely escaping during the landing skirmish, he established clandestine operations in the Sierra Maestra in eastern Cuba. He recruited *campesinos*, peasants, from the surrounding countryside, broadcasting his revolutionary philosophies from a makeshift radio station known as *Radio Rebelde*. As the momentum of the July 26th Movement grew, the orchestrated guerrilla attacks against the Batista government became more frequent and widespread.

Bombings and assaults were now a common occurrence all across Cuba. Explosions rocked government buildings, trains were derailed and telephone and power lines were cut. Even the sugarcane was set on fire before harvest. I can still remember the ardent flames and eerie smoky glow from the vast burning fields between Cárdenas and Varadero as I peered from my back seat window while Tía Gladys sped home late at night from a weekend at the beach.

Going out, especially in the evening, became too risky; bowling alleys, movie theaters and public gathering places were all targets. Our sense of neighborhood community was being destroyed; fun had given way to fear.

Even with a pervasive military presence and round-the-clock street patrols, Batista's army could not contain Castro's guerrilla attacks and the growing civil unrest. It was believed that Batista killed or tortured thousands of dissidents in his attempt to suppress the revolutionary movement. Horrific rumors circulated about the brutal methods used, such as slicing off tongues and ears, chopping fingers, breaking bones and pulling out fingernails with pliers.

My mother's cousin, Gilberto Pastoriza, narrowly escaped one such military crackdown. As the urologist on call at the emergency room at Covadonga Hospital in Havana, he was assigned to treat a *Fidelista* who had been savagely kicked and beaten by the police. In order to save his life, Gilberto had to remove the rebel's hemorrhaging testicles.

After the emergency surgery, Gilberto was leaving the hospital when he was hustled into the back seat of a police cruiser, flanked on either side by members of the SIM, the military secret police. In the front seat sat Lt. Colonel Esteban Ventura, Havana's most feared police official, infamous for his brutality. "I've wanted to meet the *mediquitos*, the little doctors who take care of these sons of bitches."

Gilberto replied, "I'm a doctor, I'm not in a political position. I follow my Hippocratic oath to help anyone who needs medical assistance."

"You mean to tell me if I were ill, you would treat me too?" Lt. Colonel Ventura asked.

"Of course. If you call the Minister of Health, Eduardo Borrell Navarro, you would know that I am the physician for many government officials as well as his own family."

"I don't need to call anybody!" the vindictive colonel snapped.

Fortunately, a nurse's aide had witnessed the abduction and had called Gilberto's mother. Seeking help, Benita Pastoriza immediately called Eduardo Borrell at home. Borrell then called President Batista, who instructed an aide to page the squad car. "Palacio (the code name for the president's office) has a direct order! Dr. Pastoriza is not to be harmed. Release him immediately!"

All this happened in a matter of minutes. Gilberto was relieved as he overheard the presidential command to set him free, and the ruthless colonel's demeanor changed instantly.

Although rebel cells were terrorizing the cities, most of the combat initially took place in the eastern, rural part of the island. By the spring of 1958, Raúl Castro, Fidel's brother and comrade, had established a second front in the Sierra Cristal in what is now the province of Holguin. Ernesto "Che" Guevara, Fidel's first commander and an expert in guerrilla warfare, was moving further west, finally capturing Santa Clara in central Cuba on December 29, 1958. Guevara derailed the trainload of Batista's army reinforcements headed east, taking one thousand prisoners, their guns and ammunition and cutting off their access to Fidel's base camp in the Sierra Maestra.

This was Batista's death knell. The *Fidelistas* now controlled eastern Cuba—splitting the island in two, they rapidly advanced westward toward Havana. Realizing his imminent demise after years of terror and tyranny, the dictator fled the country with an entourage of relatives and cronies right after an extravagant New Year's Eve party at the presidential palace. But Fulgencio Batista left with no concerns about continuing his lavish lifestyle. In addition to the millions he had squirreled away from mafia bribes to operate the world-renowned Havana casinos, Batista also had systematically drained the National Treasury as if it were his own piggybank and escaped with suitcases full of cash.

Castro and his revolutionary regime immediately assumed power. *Los barbudos*, the bearded ones, marched triumphantly down from the hills and out of the woods as the liberators of the Cuban people, waving the Cuban flag as well as the red-and-black flag of their July 26th Movement. They were wearing the army-green militia uniforms that had been hand-sewn in secret with donations from across the country as well as from abroad, including the United States.

Chants of "*¡Viva Fidel!*" echoed throughout the island as citizens hailed *los barbudos* in jubilation, regarding them with reverence as though they were saints, with Castro as their Messiah. With unkempt long hair and beards, they were decorated with both rosaries and *Santería* beads, vainly displayed with their shirts unbuttoned, like half-dressed heroes glowing in the sun. Euphoric about their victory and the broad support of the Cuban people, *los barbudos* were loud, proud and arrogant. These images forever branded in my mind a dislike of facial hair and its association with guns and violence.

Los barbudos paraded down streets in cities across Cuba, welcomed by supporters showering them with confetti and cheering wildly from balconies decorated in red and black, the colors of the revolution. Many had the movement's insignia "M 7-26" painted on their foreheads. Military trucks, jeeps and convertibles blowing their horns overflowed with rebels, shouting "Victory or Death!" while holding their weapons high and tossing bullets like candy to the edges of the road, where the tumultuous crowd grabbed the pernicious souvenirs.

These parades went on for days as Fidel and his military entourage traveled across Cuba in a weeklong victory tour, greeted at every stop by frenzied masses. Along the way he deputized a loyal *Fidelista* in every town—assuring him jurisdiction over the island as he traveled westward. This five-hundred-mile journey originating in Santiago de Cuba culminated in Havana with a triumphant celebration. On January 8, 1959, in front of hundreds of thousands of supporters and broadcast on national TV, Fidel Castro officially proclaimed the victory of *La Revolución* to the Cuban people and to the rest of the world.

Even I had to wear a *barbudo* outfit in the school parade honoring the revolution. Mami had made it for me, with the black and red "July 26" badge and a fake beard to boot. She thought it was best for me to maintain the status quo, and we agreed not to tell Papi. He had nothing good to say about Castro nor his revolution; Papi was a *Batistiano* to the bone. Fortunately, he never saw my *miliciano* garb, or else he would have had a volcanic eruption.

But in the following months the bloodshed continued, as the new regime eradicated any remnants of Batista's organization. During the first ninety days of Castro's rule, nearly five hundred former government officials and military officers were imprisoned, tried and publicly executed by a firing squad. These tribunals and executions were broadcast live on radio and television like a twentieth-century Roman circus. "¡A el paredón! To the wall!" became the vengeful daily cheer of the Revolution.

My infamous barbudo *outfit*

Fortunately for us, these trials were held primarily in Havana, while we spent most of our time at Varadero, where it was politically quiet. Like a golden goose, the resort was spared. We did have a few anxious times—my father was detained and questioned twice. But even though Papi had been a *Batistiano* and he did not trust Castro, he was not involved in any resistance movement and had always been a conscientious public servant. The people of Cárdenas were very fond and protective of him and the Neyra family.

The Revolution Within

My greatest challenge was not surviving the Revolution but staying in school. By the fifth grade, I already had attended three. My first dismissal was from *El Apostolado*, a private, coed Catholic school that Melba and Lalita also attended. The same nuns who so adored my sister gave me the boot after I refused to do my schoolwork, got into fights and pushed other students at recess.

La Parróquia was the next school, but things did not go well there either. Ramoncito, a big, chubby bully, tried to intimidate me out of my *merienda*, snack, on the very first day. Surprisingly, my father happened to be home that night, so I told him about it. Of course, his response reflected the Neyra pride: "Punch him out and he won't dare take your food again."

When I returned to school the next day, Ramoncito tried to grab my snack bag when I lifted the lid of my desk, but I pushed him away. He tried a second time as we stood up to walk toward the courtyard for recess. I waited for the teacher to leave the room, who was leading the

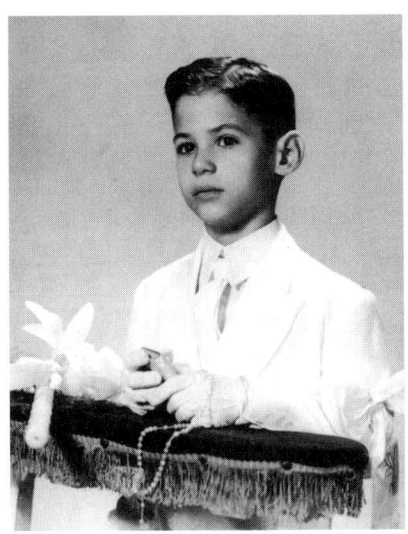

My First Communion and last year at El Apostolado

class in a single file. As soon as she was out of sight, Ramoncito once more reached for my snack and I connected a solid right to his left eye. He fell sideways, cut his brow on the corner of the desk, and his tears diluted the blood running down his face.

The news quickly traveled to the front of the line and reached the teacher, who ran back into the room to settle the matter. Since Ramoncito had a reputation for being a bully, and my classmates corroborated my story, I was not punished. That was the end of his free food and my fear of bullies.

But *La Parróquia* was still not a safe place. The boys were split into rival packs, and there were fights nearly every day; you had to choose a side just to survive. I had to come to school each day alert and prepared with my peashooter and ammunition to avoid an ambush. I kept a few peas in my mouth during critical times, like during recess or walking to my next class. When the peas got too soft or a teacher got too close, I would spit them into a plant or a drain and then reload from my stash in a gutted pen casing or other strategic hiding place.

As in most conflicts, the situation escalated, and the armaments became more lethal. The teachers learned to look for thin tubes so our next weapon of choice was a heavy-duty rubber band that we pretended to use to hold our books together, but in reality was used to launch projectiles. We would tightly wrap the band around our thumb and index finger and stretch it like a slingshot. Paper clips began to fly. Then we began to make our own ammunition from stiff wire that most of us could find around our homes. The only tool needed was a pair of pliers to cut and fold the metal into a U-shaped bullet.

Reluctantly starting off the new school year at La Parróquia, *while the girls returned to* El Apostolado

The new weaponry required practice for accuracy. At home, in our yard, whenever Mami was not looking, I would place my targets and refine my aim. But one day I took it too far. Pepa, the helpful lady who washed our clothes by hand, had filled a large wooden tub with hot water and was vigorously scrubbing under the shade of the carport, stopping only briefly to flip the garment, stroke it with a bar of soap and then mop her brow. The next thing I knew, I had hit Pepa in the forehead, right between the eyes. Her skin had been cut, and she was bleeding. I was shocked, scared. I felt terrible. How could I do this to such a nice woman?

Pepa yelled for my mother. "Cuca, come here!" Pepa was very forgiving about the incident, but Mami was furious with me. "You could have taken out her eye! Why would you do such a thing?" she demanded. During her interrogation I revealed what was going on at my school, and she realized that perhaps it was time to make yet another change.

But it turned out not to be a matter of choice. Not long afterward, I had a run-in with a teacher who would not grant permission for me to go to the bathroom. I stood up in class, opened my zipper and urinated on the floor right at my desk. Sure enough, I was immediately hustled to the principal's office, then on to another school.

I regularly got into fights, but none of the punishments at any of the schools ever seemed to stop my aggression—not even being put in the corner of the classroom to kneel on hard corn kernels for an entire period. Often, my poor mother would get a call from Tía Nina, who lived near the park where I would rendezvous to settle a score.

But the fight I remember most vividly was near our house. I had volunteered to deliver powdered milk to a needy family through a program offered by the school. I stopped at home to drop off my books and let my mother know where I was going. On my way, I came across a young boy who had dropped a *peseta*, a twenty-cent piece, on the sidewalk, and it had rolled into a courtyard. He was asking permission from a much older boy to be allowed into his yard to retrieve his money. But the bully stood guard at the gate and would not allow passage. As I walked by and overheard the conversation, I peered through the wrought-iron fence and spotted the coin.

"I see it!" I shouted. "Why don't you let him get his *peseta*?"

"Stay out of this! It has nothing to do with you!" he angrily retorted.

"Let him get his money!" I demanded.

The bully then asked the wrong question: "Are you going to do something about it?"

"Yes, but first I have to deliver this package. You can be sure I'll be back to help him get it!"

"*¡Bueno! Te espero.* Good! I will wait for you."

I was scared to death. This guy was older and a lot bigger than me, but I had no choice except to keep my word. It was now a matter of pride and neighborhood survival.

On the way back after I had made my delivery, I was hoping that the dispute had been resolved. No such luck. The bully was still standing guard, ready for a physical confrontation with his fists clenched. I whispered to the younger boy that as soon as the fight began he should run into the courtyard and get his money. "*Está bien,*" he answered gratefully.

The fight began in the traditional Latin way, by trading insults. *¡Cabrón, tú eres un come mierda!* which implied I enjoyed eating excrement. Next, it escalated to a word challenging my masculinity, *maricón*. Then I heard the unforgivable barb, *hijo de puta*, son of a whore. That was all I needed to hear to start swinging.

Finally, I broke the number-one rule of street-fighting tactics: If your opponent was smaller than you, move in close; if bigger, keep your distance, punch and retreat. But I could not get him to engage, so I dove in close. Of course he slammed me to the ground, and off we went, rolling onto the sidewalk, over the curb and into the street. Traffic screeched to a halt and a crowd gathered. We grappled on the pavement, scraping our elbows and knees raw. I was bleeding profusely from my nose and from a cut above my eye. No one got involved in breaking it up until there was a sure winner, and the onlookers were satisfied. Of course I lost the fight, but the *peseta* and my pride had been retrieved.

My third school, *La Progresiva*, was an academically driven Protestant school founded in 1900. Why they let me in, I will never know. It was unusual for a Catholic to attend, my grades were not good and my disciplinary record was even worse. I vaguely recall having to promise to behave. I knew this school would be tough on discipline, but I was so glad to be in a new environment that I stayed out of trouble. My report card improved, and I loved participating in athletics. It was an unusual setting, for most of our sporting events were held on the red-tile rooftop under sunny Cuban skies.

Ironically, I had finally started to succeed in school, but now *La Revolución* ensured that my attendance at *La Progresiva* would also be brief. The political climate began to influence everything we did, everything we thought, everything we talked about. All segments of society came under scrutiny from government-organized groups—which you were expected to join. Failure to do so was a sign of being a counterrevolutionary and therefore suspect. There was no way to stay neutral or uninvolved. Even the Boy Scouts had been turned into juvenile vigilantes, trained to tell on their family and friends. Needless to say, my family was very worried about what else the future would bring.

THE WAITING GAME

On the morning of April 17, 1961, while sitting at my desk in my fifth grade classroom at *La Progresiva,* I was paged by the principal's office and summoned to the front lobby. I feared my grandmother had died. As I hurried across the school courtyard, the crackling loudspeaker suddenly announced, "The city is on high alert. Classes are canceled. *La Progresiva* is being evacuated." As I reached the entrance, now clogged with other students and their frantic parents, Tío Hevia, Elena's husband, was waiting for me, and his face was contorted in distress.

"*¿Qué pasó, Tío?*" I asked my uncle, who lived next door to us.

"*¡Una invasion!*" he breathlessly explained. "The United States has invaded Cuba. I was closest to the school so I am taking you home." I arranged my books on the rear rack of his bicycle, hopped sideways on the top tube and held on to the center of the handlebars as he quickly pedaled me home.

The streets were mass confusion with sirens blaring and people rushing in all directions. My extended family was gathered at our house, the crisis control center. I helped fill every empty container we could find with water, and the adults went to nearby stores to buy whatever canned goods were left on the shelves. The radio and television kept broadcasting the urgent need for blood.

The days before the invasion had been frightening, with air strikes to disable the Cuban Air Force. At night, with a deafening roar, low-flying U.S. planes dropped leaflets that looked like large confetti raining down on Cárdenas. I would rush outside to scoop them off the pavement and run back inside with the contraband propaganda to secretly read the message encouraging citizens to revolt against Castro. Immediately, there was a major crackdown, and Castro ordered his *milicianos* to round up anyone remotely suspected of being a dissident.

In less than a week, more than two-hundred thousand people reportedly were arrested. The jails were soon so crowded that those who were considered low risk were detained in stadiums, schoolyards and even chicken coops. Such was the case for my mother's cousin, Manolo, who told us stories of his incarceration. "The worst part was the smell," he recounted. He was shortly released, never really knowing why he had been apprehended.

It was a very tense, terrifying and divisive time. Some Cubans had an intense fear of the most powerful nation in the world attacking our island. Others, including my family, believed U.S. military might was the only way for the now Soviet-backed revolution to collapse.

For months, there had been a secret military buildup in Cuba financed by the Soviet Union. But the United States was hoping to disable Castro before his Russian MiG fighters were delivered. A Cuban exile brigade trained by the CIA in Guatemala launched an attack at the Bay of Pigs, a narrow, fingerlike inlet on the southern coast of Cuba, just fifty miles directly south of Cárdenas. But the mission was doomed. Castro had been tipped off and was ready with an overpowering force of troops, tanks and heavy weapons under his personal command. Furthermore, the U.S. air support promised by President Kennedy was abruptly aborted, and the small invasion brigade was defeated and imprisoned within seventy-two hours.

After this disastrous invasion attempt, military bases were on full alert and Castro mobilized his army to closely guard bridges and government buildings. He used the invasion as a pretext to escalate his crackdown by closing all schools and forcing priests and nuns out of the country. Cuban parents were alarmed, recalling the Civil War in Spain in the late 1930s when the Republican Army kidnapped the children of Nationalists and used them as leverage to flush out their parents.

So many social changes already had taken place that nothing sounded implausible. According to information circulated by the underground opposition to Castro, a government decree would soon severely restrict the rights of parents. Children would remain in their care only until age three. Then they would be turned over to the *Organización de Círculos Infantiles* for physical and intellectual education—basically, state-run indoctrination where they would live in government dormitories and be permitted to visit their parents on a strict schedule. Older children would then be separated by intellect and ability—which meant a gifted student or athlete could be shipped off to a Russian school and perhaps never seen again. All these fears had thousands of parents searching for ways to send their children abroad before the government could forcibly take them.

In the year leading up to the invasion, the Cuban government had taken many actions that heightened these concerns. The program was called *intervención*—but what it really meant was confiscation. In June 1960, the oil refineries had been seized. In July, the expropriation of all U.S.-owned property in Cuba had been authorized. In August, the Cuban government had taken over all U.S. business concerns, including sugar mills, manufacturing plants and tourist properties. In October, the Urban Reform Law had been enacted, confiscating all urban rental units.

By then Tía Gladys already had begun a strong campaign within the family to send Lalita, Melba and me to the United States. She suggested that the adults should stay behind to hold onto whatever assets they could until things returned to normal—hopefully, a few months at most. Like many Cubans, my family truly believed that there was no way that mighty America would ever tolerate a Communist neighbor and that Castro's regime would not last long. But Papi was completely against the idea of us leaving, and he used his resistance as leverage against my mother.

Amid all of this chaos and uncertainty, I was stunned to overhear Papi threaten to leave Mami once the children were gone. It scared me to think of her being left all alone. How could I abandon my beloved mother now? But there was nothing I could do about it; I knew our departure was already set in motion. Still, I felt like I was betraying her, a haunting thought that I could not tell anyone. Throughout all of our preparations to leave, there was never any discussion about the details of us children leaving home. I guess it was something too painful to talk about. So we never did.

Children entering the United States had to be vaccinated for smallpox, so the telltale skin reaction was like a billboard advertising our imminent plans to leave the country. Children with this distinctive scar were often harrassed by supporters of the new regime, which is why I was always careful to hide mine. To make matters worse, my inoculation site became infected, and the crusty thick scab was the size of a *peseta* coin.

We spent the rest of our time in Cuba at Varadero. Most of our friends arrived at the beach early that summer of 1961 with no intention of going back to the city. Since the schools were closed, and we did not know when our visas would arrive, we had the dubious pleasure of an indefinite vacation. An endless summer…

Even amid all the turmoil, our final eight months in Cuba were carefree at the politically insulated Varadero Beach. Every day a large group of

Fun days during the endless summer at Varadero Beach

kids would gather and decide what to do: ride bikes, go horseback riding or water ski. Afterwards, we would usually end up at the beach in a huge circle, standing in chest-high warm water while telling stories. In the evenings after dinner, we would reunite for bowling, play hide-and-seek or go to the movies. The wildly popular theme from the romantic movie *A Summer Place* was etched in my memory as the musical score to our good times.

Although I was one of the youngest kids, the older ones tolerated me, and we all got along. Besides, I knew too much about who secretly liked whom and who had been kissed, information that I used to my advantage. Lalita and Melba tried to keep things from me, but I was always right there, trying to find out what was going on that night. I can still see them, rolling their hair in plastic curlers large enough to be underground pipes, holding hairpins in their teeth, making plans—plans they did not want me to know about.

Standing chest-high in the warm water with the gang

They used a coded conversation that drove me insane. I think they mainly did it to see my reaction and make fun of my frustration. They would use a "chi" sound before every syllable and rattle off a sentence that I could not understand. The only word I ever figured out was my name: "*Chi E, chi du, chi ar, chi do.*"

It seemed as if we had unlimited time and certainly a lot of freedom, as long as we behaved. But of course that was not always possible since my buddies and I occasionally stirred up trouble in the neighborhood. Among the guys in the group were the three Torres brothers and their cousin. Their family also owned a hotel in Varadero, and they lived there all year round. I used to hang out with them even though they were a few years older.

One day we got into an argument that turned into a rock-throwing fight. I got hit in the head and was really angry, so I ran unseen to the side of their home, placed the garden hose through the window and turned it on. Soon their living room was flooded. They chased me and grabbed me by my arms, ramming my head against the corner of the square pillar of their front porch. I rushed home with a big gash, blood all over my face and a throbbing headache I will never forget.

We used to run behind the city jeeps that sprayed insecticide to minimize the rampant mosquito problem, breathing the nasty fumes that we thought smelled good then. The chemical penetrated the fibers of my clothing and stuck to my skin. As we closely trailed the truck, we were hidden in its thick noxious cloud, which we used as cover to bombard people with eggs and rotten fruit stolen from the hotel kitchen.

Although Varadero held many fond memories for me, there were also some dangerous episodes. One day my friend Nelson sought my help to assist his brother and our neighbor, Jesús, who planned to leave the country in a small boat during the complete darkness of a new moon. Bit by bit, we took turns cutting out the back of their wood-framed garage so they could sneak the small craft out the rear, which faced the ocean, and escape undetected. This project took several weeks while waiting for the right weather conditions.

During this time I also periodically delivered food and cigarettes to a man in hiding, a former official in Batista's government who was going to escape with Jesús. I was not allowed to see his face, nor was I told his name. There was no better decoy than a child wandering the streets with a lunch bag, but if I had been caught, I might not be here today. Even more audacious was that we accomplished our secret mission right under the nose of the G2, Castro's secret police, who had informants in the neighborhood and kept an eye on the streets from their office in the apartment building next door which Jesús managed.

Jesús was like an uncle to me and he became very concerned when he noticed one of his apartment tenants, a beautiful brunette in her thirties, trying to befriend me. She would invite me up to her apartment for lunch while her husband was out of town and her two young daughters were at the beach with their nanny. When Jesús saw her rubbing my back with her perfectly polished red talons in the parking garage, he pulled me aside later and gravely cautioned me, that although Lola was extremely attractive, her intentions were not. He told me she was sleeping with the chief of the G2 office, and was trying to seduce me to extract information.

On the night of their daring departure, my job was to stay awake past midnight and flicker the lights on the top floor of the hotel for a couple of hours as a navigational aid, while they silently rowed to a safe distance far from shore to start the motor.

It was exciting to help someone escape. My problem was the hotel's night watchman. He was an old, retired guard who usually fell asleep in a rocking chair behind the glass entrance to the restaurant. But on this particular evening, he was alert and agitated. As he saw me running around, he thought I was playing yet another prank. I would turn the other lights on the property on and off to keep him distracted. Then I would resume the assignment of flashing the beacon that was guiding my friends to freedom.

Jesús and Nelson's brother made it to the United States. Others in their boat were not so lucky. One woman and a man died; another had severe burns from spilled fuel in the intense sun. Fortunately, a Shell Oil tanker rescued the survivors at sea. Jesús ended up in Dayton, Ohio, where years later he would help my parents with temporary refuge.

By the end of the summer of 1961, we were feeling sentimental. Most of our friends were also processing the necessary paperwork to leave the country, and we knew our time together would soon end. But we never talked about it. Many mornings, my beach-bumming buddy Tony Caravia and I would wake at dawn to go water skiing in the flat-as-glass, early morning Caribbean waters. My mother would watch from the patio hoping our instructor would not take us too far or too fast in his speedboat. As we walked down the beach, Tony and I would sing a parting song by Carlos Gardel, the Argentinian tango idol, with our arms wrapped around each other's shoulders like a couple of drunken sailors:

Adiós, muchachos, compañeros de mi vida.
Barra querida de aquellos tiempos,
Me toca a mi hoy emprender mi retirada.
Debo alejarme de tan buena muchachada.
Adiós, muchachos, ya me voy, no me despido,
Es mi destino nadie lo escapa.
Me toca a mí hoy emprender mi retirada.
Debo alejarme de tan buena muchachada.

Good-bye, friends, companions of my life.

Loving group from those days,

It is my turn today to begin my departure.

I must distance myself from such good friendship.

Good-bye, friends, I am leaving now. I will not say farewell.

No one can escape his destiny.

It is my turn today to begin my departure.

I must distance myself from such good friendship.

Tony and I must have sung those lyrics a thousand times. Although we often got silly with deepened voices and exaggerated gestures as we performed it to an audience of hotel guests, we were already wallowing in the sadness of our impending loss. Every moment was precious now. Our departure visa notifications via *los telegramas* could come at any time, and then our farewells would take place within days.

In the evenings, I would sit on the patio seawall facing the ocean, admiring the glowing sunset, listening to the surf and looking across the sea, knowing my new home was far beyond the edge of the horizon. Varadero was the closest point to American soil, only ninety miles to Key West—but to me the United States was still a whole world away.

Soon I would be heading toward a new country, a new city, a new home. The thought of no longer living in my paradise island overwhelmed me with contradictory emotions. Although I was frightened, I was also excited and curious about what my journey would bring. I felt guilty and sad about leaving my mother but challenged by this early initiation into manhood and responsibility. The crashing of every wave echoed the inner turmoil of my conflicting feelings and doubts. But there was one thing I knew for sure—soon nothing would ever be the same. No beach-bumming buddies. No aunts, no uncles. No grandparents, no Papi.

No Mami.

Gusanos

We received the dreaded telegramas *during the Christmas holidays of 1961.* Noche Buena, the Christmas Eve celebration, now took on a somber tone, and we spent the rest of the shortened holiday exchanging our final good-byes. We would also miss *El Dia de los Reyes Magos*, the traditional day for exchanging gifts, but it did not matter anyway, since we were not allowed to take anything but clothing with us.

On January 3, 1962, my family rose early and left for Havana, which was less than two hours away. The highway route followed the scenic coastline so I gazed at the beautiful countryside and the endless ocean that I might never see again. I was silent as we rode and tried to capture my own last mental snapshots of Cuba's natural beauty.

We drove across Cuba's highest bridge, the Bacunayagua, which spans the Valley of Yumurí. The huge royal palms had never looked lovelier and the view was breathtaking. In the valley, animals grazed in the lush pastures and the little *bohios*, square huts with palm frond roofs, baked in the sun. I can still see the children playing outside in the rich, red Cuban soil and the laundry on the clotheslines, flapping in the breeze, like scenes from a photo album.

Yet one of my most lasting impressions was of the potholes at both ends of the bridge, deliberately dug in a staggered grid pattern across the full width of the four-lane highway. The two-foot square holes were filled with sand to help absorb the impact to vehicles that did not slow down. But these cavities could also be quickly loaded with dynamite by soldiers guarding the bridge, who could blow it up immediately to immobilize any potential invaders.

When we arrived in Havana we checked into the Riviera, a high-rise hotel near the sea that stood tall in the city's skyline with a distant view of the entrance to the Havana harbor. The opulent Riviera was originally built with a lavish casino in 1958 by America's mob mastermind, Meyer Lansky, with Batista's blessing. But the Revolution had no tolerance for gambling and organized crime. On New Year's Day, 1959, Castro's angry supporters had looted the Havana casinos, smashed the slot machines with baseball bats and piled the furniture in the streets to burn in huge bonfires. The Riviera had since been restored, and although the casinos had been converted into meeting rooms and shops, the swank hotel still remained as a testament to the decadence and corruption of the previous decade.

All the conflicting emotions that had haunted me for months while waiting for this departure were compounded that day. I was anxious to be leaving the only home I had ever known, but there was a sense of excitement since Havana was a busy, vibrant city of more than a million people, and I had only been there just a few times before. I was trying to inhale the sights, sounds and smells I was leaving behind, hoping to brand them into my heart and soul like an emotional souvenir to keep me company on my upcoming journey.

My excitement was soon churned into apprehension from the constant traffic of military jeeps and trucks loaded with armed *milicianos*. Tanks protected government office buildings and barricaded monuments. Major intersections and large gathering places were under around-the-clock surveillance. My last impressions of my country were of guards, guns and gates, and I dreaded leaving my mother behind under these threatening conditions.

At the end of this long day, Tía Gladys again reviewed our paperwork to verify one last time that everything was in order. As I watched her neatly fold each document, I realized my destiny was cryptically concealed within this stack of red tape.

Finally it was time to go to bed, but the night was filled with fears. What would my new home be like? Where would I go to school? How could I make friends without speaking English? What would it be like to live with our guardians in Cincinnati? Just how cold are snow and ice?

Would I ever see my parents again?

We awoke the next morning knowing this was finally the day we had long dreaded. Our *gusanos*, lightweight vinyl duffle bags, were packed and ready to go. *Gusanos* literally means "worms," which was a descriptive term characterizing the thin, long bags. But it had also become the derogatory slang term hurled at anyone perceived to be anti-Castro, including those of us fleeing the country.

Wrestling our *gusanos* and navigating through crowded hallways at the airport with a great sense of urgency and insufficient directions seemed more formidable than we had expected. Every step involved paperwork that required certification by the department head of one office or another. There was also the fear of knowing that any error, missing signature, misplaced copy or absent seal or stamp could easily keep you from leaving the country. This process took hours, with long lines and every procedure enforced by an uncompromising government agent looking for an excuse to complicate your departure. We had been instructed to be respectful and avoid confrontation, to provide only short answers without volunteering any additional information. The mission was to get out.

The airport was packed. Family and friends had come to say good-bye to their loved ones—and in Cuba, *familia* also included every uncle, aunt, cousin and grandparent. It was quite a crowd. The frightening feeling of imminent separation was palpable, so the noise and busyness were welcome distractions to me.

It was my turn to go through the paper maze—but suddenly there was a snag that might prevent me from leaving. Although all of my documents were in order, an overzealous clerk noticed on my passport that I would be turning twelve years old in just five days. At that time, twelve was the benchmark for an adult fare. Since I was still eleven I had only prepaid for a child's ticket. But all laws were now subject to the interpretation of those in charge, and we were informed that I could not leave.

I briefly wondered if perhaps I was not meant to go, and I was temporarily filled with relief. But Mami was determined that I would be on that plane. She knew that by age fifteen, I would be required to register as a *miliciano* in Fidel

Castro's Revolutionary Army, and by sixteen, I could be called to active duty. If I had stayed another year or more, I would have been past the age permitted to leave. It would be years before I fully realized the reason for her prophetic urgency. We also had no way of knowing that within nine months, all flights would be canceled due to the Cuban Missile Crisis.

Tía Gladys quickly called her cousin Julio Pastoriza at his law office in Havana. Julio, known as Toto, was an articulate, successful attorney who had mastered the art of intimidation with his intense bulging eyes and deep, powerful voice. His wife, Emilita, and his children already had fled to the United States and he already had been instrumental in helping us, too.

Once at the airport, it took Toto nearly an hour to get the uncooperative immigration officials to realize we would not give in to their harrassment. Being a lawyer, he understood the importance of not caving in to the temptation to pay the extra fare to silence their unfounded objection—thereby courting the possibility that I might not be allowed to leave at all. I would have had to start the application process all over, a series of steps that already had taken nearly a year. Toto's persuasive arguments finally got the best of the stubborn clerks, and they cleared me for departure.

Toto helped me escape through a very narrow window of opportunity. And now I was behind the impenetrable glass wall of *La Pecera*, awaiting the final security search to make certain that no *gusano* left the country with any money, jewelry, or even a family photograph. I was terrified. I had heard frightening stories about people being taken to private rooms to have their body cavities probed. Even clothing hems were torn open to look for hidden valuables. Luckily, I was only patted down and cleared for departure.

EDWARD J. NEYRA

CATHOLIC WELFARE BUREAU
DIOCESE OF MIAMI

REV. FATHER BRYAN O. WALSH, S.T.L.
EXECUTIVE DIRECTOR

REGIONAL OFFICES
MIAMI · FORT LAUDERDALE

395 N. W. FIRST STREET — SUITE 207
MIAMI 36, FLORIDA
FRanklin 9-2893

Octubre 1961.

A QUIEN PUEDA INTERESAR:

Se hace constar que a *Julio Eduardo Neyra Perez* le ha sido concedida la "Visa Waiver" por el Departamento de Estado a peticion del Catholic Welfare Bureau, Inc.

Pan American y K. L. M. han sido notificadas. El solicitante debera dirigirse a dichas oficinas para hacer la reservacion y comprar su pasaje.

Si Pan American y K. L. M. en la Habana no hubiesen recibido la confirmacion de la "Visa Waiver", el solicitante debera de esperar unos dias y tratar de nuevo.

Bryan O Walsh
(Rev. Fr.) Bryan O. Walsh
Director

MEMBER OF THE UNITED FUND OF DADE COUNTY
MEMBER OF THE UNITED FUND OF BROWARD COUNTY

My visa waiver signed by Fr. Walsh

ACCLIMATION

*L*ooking at all of the snow-covered ground, I thought we must have landed somewhere near the Arctic. I will never forget that first stinging slap of bitter cold as we stepped out of the airplane in Cincinnati. The sharp, frigid wind numbed my face, paralyzed my lips and stung my eyes, flooding them with tears. I had never been exposed to anything much cooler than a Caribbean breeze from *el Norte*, and the only white-covered ground I had ever walked on had been the warm, soft sand of Varadero Beach. Even my cousins' taunts about the cold during our short stay in Miami had not prepared me for this.

We had arrived from Miami late in the afternoon. I had been restless during our long flight, trying to imagine what Ohio would be like. I drank Coca-Cola and tried to listen to the conversations as Mr. Bass, our new guardian, and my sister translated, but I still felt disconnected and isolated from hearing words I could not understand.

I kept looking out the windows, soliciting reassurance from Melba that we were not lost and heading for the North Pole. The plane was not full, so I traded seats, hoping to find something better and brighter outside a different window. But it all looked hopeless. Far below, the trees had no leaves and the ground had no grass.

Kendrick and Eleanor Bell, whom we also knew from their vacations in Varadero, were lifelong friends of Herbert Newman and Quincy Bass and were waiting for us at the airport. Mrs. Bell tried her best to convince me via Melba that snow could actually be a lot of fun. She chattered about sled riding and snow skiing. I could only think of boat riding and water skiing. While we waited for our luggage, she suggested going outside to show me how to make a snowball. The thought of venturing into the cold for entertainment seemed *loco*. We darted out briefly, though, and gamely tried to pack snowballs—but I soon discovered that snow melts into your gloves and shoes and makes you even colder, if possible.

We had had heavy winter coats made for us back home, but finding insulating fabric in Cuba's warm climate wasn't easy; several layers of a blanket-like cloth had to be sewn together. I made fun of Lalita's and Melba's matching coats with big collars and giant buttons around the neck—apparently without a clue as to how foolish my own winter gear looked. But they were no match for *el conjelador*, the freezer.

My luggage had been lost and the airport officials promised to deliver it to our new home within a couple of days. I was very concerned, for I figured that I would need to wear six layers of pants and a dozen shirts to survive the cold.

We all piled into Mr. Bell's 1957 Chevrolet station wagon. The roads were still being cleared from the snowfall earlier that day. I was intrigued by how the snowplows worked, but as they scraped the white powder off the street, it mixed with the grime from the pavement, piling the dirty muck against the curb. What an ugly mess! I then looked at the lifeless, leafless trees and wondered aloud, "Would they ever turn green?"

Everyone laughed. Mrs. Bell explained, "Eduardo, it will be lovely come spring. And summers will be as hot as Varadero Beach!" she added.

I certainly doubted that.

It was rush hour by now, and traffic was getting heavy. I just could not believe that people lived in such severe conditions and drove in this slippery slop. Mr. Bell was telling us that a new bridge was being built, so we would have to take detours. While in the midst of the traffic jam, I realized that the sun, which had been dimmed by a curtain of solid gray clouds, was now completely gone. As we drove through downtown, I was also disappointed at how gloomy and dingy the buildings looked.

We arrived at our new home and walked into the large, dark living room filled with heavy antique furniture, Oriental rugs, and two Steinway grand pianos. It all looked foreboding and foreign; any excitement about this adventure had come to an excruciating halt. A crushing sense of hopelessness overwhelmed me as I plopped down into a high wingback chair covered in somber damask. As I sank into it, so did my sense of security—and all the pent-up despair broke loose and flooded me with tears.

I cried uncontrollably, and Mrs. Bell tried to comfort me. She put her arms around my shoulders cooing, "Eduardo, things are going to work out fine.

We will look after you." After a long, hard wail, my sobbing finally subsided. As I caught my breath, Mr. Bell suggested that we go out and get something to eat, but we were all too tired. He then volunteered to pick up dinner and bring it back home and insisted that I accompany him. I did not want to go back out into the cold, drive in those sloppy streets or stop at a restaurant without my translator Melba. He assured me that it would not take long, and everything would be all right. With great reservations, I finally agreed.

We drove a few blocks to Peebles Corner, a nearby business district, and brought home Frisch's Big Boys, fries and chili. Of course, I was accustomed to eating beans and beef together, but the tomato sauce was a brand-new experience—as was the cheeseburger with tartar sauce. After the first few bites, I was immediately converted.

Once we finished our meal, Mr. and Mrs. Bell left, and we were given a tour of our new home. I helped the girls carry their luggage upstairs. They shared a bedroom, and I had my own next door. Both large rooms were furnished with antique furniture, Oriental rugs and a fireplace. My bedroom even had a grand piano. Our guardians' rooms were directly across the hall and they instructed us to knock on either of their doors if we needed anything. Then we all said goodnight.

I entered my room, closed and locked my door, and tried to think about the events of the day, the month, the year; but I was too physically exhausted to allow any of my apprehensions to keep me awake.

When I awoke the next morning, a midnight storm had smothered the dreary landscape with another thick layer of snow. I was surprised to see the way it clung to everything, especially the branches of the bare, winter-beaten trees. Cuba had become very distant very quickly. Facing the grim reality of this new life, I felt imprisoned by shackles of fear and doubt; my self-assurance had surrendered. I tried to focus on my conditioning from home. I could still hear my father's voice, "Be strong. *Los Neyras no lloran*—Neyras don't cry." Somehow the proud promise that I had made to be self-reliant kept me from drowning in despair.

After a couple of days my *gusano* finally arrived, and I was eager to unpack and change into fresh clothing. But rough handling in the bitter cold had ripped open the thin vinyl duffle bag, and most of my clothes from home were missing. Our guardians' friends immediately came to my rescue and brought over their own children's clothing for me to wear. I was grateful, but I could not help feeling like an orphan.

I spent most evenings alone in my room staring out the window, leaning on the radiator to stay warm while listening to music on the radio, trying to learn English by memorizing lyrics to popular songs. I still know all the words to "Duke of Earl" and "The Twist" and many more from that repertoire of early 1960s hits. Even today when I hear one of those classic oldies, I feel a twinge of loneliness.

I also liked to go to bed early. I would pray for my parents and then lie awake to think about how I was going to direct my life. Such a burden of responsibility burned like a beacon. I was obsessed with formulating a plan, not just for my survival, but for a productive and successful life as an adult. I was only twelve years old, but for me, childhood was over.

CARIBBEAN CRISIS

Not even a month after our arrival, the relationship between the Unites States and Cuba had deteriorated dramatically. On February 7, 1962, President Kennedy imposed a total embargo on all Cuban imports. The U.S. government, under corporate pressure, was retaliating for Castro's *intervención* of American-owned property in Cuba. The enormous gulf between Cincinnati and Cuba widened even further.

Soon afterward, telephone communication to the island was suspended and the weekly calls from our parents on Sunday aftenoons ceased. Letters were delayed months due to censorship, and often not delivered at all. Even telegrams were now difficult. Sadly, contact with home became exceedingly rare.

Since we were now isolated from our parents, Tía Elena came to visit us that first summer in Cincinnati. She had been living in Caracas, Venezuela, since 1960 with Tío Hevia and her two daughters, Teresita and

Pocha. Pocha had married Arturo, a corporate executive, and they were living a very successful life in Latin America. In fact, Tía Gladys and Mami had once considered sending us to Caracas, but they believed the United States would be much safer.

Tía Elena wanted to see how we were adapting to our new American life. She arrived with her arms full of gifts, but unfortunately, she also delivered disturbing news about what was happening in Cuba.

The Imperial at Varadero Beach had been a victim of *intervención*. Seized. Confiscated. Government owned. Benito, the knife-wielding chef at the hotel who had once defended me, had turned on my family. He had become *un revolucionario*, a member of the CDR, the Committee for the Defense of the Revolution, and had snitched on Tío Ramón, who had removed an air conditioning unit from the hotel for repairs. Under the rules of the Revolution, you could not remove any company-owned assets from your property without government permission. Within twenty-four hours, a convoy of military jeeps encircled the hotel, and the armed *milicianos* entered the lobby to seize the Imperial. My summer place was now gone forever, and so was any hope of ever returning to the turquoise blue waters of Varadero Beach.

I could only imagine the pain and loss that my family was going through, especially Tío Ramón and Tía Gladys, who had worked so hard to build their tropical jewel. Mami and Papi, Tía Gladys, Tío Ramón and Abuela had been forced to consolidate their households and were now living together in Cantel, where Tío Ramón had added an upstairs to the country villa he owned there.

Cantel was a tiny, quiet countryside town midway between Varadero and Cárdenas. Tío Ramón had thought it was a good idea for us to spend a week or two at the villa to experience rustic surroundings before we grew too accustomed to oceanfront luxury. The home was on a farm, which grew the most delicious mangos, guavas and oranges. I loved to pick the ripe, juicy fruit right off the trees and eat them under the shade in the gentle Cuban breeze.

Tía Elena informed us that things were now very tense in Cuba, and it was difficult to leave. She assured us that they were trying very hard through political connections in Venezuela to get our parents out. The brief comfort we felt during her visit diminished quickly.

The news held constant reminders of the strain. Our guardian Herbert Newman was a well-informed man and read two local newspapers every day and the *New York Times* on Sundays. Each morning he would rise before dawn, percolate a pot of coffee and read the *Cincinnati Enquirer* from front to back. In the evenings, if the *Cincinnati Post* had not been delivered, I would pick one up for Mr. Newman from the box at the end our street.

I would struggle to read the articles about the Cuban Missile Crisis as I slowly walked back home, clutching the cold paper in my shivering hands. The headlines intensified. Finally, on October 22, 1962, President John F. Kennedy announced the confirmation of Soviet nuclear missile installations in Cuba and his decision to blockade the island. The United States and the Soviet Union threatened the world with a nuclear confrontation.

"That son-of-a-bitch, Kennedy!" Mr. Newman exclaimed. "He is not equipped to handle these crises." Herbert Newman did not like JFK one bit.

He thought he was too inexperienced, too spoiled and not very smart. "A horse's ass," he would say. Mr. Bass would remind him that children were present, but when it came to politics, Mr. Newman did not hold back—especially in front of Mr. and Mrs. Bell, who were both Kennedy fans.

We would intently watch the evening news to follow the latest developments on the Cuban Missile Crisis. The aerial footage of the powerful U.S. naval ships racing to Cuba to blockade the island before the Soviets could unload their deadly cargo made me shudder.

I was horrified to think what would happen to my family if a nuclear war broke out. A military base designated for Russian armament had been built in Cantel, just a mile away from Tío Ramón's villa. Playing in the yard two years earlier, I had heard the bulldozers begin to clear the land and jumped on my bike to ride past the new construction site. Now my family was trapped living next to an obvious military target. It was all so frightening.

By October 1962 all flights from Cuba to the United States had been canceled indefinitely, and for the first time the meaning of the Iron Curtain was painfully clear to me: Cuba was on lockdown. I was now facing my greatest fear—that our parents would never get out and that we would never return.

New Kid in Town

Immediately after our arrival in Cincinnati, we were enrolled at Holy Name School which was just down the street from our new home. Our guardians were not religious but they respected the fact that our family wanted us to attend a Catholic school. Mr. Newman even attended church with us and provided money to place in the collection basket. That first Sunday he took us to Mass, I could see him wiping the tears from his eyes as we returned to our pew after receiving Communion.

Holy Name was a co-educational parochial school and was supervised by the Ursuline Sisters of Cincinnati. But we only went there that single semester, and it seems a blur in my memory; I never really talked to anyone, so my short stay was not conducive to building friendships. Although not knowing English was certainly a disadvantage, I developed a great sense for body language and an instinct for perceiving people's intentions.

Because of my poor English, I was initially placed in third grade even though I was twelve years old. I had to walk in line with much younger children and was always at the end because of my height. I felt humiliated, very much on display, like everyone was staring. It was a great incentive to learn the language fast.

The Ursuline Sisters of Cincinnati who ran Holy Name also directed St. Ursula Academy, a private school that had given refuge to several Cuban nuns from the same order that operated the orphanage in Cárdenas. For many years Tía Gladys had fulfilled her *promesa* by closing the Varadero Beach resort on Lalita's birthday and inviting the orphan children to join our family and friends for a full day of fun. The Mother Superior at St. Ursula had been informed of the connection and called our guardians with the offer of free schooling at the St. Ursula Academy the coming fall.

I quickly made friends at St. Ursula, but soon tragedy struck again. I had developed a close relationship with a classmate named Donald. But

Celebrating la promesa *in Varadero Beach in 1958*

one Monday morning when I arrived at school, he was not there. Over the weekend, he had been hit by a car while chasing a ball into the street and was tragically killed. I felt an intense loss, but by then I was in the habit of repressing my feelings in order to survive. The following week, a package was delivered to me at school. Donald's parents wanted me to have his baseball glove and his piggy bank, full of his savings.

The Academy was a very nurturing school, with caring teachers, appropriate discipline and friendly classmates. I no longer needed to misbehave as I had in Cuba in order to attract attention. I already stood out—my goal now was to fit in. After a couple of summer school sessions, I was able to catch up with my age group.

In eighth grade I was blessed to have an extraordinary English teacher, Sister Monica. She was enthusiastic, energetic and had written a book titled *The Professor of Phonics*. Besides being an expert in teaching children to read, she took great interest in her students—me in particular. She was a motivator, instructing her students in composition, "Don't procrastinate, just start writing! Don't worry about the perfect beginning."

In a class of twenty-one girls and only six boys, there were plenty of opportunities to be disruptive, but she was a four-foot-ten-inch dynamo who kept the group under control at all times with her strict discipline. Sister Monica was also our science teacher, with very creative lessons—including one where she choreographed revolving students to illustrate our solar system. With her visual teaching style I grasped everything quickly and easily.

She was amazingly open about sex and boy-girl relationships, which was surprising considering both the times and the Catholic tradition.

Scientific in her approach, she utilized graphs, diagrams and three-dimensional models of the reproductive organs to make sure we understood exactly how they worked. No one in the classroom dared to giggle during these presentations.

Aside from being my favorite teacher, Sister Monica also took great interest in my personal development. She was my protector and often took me aside and gave me advice about American girls. "They are very forward," she warned. "Be careful."

One day she confiscated a note thrown from the second-floor window while we were walking single file to lunch. I was in the eighth grade; the note came from a sophomore. It had a name and phone number for me to call for a date. "I can drive and pick you up," the note instructed. Needless to say, my admirer was called to the principal's office and reprimanded.

I had a great relationship with Sister Monica. I was the only student who could kid around with her. Since she knew she could trust me to keep order, Sister Monica would leave me in charge of the class when she had to step out of the room.

One day she instructed me to fly over to the chapel and deliver a note to the principal. I stared at her and laughed.

"I can't 'fly over' to the chapel," I said.

"Why not?" she demanded.

"I don't have wings!"

After we both laughed, I explained why English was so difficult.

"You say so many funny things; it's confusing. 'Fly over to the building,' 'Spill the beans,' 'Let the cat out of the bag.' English is a crazy language!"

I always kept in touch with Sr. Monica. Here, I was proudly picking her up to go to a fundraiser at my home in 1988.

ASSIMILATION

i was always nervous about going to church at our school. Attending services included Holy Communion, receiving Communion required going to Confession, and Confession meant revealing myself to the priest. Even though I was inside the dark anonymity of the confessional, I knew that the priest could easily detect my accent; no one else in school sounded like me. I felt very vulnerable, knowing that if we met in a hallway he could stare me down, aware of all of my sins. Besides, to survive the Revolution I had been trained not to tell my secrets to anyone, not even a priest.

Although learning English was my greatest challenge, I thought I would never get used to the winter weather or to American food. It was all hard to swallow without those wonderful Cuban seasonings. Even Abuela's meals were now elevated to a grander place in my memory once I tried broccoli, spinach and cauliflower.

Herbert Newman's German heritage introduced us to many

unpalatable dishes like boiled brussels sprouts, which tasted even worse than they smelled. And sauerkraut—appropriately named since it was sour. To top it off, he would occasionally serve cow tongue or brains. And the cook, Alma, occasionally tried to get us to eat her favorite Deep South delicacy, pickled pig's feet. But fortunately, not every evening featured one of these dreaded dishes. For the most part, we ate well-balanced, hearty, home-cooked meals.

Dessert was allowed only in moderation, so we sneaked sweet snacks. Often after school, before our guardians arrived home, we would walk a few blocks to the neighborhood drug store and spend part of our allowance on Hostess chocolate cupcakes. They were worth the walk, even in the cold.

I had even finally warmed up to the idea that playing in the snow could be fun. On a cold and blustery evening during the holidays, Mr. Newman took me to Sears & Roebuck so that I could personally select my very own sled as a Christmas gift. I proudly walked out of the store with it in tow, gliding across the slush-covered parking lot, discussing the different hills near the house where I could christen my new sled.

After the next heavy snowfall, my friend Phillip and I rushed to the park to go sledding right after school and before it got dark. Phillip didn't want to waste time to go home to get his own sled, and since I lived closer to the hill, we decided that we could have just as much fun riding together on my brand new one. He showed me how to make the sled go faster, so before every run I pulled a bar of soap out of my pocket and greased the rails yet again.

"This is fun, Phillip, but wouldn't it be even better to slide across the frozen lake at the bottom of the hill for a much longer run?" I cajoled him.

"No way," Phillip insisted. "I will jump off if you head toward the lake."

"Chicken!" I yelled all the way down, but with my Cuban accent it sounded more like, "Shicken!" He kept repeating it, laughing, shaking his head and telling me I was nuts. "*¡Cubano loco!*"

At the foot of the hill, right before we hit the slick surface, Phillip leaped off, still laughing. As I approached the center of the lake, the sled began to slow down and then came to a sickening halt. Still belly-down, I broke through the ice and sank fast in the frigid water. Fortunately, it was only knee-high, so I was able to scramble back toward the bank. With every step my boots broke through the frozen crust. Within seconds, I was so cold and numb that I could not feel my feet.

Just as I reached dry land, I realized that I had left my brand new Christmas gift behind. Phillip was still laughing. I yelled to him that I had to go back to rescue my sled, because I was not about to tell Mr. Newman how I had lost it. Shaking, I retraced my steps on the wake of broken ice. Once more I had to submerge my upper body in order to grab hold of the sunken sled.

Fully dressed, soaking wet and freezing, I climbed the slope up a quarter-mile incline to the house. I went to the back door, but Melba and Lalita could not hear me knocking. I trudged to the front door and rang the doorbell. However, we had all been instructed not to respond or let anyone in. Finally, I desperately returned to the rear entry, banging on the door and screaming at the top of my lungs until Melba answered.

By the time I entered the house, I was blue and shivering so fiercely that I could hardly talk. Once upstairs, I stripped down, wrapped myself in a blanket and began running a bath. As I lowered myself into the tub, I could barely resist screaming from the pain of the hot water on my frozen skin. I soaked for nearly an hour before I felt normal again.

With our guardians, Herbert Newman and Quincy Bass, at our new home in Cincinnati

Guardian Angels

*h*erbert *Newman and Quincy Bass were bachelors, professors at the University* of Cincinnati College-Conservatory of Music. They were very kind and generous substitute parents who provided us with a safe, comfortable home and introduced us to their creative, civic-minded circle of friends. Although Mr. Newman and Mr. Bass were both caring and committed, Herbert shouldered the brunt of the responsibility of raising us.

I was always treated with respect. Mr. Newman would often give me informal English lessons in the kitchen as I helped him put away the groceries—the object was to learn the name of each item. Then he would ask me to teach him the words in Spanish. It was his clever way of motivating me and protecting my dignity.

The house rules were strict. Homework was to be completed before we could ever watch TV or use the telephone. Even those priviliges were limited to fifteen minutes on the phone and one TV show each evening.

My favorites were *Leave It to Beaver* and *Ozzie and Harriet*—both idealized portrayals of two brothers and the happy family life I longed for.

Mr. Newman was firm, but also fair. If I ever was invited anywhere with a school friend and his family, my considerate guardian always reminded me to be polite. A stickler for etiquette, Mr. Newman taught me the proper way to greet a new acquaintance—with a firm handshake, direct eye contact and a respectful greeting, "How do you do?" He also expected me to make prudent decisions. I always followed his advice and never gave him any reason not to trust me. In my young teens, I was even given adult privileges and allowed to have a weak mixed drink with the grownups. On warm summer nights, we often sat on the back porch and listened to stories about our guardians' childhoods or laughed at Quincy's lame jokes.

Herbert Newman hailed from Versailles, Kentucky, and pursued a career in music—much to the dismay of his physician father, who also owned several tobacco farms. One of the farms had the perfect spring water for making bourbon. Mr. Newman liked his Echo Spring Bourbon, turning him into the life of the party as he played the piano and sang with his friends.

Although he was very educated and well-spoken with a Southern gentleman's demeanor, once in a while he could be quite defiant. One spring Mr. Newman generously took Melba downtown to buy her prom dress at Gidding Jenny, at the time Cincinnati's most exclusive women's clothing store. While he waited for Melba as she was trying on dresses, he lit up a cigarette and went looking for an ashtray.

"Sir, you are not allowed to smoke in here!" commanded the salesperson.

Without an ashtray, he proceeded to grind the cigarette out in the glass coffee table in the waiting area and marched out of the store to buy Melba's dress somewhere else.

During that first summer of 1962, Mr. Newman surprised us by renting an oceanfront house in Daytona Beach, Florida, for six whole weeks. Since we could not return to Cuba, he thought we would all enjoy taking a summer vacation at the seashore. At the end of our first day's trek towards the Sunshine state, we checked into a motel in Knoxville, Tennessee, cranky and hungry.

We noticed that the restaurant was very crowded—the local Rotary Club was holding its monthly meeting—so Mr. Newman asked the host if it would be a problem for us to be served. Of course not, he was told. But after a half hour of waiting, Herbert finally had enough. As the club members departed, Mr. Newman brought over to our table the baskets of fried chicken, rolls and extra bowls of mashed potatoes that had not been touched from their meeting. The waiter finally showed up just as we were finishing our meal. He reprimanded Mr. Newman and slapped a check down on the table. Herbert sharply responded he had no intention of letting the restaurant charge twice for the same meal, especially since we had to get our own food. Mr. Bass, on the other hand, just went along and did not say much, as usual.

Mr. Bass was originally from Boston. His full name was John Quincy Bass, and he was a descendant of John Quincy Adams—although he seemed somehow disconnected, without any family ties. He rarely spoke of his family and never went to visit.

Quincy Bass was not as engaging or connected to the three of us, although he was very kind and sometimes helped with our homework. Mr. Bass was fluent in Spanish and understood French and German, in addition to his flawless command of English. He always patiently corrected any grammatical mistakes we made when speaking our new language, but was never critical of our heavily accented pronunciation. In addition to his exceptional linguistic abilities, Mr. Bass was also very knowledgeable about art, history and science and could finish the daily newspaper's crossword puzzle in record time.

Quincy Bass was a musical genius and had what they call "a perfect ear." Mr. Newman would readily admit that Mr. Bass was the better musician—in fact, he said, "one of the best." Mr. Bass never paid much attention to compliments. He turned down a contract to play as a concert pianist in New York because he did not like the attention that accompanied public performances. He retorted, "Fools' names and faces are seen in public places."

Quincy Bass also consumed his share of bourbon, and he would slap on Old Spice aftershave on his way out the door to mask the reek of alcohol. Unlike Mr. Newman, Mr. Bass' drinking made him somber and withdrawn. I don't think I ever saw him have much of a good time. He was rather analytical, caught up in the intellectual side of things.

Lalita seemed to be a little closer to him than Melba or I. Mr. Bass was trying to teach her how to drive while vacationing in Daytona Beach where you could drive on the hard-packed sand. Lalita was doing fine there but became hesitant to make a turn as they approached softer sand. She warned

Mr. Bass, but he insisted that it would not be a problem. No such luck. They got stuck and had to be towed.

I once approached Mr. Bass to help me with a poem I had written. The fifth-grade assignment was to compose a verse about our home. I had worked on it for quite a while, but I thought with his mastery of the language, he might be able to suggest some improvements. When he read it, I heard one of his rare laughs. "Eduardo, I think it's great, you don't need my help!" It was so amusing to him that he often repeated it to his friends:

I live in a house, which is very old
In the summer it's very hot
And in the winter it's very cold.
This is the saddest story
That I have ever told.

Mr. Newman and Mr. Bass had hired help, Alma and Cleve, to take care of their historic home on Auburn Avenue, which had been one of the first in Cincinnati to be built away from the river. It still bore an identification plaque above the front door from the fire department. In the old days you had to buy fire protection, and the sign signified you were a registered customer in good standing. I always wondered if they would really let your home burn if you had not paid the bill.

Cleve was a tall, kind, old man from Alabama with a deep Southern drawl. Since I had a thick Cuban accent, we never understood each other very well. But that didn't stop us from trying to talk, and he would laugh with a high-pitched yelp, a shrill "hee hee hee hee," which would make me laugh even though we were both clueless about most of our conversation.

Since the house was located in an urban neighborhood, there was not much of a yard, no front lawn and the narrow, deep backyard was a steep downhill slope and rather overgrown. Cleve would show up about mid-morning and sweep the sidewalk. After lunch he would help Alma do the dishes as she prepared the evening meal. Then they both dipped into the bourbon and diluted it with water in the hope that Mr. Newman would not notice how much had been consumed. By mid-afternoon, Cleve let the dog outside to relieve herself before he and Alma headed home.

Puppy Dog was a dachshund with a terrible disposition. She would eat only boiled kidney cut in thin slices. She was usually corralled in the kitchen but would occasionally be allowed in the living room, where she would spin and chase a two-tone rubber ball with a bell inside for hours. She had even worn a threadbare spot in the expensive Oriental rug with her compulsive habit.

One year during an Easter party, Mr. Bass let the dog out of the kitchen to stop her barking. When Puppy Dog entered the living room, Mr. Newman asked that no one try to pet her, because she was a biter. One of the guests, a former student of Mr. Bass who was now a local TV piano celebrity, insisted that he had a way with animals, but Mr. Newman emphatically requested that he leave the dog alone. The guest persisted and reached under the couch to pet her—and was bitten severely on the hand. Mr. Newman was furious. He called the man an idiot, said he got exactly what he deserved, and that he really should leave. Mr. Bass was more sympathetic, and brought him a towel to bandage his hand, suggesting he should have it looked at by a doctor. Even though this animal was clearly neurotic, Herbert, Quincy and Alma all spoiled Puppy Dog. We kids could hardly go near her.

Alma had worked for Mr. Newman and Mr. Bass for more than thirty years. She did only what she wanted to do, knowing "Mr. Herbert" was never going to interfere; they had too deep a friendship. Alma was not particularly thrilled about having three children suddenly show up and add to her daily chores. Although she continued to wash our bed sheets, it was not long before she taught us how to operate the washing machine and iron our own clothes.

One humiliating moment for me was when Alma discovered that I still occasionally wet my bed. It was something I was terribly embarrassed about. I used to avoid staying overnight at friends' houses and even used to worry that it would prevent me from ever getting married. Alma earned my trust by never mentioning it. In return, I kept quiet about the bourbon bottles.

Alma never squealed about the time I almost set the house on fire. In an effort to make the girls' bedroom warmer on a cold winter day, I had started a fire in their fireplace. Unfortunately, I did not even know there was a flue, which Cleve had closed. He had also stuffed the chimney chock full of old crumpled newspaper to prevent drafts. As the smoke from the choked fire billowed out of control, I frantically stomped on the burning embers swirling in the room to prevent the Oriental rugs from catching on fire. Alma heard all the commotion and rushed upstairs to see what the problem was. She found me putting out the last bits of the burnt paper.

"I hope you plan on cleaning up this mess, Eduardo."

"Yes, ma'am, I will," I stammered.

"You might want to open a window to vent the room," she kindly suggested. And that was the last she ever said about it.

Mr. Newman and Mr. Bass had many friends who were kind and generous to us. We often were invited to fun activities including the zoo and baseball games at Crosley Field. My favorite place was Coney Island, an amusement park on the east side of Cincinnati with the largest recirculating swimming pool in the world. They also bought us gifts and always included us in their family gatherings and parties.

Of all of their friends, no one took a greater interest in us than Kendrick and Eleanor Bell and Eleanor Allen. All three had regularly visited Varadero Beach and had known us since we were small children. Mr. and Mrs. Bell became very involved in looking after us, and we spent most weekends with them. The Bells did not have children of their own. They did have a sweet, beautiful Dalmatian named Tosca, who occasionally insisted on sharing my bed.

Mr. Bell would pick us up on Friday afternoons and bring us back to Herbert's house on Sunday evenings. We enjoyed staying at their contemporary home with a big yard in Hyde Park on the east side of Cincinnati. School friends who lived nearby came over to play, and we had a lot more freedom. Mr. and Mrs. Bell took us to movies, swimming and to visit their friends who had children our ages. They even let us have parties and invite classmates to stay overnight.

In the winter, Mr. Bell and I would build model airplanes together and in the summer, I helped him with the yard work by cutting the grass. We also terraced their sloping backyard by building dry-stacked fieldstone retaining walls. Mr. Bell was fascinating and well informed about many things. He had always been an artist and was an elementary teacher as a young man. He kept track of the latest financial reports on Wall Street to personally manage their investment portfolio and could readily recite detailed information about any publicly traded company.

Eleanor Bell was the music critic for the *Cincinnati Post*, and we would occasionally accompany her to the opera and the symphony. The Bells even took us on a few weekend trips, once to Chicago. Mrs. Bell was petite and

Enjoying an evening at home with Eleanor Bell

energetic with a very positive personality and full of fun. I would often tease her, and she would in jest make a Jackie Gleason fist, saying, "One of these days, Eduardo…!"

Eleanor Allen, a childless widow, was a dear friend of Mr. Newman and Mr. Bass, and was also very close to the Bells. She had been the dean of women at the University of Cincinnati College-Conservatory of Music and would often travel with us. Mrs. Allen was a lovely person—tall, articulate and beautiful—with a great sense of humor and very clever with words and timing. Mrs. Allen had a wonderful singing voice and, like Mr. Bass, had spurned contracts to perform in New York, although she had worked at RCA Victor in the Big Apple and had recorded "My Old Kentucky Home," one of Mr. Newman's favorite songs.

We were surrounded by music professionals, but ironically, not one of us three had a shred of musical talent. Mr. Newman had measured our hands to see whether any of us had the potential to be a pianist, and Lalita and I had the required eight-key spread. But any hopes for me were quickly dashed after only a couple of lessons. Even though I loved music, I was tone deaf. Mr. Newman would cringe with an exaggerated grin whenever we three children would join the group to sing carols at Christmas parties.

Our guardians did their best to celebrate the holidays. Mr. Newman insisted on putting up a large, natural tree. Mr. Bass would play the piano, and we would sing carols late into the night as we decorated. "Joy to the World" was my favorite. But there was not much joy in my heart as I tried to fall asleep and thought about the hollowness of the holidays without my parents.

I was often startled in the middle of the night by the mournful chime of the grandfather clock and would lie awake in my bed, staring at the ceiling. The silence of the untrampled midnight snowfall made the world feel so isolated and lonely.

Home was so very far away.

EDWARD J. NEYRA

THE CINCINNATI POST & TIMES-STAR

Three Cubans Who 'Invaded' C

Learning to eat strange foods, speak a new language, endure cold weather have not always been easy for Eduardo and Melba Neyra and their cousin, Lalita Diaz, but they are enjoying Cincinnati's Christmas sights and sounds, like the lights and trees on Fountain Square and, above, the creche in Lytle Park. From "Cascabel, cascabel, lindo cascabel," it was easy to switch to "Heengle bells, heengle bells, heengle all the way." (Photos by Byron Schumaker.)

Melba, Lalita and Eduardo read letters they left behind 11 months ago. A fire far cry from their life in Cuba which water skiing and loafing on the beac Ursula Academy. Eduardo is at St. Ursu them to adjust to their life here. The of their parents.

Our plight was featured in the holiday edition of the local weekly news magazine.

CUBA LOST AND FOUND

The Cincinnati Post and Times-Star
All Week Magazine — TV Programs, News
DEC. 22, 1962
Page 15

First Christmas in the United States

This year many thousands of Cubans' will be spending their first Christmas away from home. Many children, like the three shown on Fountain Square, have been sent here by parents whose grief at separation is assuaged by the knowledge that their children are living in a land of freedom and of plenty.

---More on Page 15

and the friends welcome, but a
swimming and
alita attend St.
nds have helped
ncinnati friends

Torn at the Seams

*O*ver time, I was awakened less often by the clanging of the clocks in the stately old home on Auburn Avenue. As contact with my parents dwindled, and I became more accustomed to the inconveniences of living in a new land, I embraced my American life with zest. Even though I tried to fit in by straightening my naturally curly hair by sleeping with one of Melba's old stockings over my head, I never encountered even a hint of discrimination in my friendly and generous new world. In fact, I was considered "exotic," since there were very few Hispanics in the Midwest in the early 1960s, which was a unique advantage in making new friends.

After my initial struggle with the language, I quickly picked up English and rarely spoke Spanish, not even with Melba or Lalita. I thrived under the stability and security that our new guardians offered and the excellent education I received. By the time I was fifteen, I had succeeded in casting off any vestiges of my Cuban culture. I proudly had transformed myself into a fiercely independent American teenager, knowing the responsibility for my future rested fully on my own shoulders.

Meanwhile, Tía Elena had kept us sporadically informed from Venezuela of any progress on our parents getting out of Cuba. Her son-in-law, Arturo, had been diligently working on a solution. Arturo was a friend of Carlos Andrés Pérez, who had been the Minister of the Interior and would later become President of Venezuela. The influential politician helped expedite the immigration process. Tragically, Lalita's father, Tío Ramón, had died of a heart attack in Cantel before he could leave Cuba with the rest of my family.

After fleeing Castro's Communist grip and losing everything they owned, Mami, Papi, Abuela and Tía Gladys lived in Caracas with Pocha and Arturo for nearly a year while the necessary residency requirements were fulfilled, and the immigration paperwork was processed to allow them legal entry into the United States. After struggling for three years to escape, my family finally arrived in Cincinnati on April 4, 1965, with little more than the clothes on their back.

Herbert and Quincy as well as Mr. and Mrs. Bell came with us to the airport to greet my family. We anxiously awaited their flight on that cool spring day from the rooftop observation deck, hoping to catch a glimpse of them as they deplaned. Papi was wearing a dark suit, and the three women were all dressed in black, still mourning the death of Tío Ramón as they shuffled toward the gate. They had aged considerably and Tía Gladys had lost a lot of weight. They all looked somber, stressed and scared, and we hurried down the steps to meet them at the doorway into the terminal. As

I hugged my mother and father, I could only imagine the grief they had suffered and the relief they must have felt to finally see us again.

We headed back to Auburn Avenue for an awkward reunion. I helped with the refreshments and found myself ill at ease with my own parents, especially my father. How was I supposed to behave? Would it offend Papi if I showed my fondness for my guardians?

Quincy tried to facilitate conversation with his fluent Spanish, attempting to fill our parents in on our lives over the past three years. But it was a stiff and contrived gathering. I was guarded among my own family, who had descended like a dark cloud, suddenly casting shadows of doubt on my optimistic American life.

Jesús, our former neighbor from Varadero, had offered my family temporary refuge at his home in Dayton. Melba and I both continued to live with Mr. Newman and Mr. Bass, although we visited my parents on weekends. Mr. Bell drove us to Dayton on Fridays, and Jesús drove us back to Auburn Avenue on Sundays so I could finish out the school year at the Academy. But Lalita remained in Dayton with her mother and was excused from the last few weeks of her junior year in high school. Lalita had been devastated by the death of her father and I think reuniting with her mother had heightened the feeling of loss and the need for the security and comfort of Tía Gladys.

I felt terrible about Lalita's struggle to reconcile Tío Ramón's death. But after having adapted to my American life, I had a much different reaction to the reunion. I struggled with ambivalent thoughts about being together again, conflicted by a tormenting obligation to remain loyal to my family which had been painfully fractured by the Revolution; to stay devoted to my parents, who had sacrificed so much and endured so many years of being apart to ensure a better life for me. Years later, I would wonder at times whether the security of living in America had been worth the chasm created by our long separation.

I had shrugged off my Latin identity in the interim, not even admitting I was from Cuba. Cincinnati was now my home. My life was secure, stable and predictable. The idea of reuniting with my family fanned the flames of my old insecurities. Where would we live? Where would I go to school? Would I have to let go of my friends in Cincinnati, and would I be able to make new ones in Dayton? Melba and I had grown up, no longer in need of parental care and supervision, and I dreaded being uprooted once more. Inside, I juggled guilt, shame and unspoken anger.

It took a while to feel comfortable around my family again. We were all different people now, causing a great deal of unease, and I am sure my parents were also dealing with the burden of guilt. We had never discussed our feelings before the departure at *La Pecera*, and we never discussed our reactions after the reunion in Cincinnati. It was all too painful. As a teenager, I tottered like a man on stilts, straddling two cultures and trying hard not to fall.

Melba was the only person who knew and understood the conflicts I concealed, but she visited Dayton less and less. She had graduated from high school with honors the year before and had been working at a bank while still living with Mr. Newman and Mr. Bass. She also had plans to marry that summer—but had not yet told our parents. Melba wanted to give them some time to adjust before breaking the news. But this was April, and the wedding was to take place that August.

As the weeks passed and we spent more time together, I began to rebuild my relationship with my parents. So one Saturday afternoon at Jesús' home in Dayton, I sat down with them and delicately explained that Melba would not be living with them. She was planning to be married and was concerned they were not ready to hear the news.

Fortunately, my parents had a great capacity to be understanding. They accepted the fact that the children they had sent away in 1962 had changed and grown up. My father was philosophical. He said he was proud of the things that we had achieved and how well we had adjusted. Papi also knew Melba had always done the right thing, although he did want to know what I thought of her fiancé.

"Is he a good man?" Papi wanted to know.

"Yes, Barry is very kind to Melba and is like a brother to me. They have been dating for a year, and we have done a lot of things together. He is also smart—a chemical engineer," I fondly replied.

Papi was relieved by my positive response. "I am not surprised. Melba is very intelligent. She has always been a good daughter."

Mami was quiet as she absorbed the fact that we would never again all live together as a family, but still she approved.

I was elated that I had helped Melba get past the hurdle of talking to my parents. When I got back to Cincinnati and told her that Mami and Papi had given her their blessing, she was ecstatic. I was so happy for the two of them. Barry was sensitive to Cuban tradition, especially since my parents barely knew him, so just three weeks later, I was the translator when Barry formally asked my father for Melba's hand in marriage. I loved to kid him that he had needed my assistance in popping the big question.

Although my parents considered remaining in Dayton, I did not want to move; the thought of starting over in a new city and losing all my friends resurrected painful memories. Fortunately, my family concluded that another uprooting would be too traumatic.

Ultimately, they decided that it did not really matter where they settled as long as we were all together. So on a cool spring day, my parents, Tía Gladys, Lalita and Abuela moved to a house in Norwood, a proud, working class city within Cincinnati that was supported predominantly by a large General Motors plant that made Camaros. Our new home was in limbo—technically condemned, riddled with roaches and scheduled to be torn down at any time to make way for the new interstate highway being built—but the rent was only fifty dollars per month.

Fellow Cubans and generous American friends helped us furnish the modest home with a motley collection of used hand-me-downs, which Mami and Tía Gladys skillfully patched, painted or reupholstered. Even though nothing matched, the house was always kept spotless by my industrious aunt and mother.

But I did not move in with them right away. I had to finish eighth grade at St. Ursula, and my transportation there was already arranged from Auburn Avenue. In addition to placing a priority on my education, my parents also unselfishly acknowledged that Mr. Newman and Mr. Bass needed time to adjust to losing "their" children. Perhaps Mami and Papi knew that I needed time too, so I stayed with our guardians until late June, when they left for a summer vacation in Europe.

Living with my parents and my extended family was an enormous challenge. Every aspect of my life was altered—as many adjustments were required as when we had first arrived in Cincinnati. Even the smells of Cuban cooking spices now aroused in me a sense of agitation. Also, the only language spoken at home was Spanish—except when Lalita and I did not want anyone else to know what we were talking about.

Everyone in the family worked to save money to help other relatives who were not as fortunate. Some they assisted by financing their transportation out of Cuba, so over time our small home was crowded with relatives all talking loudly at the same time, making it difficult to concentrate while trying to study at home.

Forty years later, I have a different perspective. Those noisy conversations that irritated me back then have been filtered through time; now, I hear the compassion in their voices. The animated dialogue reflected the family's frustrations about how the Revolution had fractured our lives and their concerns about helping the others still left behind in Cuba. When I look at old photos, I see faces in pain—pain emanating from deep in their soul.

They were tough people with impenetrable loyalty in spite of their complex personalities. In their turbulent and transplanted world of conflicting cultures, they never swerved from looking after family and always putting the needs of their children first. I see it clearly now, but as a teenager, I felt the expanded horizons of my American world constricted by the Cuban culture I had discarded.

Cuba in Cincinnati

My parents, much to my embarrassment, refused to speak English. In their minds, their stay in the United States was temporary and returning to Cuba was always the goal, so there was no need to learn the language. Maybe it was also an issue of cultural loyalty and resistance to change. But their narrow-mindedness frustrated me.

Papi's reluctance to assimilate tested my patience the first time I took him to a grocery store. Once inside, he refused to use a cart. I guess he thought that would be violating some kind of manly Latin image. Back home in Cuba, in much smaller food markets, the shopkeeper would fetch the items from your list and place them on the counter while haggling over the price. I finally had to insist on using a cart.

When it was finally time to check out, I chose a lane with a very pretty young cashier, figuring it was a great opportunity to meet her. My father placed every single item on the belt one at a time, insisting that each was too expensive, wanting to negotiate the price. I was extremely embarrassed to have to translate my father's unreasonable demands to the cute clerk.

I told my father that she did not have the authority to change prices and they were not negotiable. "Everyone negotiates," he replied. He intended to give me a lesson on international bargaining techniques in the middle of an American supermarket.

Still hoping to make a good impression with the clerk, I assured her, "Don't worry, I will tell him in Spanish to put back anything that he doesn't want to pay at the price marked." Although I was able to convince my father to buy the items, and they were finally run through the cash register, I never did get her phone number.

My father was the most inflexible of all of the adults in my family and the most difficult to get along with. He wanted things done his way and on his schedule. He could not stand to be late and was obsessive about being punctual or even obnoxiously early to work, to the doctor—wherever he was expected. Except, of course, for making it home on time for dinner.

Papi was very proud and rather intolerant once he had his mind made up. Although often inconsistent, he was rarely argumentative or confrontational—but he certainly knew how to hold a grudge. He had been spoiled by being the youngest in a family of four siblings, and Mami had continued the pattern of giving in to him and enabling his idiosyncrasies throughout their marriage.

I am sure Papi was frustrated that he had been torn from his world and everything that was meaningful to him. This new situation seemed overwhelming, and he was incapable of changing it. His natural intolerance for ambiguity was only intensified by a feeling of helplessness. Papi occasionally medicated his depression by taking a few too many drinks. As a teenager, I had no empathy for his inability to adapt to a situation similar to what I had experienced.

Not only was I my father's translator, but I was also his driver. He sometimes had me take him to a nearby delicatessen where he and his American friends met in the back room after hours on the weekends for a few drinks. Although no one completely understood the other, alcohol helped as a universal language. Later Papi would call me for a ride back home. I would always confirm if he was really ready to go, but when I arrived, he would often insist on hanging out longer with his buddies. One night, I waited outside for over an hour because I did not want to get stuck translating their bull session. I went back in twice to remind him it was time to go. I was especially frustrated because I had made plans with a date. Finally, I became so aggravated I just left.

He walked the mile home and arrived shaking in anger. "How dare you ever leave me like that again!"

I shot back as I walked out the door, "You have two choices. Be ready to go when you call me to pick you up, or walk home." It was the first time that I had ever stood up to my father. Our confrontation was brief but represented a major shift in our relationship. I wanted him to realize that I would no longer accept his inconsiderate behavior.

Although Papi could be difficult to deal with at times, he was a hard worker, like all the members of our family. He worked in restaurant kitchens and on construction crews. He often took weekend jobs painting houses and doing general maintenance, and I was his assistant. Papi always paid me fairly, as if I were his partner, and was never critical.

One weekend we had been at work for about twelve hours trying to finish painting the inside of an office. Tired and rushed, I tripped and accidentally spilled a can of paint all over the hardwood floor. My father hurried to help me clean it up. Then he asked gently, "Do you know why that happened?" And without even waiting for me to come up with an answer, he said softly, "Because when you paint, you spill paint." I appreciated his calm acceptance. Although he was a perfectionist, he was oddly philosophical when it came to reprimands and very affectionate with me.

He was also an avid reader, and he stayed current with global events. Every evening he read journals, and he also listened to the news programs in Spanish on a world band radio I had given him as a Christmas gift to whet his insatiable appetite for political and international information. Over the years, his astute and prescient comments often astounded me. After the gold standard was dropped in the 1970s, he wisely predicted that now was the time to buy gold. Its price skyrocketed. And long before the fall of the U.S.S.R., he had commented, "I don't know why *los Americanos* worry about the Soviet Union. It will collapse. In the long run, the much greater concern is China—because of its population and size, its natural resources, but most importantly, its cultural tradition of strategic, long-term planning."

The women in my family had an amazing work ethic. I witnessed my mother putting in endless hours as a seamstress without a word of complaint. She would be on the bus by five each morning—never late—

regardless of sleet or snow, with her bagged lunch in hand, not returning home until after six in the evening.

Mami and Tía Gladys would then work in the kitchen to prepare dinner and clean up. Afterward they would sew together every night until past midnight, sometimes later, bending over the garments that Mami had brought home to earn extra money. I watched this day after day, week after week, year after year. They had no vacations and little recreation or entertainment. Their "fun" was the weekly venture to downtown historic Findlay Market to buy meat and produce from the outdoor vendors just like they used to in Cárdenas. They also liked to attend the Spanish Mass at a downtown church and would then continue to sew throughout the rest of the weekend.

Of all of our family members, no one was more outspoken than Tía Gladys. She was also the only adult who ever put any effort into learning English. Unfortunately, she never held back on passionately expressing her opinions in either language.

If I came home early, she would comment that I did not know how to have a good time. Why was I back so soon? If I came home late, she would inquire about my owl-like tendencies and remark that nothing good ever happened late at night. If I bought something that was of low quality, I was cheap. If I bought something more expensive, I was extravagant. It was a constant, no-win duel. Once, in frustration, I tape recorded one of our unpleasant sparring sessions and then saved the tape for just the right moment. I knew playing it back would make her very angry. But I wanted her to hear how domineering and confrontational she sounded. I was also determined to combat her efforts to make me submissive.

Despite our confrontations, I loved her very much, and I know she loved me. I was her godson, and she was always very generous with me, especially when we lived in Cuba. I can still remember Tía Gladys unloading my first bicycle from the back of her car. It was bright green with white pinstripes and rainbow streamers trailing from the tips of the handlebars.

In later years, we became very close. I respected and admired her strong character, great passion and intense drive. During the last month of her life in the hospital, I visited her regularly. We talked about old times as I lay next to her in the hospital bed. She displayed enormous courage and kept her faith, calmly reading Psalm 23 from a notecard on her nightstand during the battle with cancer, which finally took her life on May 5, 1991.

My friend and ally was always my cousin Lalita, who I really thought of as a sister. I don't recall us ever bickering much. By now her life had evolved, too; she had found a career as an X-ray technician at Good Samaritan Hospital in Cincinnati. We pretty much did our own things but always supported and cared for each other. She knew that I constantly battled with her strong-willed mother, and I was aware that she tolerated my father's self-absorption. We helped each other to get along in a home environment that was ideal for no one.

Lalita often let me borrow her car, a red Corvair, especially when I was hoping to impress a date, since our family car was an old pea green Ford station wagon with a broken heater and no reverse gear. In return for Lalita's kindness, I kept her car clean and running. Keeping a Corvair operating was no easy task.

Abuela was from the old school—tough, stubborn and judgmental.

Fortunately, I was her favorite grandchild, so she was always on my side no matter what. I was known for receiving a few speeding tickets, but my grandmother truly believed that the police simply had it in for me. Abuela was quite funny. She had no reservations about scrutinizing any girl I brought home as a friend or a date. She would stare them down and always had some disparaging comment. No one was ever quite good enough for her grandson.

Although I loved Abuela very much, when she became terminally ill in 1977, I did not want to visit her in intensive care. Mami, fearing Abuela's death was imminent, begged me to come. Abuela kept asking for me, but I was not ready to confront the possibility of losing her. When I arrived, Mami prodded me into her room. After much resistance, I finally obeyed.

As I approached her bedside with all of the tubes and medicating IVs, my eighty-seven-year-old grandmother opened her eyes. When she saw me, she slowly removed her oxygen mask, smiled and in a weak voice whispered, "I am glad you came. I have been waiting because I wanted to say good-bye." Then she squeezed my hand and died.

I tried to avoid the intense pain of losing Abuela and flashed back to funny things I could remember about her. I used to tease her by speaking in English. She would start laughing and sometimes get angry but always wanted to know what I was saying, or she would tell us in frustration to speak Spanish or leave the room. Lalita would just laugh. During the summer of 1969, when Neil Armstrong landed on the moon, Abuela was certain that it never really took place. "Propaganda!" she sneered. "Just a government stunt to manipulate the masses."

One of Abuela's blessings before she died was being able to see one of her sons, Alberto, who had remained in Cuba but had been granted a temporary visa to come and visit Abuela during her illness. I will never forget his ecstatic reaction to the displays of produce at the grocery store when Mami and Tía Gladys took him shopping. He wept when he witnessed the huge variety and abundance of apples. He fell to his knees crying, "My dear sisters, apples are my favorite fruit, and I haven't eaten one in decades!" Mami and Tia bought him a large bag, which he contentedly devoured during his two-week stay.

It seemed like the entrance to our home was a revolving door open to friends and relatives whom my family had helped flee Cuba. As a teenager I was often annoyed by the noise, crowdedness and lack of privacy. I also resented anyone that took advantage of my family's generosity, like Tía Gisela's husband, José.

José was a self-centered, unlikable character. I had learned that he had been busy drinking and womanizing in Spain with the money my family was sending Gisela and him. I could not stop thinking of the long hours I had watched Mami and Tía Gladys stitch away to afford José the luxury of spending afternoons at a bar in Madrid while waiting for their U.S. visas to arrive.

Gisela was very protective and in denial about her alcoholic, abusive and philandering husband. José contracted tuberculosis and I was responsible as the family driver and translator to accompany him to the doctor for treatment—a regular occurrence that often took many hours in the evenings or sometimes an entire Saturday morning. Normally I would have been happy to help a sick relative, but I had such strong dislike for this manipulative man. During these long sessions, I found it difficult to contain my growing anger as he played the victim, ranting on with his opinionated, chauvinistic attitude. It was a happy day for me when they finally moved out.

Eddie No Home

It was a challenge to be Ed during the day and Eduardo at night. Being at home was like wearing a heavy overcoat I had long since outgrown, but which I could not shrug off. My Midwestern preppy look must have seemed out of place once I crossed the threshold of my Latin residence, but to me, everyone else was out of place. I wanted very much to fit into this new culture that I had learned to call home, not to be pulled back into the one that had become so foreign.

My friends had nicknamed me "Eddie-No-Home," because whenever a friend called, that was my parents' standard response.

"Is Eduardo there?"

"Eddie no home."

"Excuse me, ma'am, do you know where I might reach him?"

"Eddie no home."

"Do you know when he'll be back?"

"Eddie no home."

In the fall of 1965, I had enrolled myself at Purcell, a Marianist Catholic high school in Cincinnati, with money I had saved from my summer job. I participated in sports and had an active social life—both provided a good diversion and a handy excuse to be absent from home.

In high school, the athletic director would sometimes set up wrestling matches with opponents in much higher weight classes, both as a test for me and a lesson for the other students about intensity. I never lost a match. I also set several intramural records at my high school. The athletic director called me "Blue Boy" for the many first-place ribbons I had won in various events, while the track coach's nickname for me was "Cuban Flash." Coach Shands helped me get tuition assistance so that I could continue to play sports. Although my parents were never able to attend any of my sporting events, I always appreciated it when my sister Melba and her husband, Barry, did.

My passion became American football. Although I was very fast and hit hard, I did not have the vision nor the hand-eye coordination needed for a starting position. Being a practice player and sitting on the bench was not for me. Besides, by the time I was a junior, varsity summer practice interfered with my job. Disappointed, I finally gave it up.

Although I enjoyed the camaraderie with my teammates, most of my social circle was outside of sports. Friends came easily for me, but I was never one to go along with the crowd. If I thought something was foolish or disrespectful I would walk away and just not participate. I was never judgmental, but smoking, drinking and drugs were not for me. I enjoyed dating and talking to the girls—the awkwardness that I witnessed among some friends was something I did not experience. Sometimes, I even went on double dates with Melba and Barry.

One of the guys I hung out with most was my neighbor, Pat. He attended a different high school, but we developed a great friendship. We first met when my family moved to Norwood. On that clear spring day, the windows were opened to let the gentle breeze vent the musty interior. While sweeping the hardwood floor, I was singing the Elvis Presley hit, "Crying in the Chapel."

Someone laughed loudly and shouted, "Who in the hell is trying to sing?"

"Your new neighbor," I responded. "If you don't want to hear it, come over and help or else close your window."

Within minutes Pat and his dad, Charley, who liked to be called Smiley, came over and introduced themselves. Smiley was very friendly and had also sung *a capella* for a local barbershop quartet. He quickly advised me not to waste any money on singing lessons.

From that day forward, Pat and I were friends for life. We did a lot of cruising in high school, mostly in the summers when we worked construction together. During the school year, we were both very involved in sports at our different high schools so we did not spend as much time together, except during Christmas and spring breaks.

One day, Pat's father brought home a 1957 green Plymouth, a car a friend had given away although it was still in good shape. We were only fifteen, yet for whatever reason, we figured we could drive it across a nearby field. Pat had recently seen a demolition derby on television and decided that it would be fun to plow into the trees, pretending they were competing cars. I questioned Pat before we started, but he said the car had been given to him so wrecking it would be no big deal. Within an hour of taking turns driving, there was not an undamaged square inch anywhere.

When Pat's dad saw the car parked in front of the house, Smiley was no longer smiling. It did not take long for him to figure out what happened once he followed the tire tracks to the nearby trees that were scarred and smeared with green paint.

"Are you two nuts?" he screamed.

I jumped in and tried to shoulder some of the blame. When I attempted to justify our actions, I could not think of the word "demolition," so I explained that I, too, had participated in the "wrecky derby."

As angry as Smiley was, he could not help cracking up. "What in the hell do you know? You're calling it a wrecky derby. You don't even know how to speak English! You boys are crazy!" Once Pat saw his father crack a smile, he knew we were somewhat off the hook.

In spite of my occasional lapses in judgment, my parents always treated me with respect and trust since I rarely gave them much reason for concern. Their only requests were to let them know how late I would be out so that they would not worry, and to alert them when I got home by knocking on their bedroom door, regardless of the hour.

I only violated this rule once. Pat and I had gone out for the evening and ran into a couple of young ladies whom Pat knew from his high school. It was early spring, and the Ohio River had been on the news because of its flooding. So the four of us decided to drive across town to watch the river crest under the light of the full moon.

The girls had put together a plan so they could stay out all night, and Pat and I were not about to admit that we had to be home. It was almost sunrise when we decided to stop by the local all-night hangout to get something to eat. Unfortunately, our homes were en route to the restaurant.

As we drove down our street, Pat thought he saw my family's car coming toward us. I told him not to bother me. I was busy in the back seat, and besides, no one at my house could drive. Pat insisted and I retorted, "You must be getting tired and seeing things!"

At the next red light, Pat informed me that the car was catching up; in fact, it was about to pull up right next to us. I rose from the back, and sure enough, there was Pat's father at the wheel and my father riding shotgun.

I rolled down my window and poked my head out. Pat's father asked, "Are you boys coming home tonight?"

"Yes," we answered in unison. "We're just on our way," Pat added.

"It doesn't look like it," Smiley replied sarcastically.

After quickly dropping off the girls and arriving back home, our fathers were waiting on the front porch, smoking cigarettes. All that was said was, "We're glad you're okay. Give us a call next time so we won't worry."

Pat's exposure to Latin culture left a lifelong impact. He marveled at how our family would argue heatedly, and then five minutes later hug each other goodnight. Impressed by the passion and love that we shared, he admitted he was especially envious of the affection I received from my father, as he had never seen a father who actually kissed his teenage son.

At the time, I did not always welcome my father's displays of affection, and I still harbored a grudge for the way he had treated my mother. It also seemed he made no effort to try to adjust to his new home. Papi often complained about Cincinnati—he called it a cold, two-bit cow town that folded its sidewalks after dark—but I did not fully appreciate all that he gave up to keep Cincinnati our home. He believed the language barrier prevented him from starting a business and frequently let it be known that he would have preferred to live in Miami, where the weather was warm and people spoke Spanish.

My parents worked hard to try to provide for us and had a great desire to help, but I had paid for my own education, entertainment, transportation and clothing since I was fifteen years old. There would be no financial assistance from them, and I knew I would have to make it on my own, a huge motivator that fueled the ambitious fire inside me. I had an unwavering conviction that I would be successful. I could feel it. I only needed to figure out how.

My mentor, Martin J. Byrnes, Sr.

Memories of My Mentor

I met Martin J. Byrnes, Sr. when I was just thirteen years old. I did not know it then, but he would become my mentor, providing me with both the opportunity and the guidance to succeed. His son, Marty Jr., was my friend at St. Ursula Academy. As a frequent weekend guest at their home, I enjoyed the Byrnes' big family of five children. The place was always buzzing with fun and excitement as Marty's brother and sisters also invited friends over.

Marty Jr. and I would spend hours exploring the woods of their one-hundred-acre property, taking turns at the wheel of his Desert Rat, a two-seater 1960s version of an ATV. We plowed over fallen tree trunks and up and down rocky creek banks. Our favorite challenge was to see if we could get stuck in the muck, but we never did. Mr. Byrnes often found the mud-spattered Rat parked on the driveway and would shake his head with both disgust and affection.

I visited the Byrnes' home so frequently that they fondly referred to me as their Cuban brother. By the time Marty Jr. and I were freshmen at Purcell High School, Mr. Byrnes offered me a job at his asphalt maintenance company for the summer.

I worked long hours, seven days a week, and the summers went by fast during the next few years. It was not uncommon for my social life to begin late, after already putting in a twelve-hour day in the hot sun. I kept my work clothes in the trunk of my car and would go right from my date back to the job, sometimes sleeping for only a couple of hours on the office couch. But I was never late for work, not once.

I established a reputation for being extremely hard working and productive. Mr. Byrnes knew that my projects rarely received any complaints and they were always the most profitable. In 1968, when I was eighteen, Mr. Byrnes approached me midway through the season and asked, "Do you think you are ready to be responsible for running the jobs?"

As the foreman, I received a set percentage of the gross income less the cost of labor, which I controlled. The company paid for materials, equipment and other business expenses and kept the balance as profit, a mutually beneficial arrangement. While still a high school student, I earned more during the summer months than a college graduate would in a year. After we agreed upon the details of my new job and pay, Mr. Byrnes brought up the idea of someday selling me the business and helping to finance the purchase. I told him I was very interested, but we would have to wait until I saved enough money for the down payment and was legally old enough to sign a contract.

During these years, Mr. Byrnes became like a surrogate father to me. During the summer after work, I often stopped by his home for a short visit. On the way in, I would grab his chilled martini pitcher from the glass-front refrigerator to top off his drink, always garnished with two olives.

He would welcome me from his swivel recliner on the large, enclosed back porch, shouting "*¿Como estas, Cubano?*" in fractured Spanish. Mr. Byrnes had visited Cuba many times back in the 1950s and would reminisce about late nights long ago in Havana with his buddies. He had befriended President Fulgencio Batista and his lieutenants. I am sure these relationships were the key to his lucrative contracts to pave large sections of Cuba's Central Highway that crossed the island.

Although Mr. Byrnes had an unspoken policy of not discussing business when relaxing at home, nonetheless he was always willing to help me sort through challenging work issues. Mr. Byrnes patiently dealt with pressing business problems in a composed way. His wisdom certainly had a calming effect on my personality, especially on days when my temper would flare over problems on the job site. He loved to paraphrase Proverbs 14:17, reminding me that "anger is the tool of a fool!"

A compassionate, engaging man with a great sense of humor and a ready compliment, Mr. Byrnes was very religious, and he went out of his way to help anyone he could. I once overheard him on the phone trying to find a place for a homeless person who had been written about in the previous Sunday's newspaper. He also had a subtle way of sharing his faith. "Let's stop for a visit," he would casually suggest when passing a Catholic church. Removing his hat at the entrance, he would bow his head and spend a few minutes in silent prayer before returning to the car.

Every so often, Mr. Byrnes invited me to lunch. He liked to visit small neighborhood cafés all over town, especially those known for their homemade soup. During these lunches I met other successful businessmen, including Harold Schott, a Midwestern industrialist who was a close friend and business associate of Mr. Byrnes. He would proudly boast to Mr. Schott about me, "This kid is you forty years ago!"

A couple of years into our agreement, Mr. Byrnes' bookkeeper brought to his attention how much money his young protégé was actually making. One day at lunch, Mr. Byrnes approached me about the possibility of reducing my percentage. Mustering every shred of my courage, I said, "Mr. Byrnes, we made a deal, and I'd like for both of us to honor it."

He looked at me with great admiration, almost as if it had been a test of my resolve, and he laughed, "I told the bookkeeper that would be your answer!" The issue never came up again.

In 1971, once I turned twenty-one, I decided it was my turn to take Mr. Byrnes to lunch. I wanted to discuss the conversation we had had years earlier about me buying the business. But he told me that he was not ready to sell the company.

I was disappointed but determined. "I respect your decision, but please know that I am going to start my own business. I will help train your new manager and will also make sure that all your equipment is ready to go."

"Good luck, Eduardo. I know you will be successful," he offered.

Mr. Byrnes and I always had a great rapport, and even though I no longer worked for him, nothing changed between us. Mr. Byrnes knew no enemies, and I remained close with him and the rest of his family.

I soon started setting up my new enterprise. Mr. Bell helped me design a company logo and letterhead. Equipment and material suppliers began contacting Mr. Byrnes for references on me. Of course he was full of praise in his responses.

About two months later, Mr. Byrnes called me and suggested that before I purchased any equipment, we should get together. Looking forward to seeing him, I learned at that lunch that he was now ready to sell his business. I was elated that my hunch was correct. It seemed that he always placed hurdles before me to make sure that *I* was sure. By now, he knew I was serious about striking out on my own.

"Great!" I responded. "Do you know how much you want for the business?"

"Not really. Why don't you put together an offer? Take all the time you need," Mr. Byrnes added.

I spent several sleepless nights trying to figure out how to put the deal together. I had saved quite a bit of money over the years, but deciding to part with it was difficult. I pulled together an agreement on my own without any legal counsel, working through several different scenarios, hoping to build some safeguards into my proposal.

Once I had exhausted every possibility, I called Mr. Byrnes to let him know that I had prepared my offer and was ready to discuss it. He told me to mail it to his home, and he would set up a meeting at his lawyer's office the following week.

I arrived in my three-piece suit with my shoes shining like mirrors. Mr. Byrnes could not help smiling—he noticed that I had cut myself shaving in several places.

"What happened to your face?" he teased.

"I used a new blade for a close shave," I admitted.

"Are you sure it wasn't a machete?" Mr. Byrnes joked, and then added some fatherly advice, "You might want to slow down and take short strokes next time."

Mr. Byrnes then informed his attorney that we were meeting so he could sell his company to me. This was news to his legal confidant, who wanted to know if we had discussed any details.

"Yes," Mr. Byrnes responded. "I have the agreement in my pocket."

His attorney appeared stunned. "Why haven't I known about this?"

Unfazed, Mr. Byrnes pulled the envelope out of his suit coat and asked to borrow my pen. He unfolded the contracts and without even reading a word, scribbled his signature on both. He handed one to me, and gave the other to his lawyer to file.

Prepared for some tough negotiating, I sat speechless, amazed that the whole deal had taken less than five minutes. I had wasted a lot of energy on mentally rehearsing rebuttals to objections that never materialized.

Mr. Byrnes invited me to lunch. I was still in shock over the speed of the transaction, and wondered if I had indeed made a good deal. I asked him, "Did I pay too much?"

"You will never know, my boy!" he said and smiled enigmatically.

It took me years to realize that the "sale" was nearly a gift.

Mr. Byrnes continued his support even after I bought his company. He would frequently call me with leads for new accounts. I continued to seek his advice as my business grew, and the following year he helped me finance expansion plans. Once, I became frustrated by a situation where a supplier that I represented had threatened to bypass me and sell directly to an account I had acquired for them. Mr. Byrnes volunteered to drive me to the vendor's office three hundred miles away. His experience and industry clout resolved the situation immediately.

Mr. Byrnes taught me many things, but the one I practiced most often was, "Don't belabor the small decisions but always sleep on the irreversible ones." Marty was also a man who practiced the early-to-bed, early-to-rise adage. "Things always look better in the morning after a good night's rest." And my favorite, "Make friends, not enemies, for you never know who will be the guard at the gate."

I always maintained a close relationship with Mr. Byrnes as well as his family. Several years after I had bought the business, Marty Jr. called to let me know that his father had suffered a heart attack while he and his wife, Marge, were vacationing at their Florida condo. I called and talked to Mrs. Byrnes, who assured me Marty was doing well. Although I wanted to visit him immediately, she insisted I wait until he returned home to Cincinnati.

Although I respected her request, my instincts warned me that I might never see Mr. Byrnes again. Martin J. Byrnes, Sr. died the very next day at the young age of sixty-two.

It was painful and lonely for me to think about life without my mentor. I truly believe that without Mr. Byrnes' friendship and guidance, my life would have turned out much differently. I have always wished he had lived longer to witness the success for which he helped lay the foundation. But I am certain that from his heavenly vantage point he is aware of it—and of my immense love and gratitude.

On My Own

I had enrolled at the University of Cincinnati back in the fall of 1969 while working for Mr. Byrnes, taking business classes toward a degree in industrial management and marketing. Although I did well at the university, I never really felt much a part of it. I had considered a partial swimming and track scholarship, but I was not willing to make the commitment since it would have taken too much time from work. Although my income exceeded that of all my friends, so did my responsibilities. I was living an adult life—which created distance between us.

My college years between 1969 and 1973 were a difficult period in U.S. history—the Vietnam War was at its peak, tearing America apart. I had witnessed the destructive consequences of social unrest as a child in Cuba, and the idea of large crowds waving signs and shouting at guards with guns carried no appeal for me. Peace movement demonstrations became more and more violent, and the Kent State killings by the National

Guard on May 4, 1970, were especially disturbing. The quarter ended early that spring due to the shootings, and we all received full credit without even taking final exams.

From my viewpoint, the theme "Make love, not war" was merely an excuse for many young people to sink to new levels of disrespect. Students came to class shoeless and with unkempt hair. Many girls wore very short, frayed jeans with cutout side panels, the large gaps woven with shoelaces—and no underwear. So there I was, wearing tailor-made suits, going to class with hippies.

I felt out of place not only at school but also at home. Even though Tía Gladys, Lalita and Abuela had recently moved out, and I was now living with just my parents, I hungered for independence. I knew it was time to get a place of my own and found the perfect one-bedroom apartment with a rooftop pool and a distant skyline view of downtown Cincinnati. Best of all, it was only ten minutes from my office as well as the university. I started buying things for my new place and storing them at home. I am sure Mami was putting the pieces of the puzzle together, but we never talked about it.

One evening while I was assembling a bookcase in the dark, dingy basement, she came down the stairs and asked what I was up to. It was only then that I summoned the courage to tell her I was moving out. Her eyes filled with tears, and for a moment she said nothing. She gave me a kiss and told me, "I am so proud of you. After all of the time we've spent apart, I hoped this day would never come, but I knew it was inevitable."

Although I was not harnessed by my parents living at home, their constant presence represented the Cuban culture that was suffocating to me. I craved peace and solitude. But I felt that old guilt from once again abandoning my mother—leaving her alone with my father in a marriage that seemed to me like a one-way relationship. I gave Mami a hug and a kiss and said, "*Te quiero*, I love you." I wanted to tell her so much more, but I did not know how to express it without breaking down emotionally; I regretfully let that opportunity slip away.

It was nearly midnight, and she asked me how much longer I would be working. "For quite a while longer," I said. "I plan to finish this tonight." There was a brief silence.

"*Hasta mañana*, Until tomorrow," she sighed. Then she went upstairs to bed.

I knew even then that my new apartment was more than a place to live. It represented my freedom, and I finally had quiet privacy. Although I continued to visit my parents at least once a week and helped them with anything they needed, I was relieved to escape the confining clutches of what had long since become a foreign culture.

The Thrill Seekers

I had little interest in joining a college fraternity, but my friend Jim kept recruiting me. "We have a great group of guys. You'd fit right in."

"I'm not participating in any of that hazing nonsense!" I objected.

"So why don't you join at midyear, when there's less emphasis on initiation?" Jim suggested.

I relented. Halfway through my sophomore year I became a member of ΣAE, the Sigma Alpha Epsilon fraternity. It turned out to be a rewarding source of many lifelong friendships—and a lifetime of hair-raising adventures.

One fellow frat brother was Carl. We met during a water fight that involved a mad chase through the fraternity parking lot. Later that evening we pledges had to take "Oscar" downtown and gave him a physical beating on Fountain Square. It was a traditional prank—Oscar was a six-foot male mannequin. The objective was to snag the attention of passers-by until someone called the police. So Carl and I began our friendship by trying to stay out of jail in downtown Cincinnati.

Like me, Carl was fascinated by all physical challenges. It wasn't long before he started including me on his adventurous trips. A group of us would go canoeing, which usually turned into a race to the finish. We went rafting on the Lower New River in West Virginia and even filmed ourselves to see which team best maneuvered the most precarious run through the Class V rapids. When skiing out in Snowbird, Utah, we raced down the steepest, most rugged double-black-diamond slope to see who was first at the lodge. We hiked the Grand Canyon's Boucher Trail in the moonlight, only to realize at dawn that we had walked on a two-foot-wide trail on the very edge of the cliff. The more difficult the terrain, the more we liked it.

One evening before a campsite dinner, Carl broke out of his backpack gifts for each of us—brass grub cups inscribed with the words "Thrill Seekers." The group had grown to eight of us, all intent on adventure: Carl, Jim, Tommy, Randy, Jack, Dave, Jeff and me. Not everyone participated in every trip, so our numbers varied. But the friendship, camaraderie and tall-tale bragging rights remained constant. We had been stared down by eagles, howled at by wolves and had our tents trampled by herds of caribou. But the tales we have told and retold most often are those of our encounters with bears.

The Thrill Seekers had set out to find the mysterious Lost Dutchman Gold Mine in the Superstition Mountains near Apache Junction, Arizona. One night while eating dinner at camp, I peered into the forest, and I spotted a bear.

"Boys, stay calm," I instructed. "There's a bear."

Randy squinted and confirmed, "I see two of them."

"I see three," Tommy chimed in. "Mama Bear, Papa Bear and Baby Bear."

"Make sure we aren't trapped between them and the food," Carl warned.

As the bears moved closer, the Thrill Seekers began to spread out and make noise. Carl darted forward to chase off the beasts. He was the most experienced among our group of city slickers; he already had stood his ground on an earlier trip when a bear had tried to steal his catch of the day. "We can't let them know we represent food," he continued, "or they will keep coming after us."

"That sounds great, Carl. Go get 'em." I headed toward a tree. Carl began to laugh, "Eddie, you may think you're fast, but any bear can outrun and outclimb you, buddy."

After the bears finally moved on, we sealed our food in plastic bags to confine the smell and then hoisted them high on tree branches. When it came time to call it a night, I said, "Boys, I'm not sleeping surrounded by all these bears."

"Don't worry, Eddie," Randy reassured me. "They don't like Cuban meat."

"Well, you might be right, Rojo," our nickname for Randy because of his reddish hair, "But I'm not taking a chance. I'm hiking back to that abandoned shack we passed about a mile ago."

"That's not a bad idea," Rojo responded. "I'll go with you."

Before long I could hear the other Thrill Seekers creeping into the room one by one and spreading out their sleeping bags.

The next morning, I awoke to find that most of my trail-blazing friends already had headed back to our camp for breakfast. I rolled up my sleeping bag and headed down the trail singing a rusty rendition of "What a Wonderful World." Somehow I had the feeling that my buddies were up to something. They would probably hear my singing and try to trick me into thinking that a bear was near. My habit of singing on the trail was well known; one night I had performed a cover of James Brown's "I Feel Good" while dancing around the campfire doing my imitation of the Godfather of Soul. During an attempted spin, I found out hiking boots make lousy dancing shoes when I tripped and fell flat on my backside, almost landing in flames—a pratfall my camping buddies had never let me forget.

Halfway to the camp I began to hear rustling noises in the thick brush lining the trail. Then suddenly came the warning, "Eddie, there's a bear near you!" Ha—and they thought they could fool me!

"Eddie, we are serious! Look to your right!"

I kept walking, not even flinching, convinced that these guys were pulling a prank. But the noise grew closer and louder, and the shouting grew more intense. "Get the gun!" I heard someone say.

It was Tommy's distressed voice that finally convinced me to pay attention: "Eddie, it's not a joke! He's coming right at you!"

My first instinct was to run and climb a tall tree. But Carl had already warned me that was no protection. Suddenly, I caught a glimpse of the large beast behind a thicket. It stood tall on its hind legs in charging position, staring right at me less than fifty feet away.

My buddies desperately tried to distract him by yelling, clapping and firing gunshots as they chased the thousand-pound beast—all except for

Carl, who was filming the entire event! Fortunately, the bear decided I was more trouble than I was worth and shuffled away.

I was swept with relief that my buddies had come to my rescue. Still shaking, I turned to yell at Carl, "But you were more interested in documenting my death than in saving my life!"

"Well," he shot back, "I am in the insurance business. We like evidence."

Another unusual adventure took us to the extreme north. We landed in the tiny town of Deadhorse, Alaska, where we were to meet our guide. The small airport terminal was buzzing with alarming warnings about grizzly bear attacks. We were told about Joe Want, a legendary character who supposedly fended off one of those powerful creatures with a single knife, a small gun and his bare hands—but we should not count on being so lucky. Carl immediately adopted the legend's last name and started calling himself Carl Want.

I showed the guide the large revolver on my hip. He shrugged, "Trust me, that gun you're packing won't do much to a charging grizzly."

"Sure, it will," I countered with a straight face. "See that tall blond guy over there?" I pointed at Carl. "That's my buddy. My plan is that when the bear charges, I shoot my friend. While the bear is busy having him for lunch, I take off running."

The guide warned, "Good luck in the woods—but be careful. You may want to save that last bullet for yourself."

When our week of rafting and fishing was over, the pontoon plane arrived to pick us up, and the pilot docked at the water's edge. The rest of the group had decided to go fishing one last time. But I stayed behind, looking forward to an afternoon nap in the back seat. The pilot dozed in the cockpit while I lounged in the rear, holding the door open with my feet propped on the windowsill. I quickly fell asleep in the clear Alaskan air.

Suddenly I was awakened with a sharp jerk. My eyes popped open to see a bear just a few feet away, gripping the wing and rocking the plane.

"Hey," I yelled.

The pilot barely opened his eyes.

"Look! A bear!" I exclaimed.

"Don't worry. He'll go away."

"Easy for you to say. You're up there protected in the cockpit. I'm back here with the door open and he's close enough to take a bite!"

He calmly assured me, "They're here to fish. Look, there's another one!"

As I closed the door, I looked up just in time to see a bear grab a fish in midair. It was amazing to see how fast the reflexes of this powerful creature were.

Alaska was so wild and beautiful that we returned several times. Our trips there were always full of excitement—and some unexpected surprises. One time Jeff and I were walking on the tundra. It was cold and wet and slow going as our feet fell into the uneven crevasses beneath the surface. It did not take long to wear us out. But Jeff and I got excited as we spotted a light gray object up ahead. The closer we got, the more incredulous we became.

"What do you think it could be?" I asked.

Jeff gasped, "We could be standing where no human has ever set foot—I think this is a mammoth tusk! Let's take it back to camp."

Jeff and I hauled our ancient relic. The other guys could not believe it. There was some argument as to whether it really was a mammoth tusk. So we brought it home and then took it to the natural history museum, where they confirmed that it was indeed authentic.

I suggested that since Carl had been the one who had made all of our trips possible, we should give it to him as a gift of appreciation. I had a walnut display case built with the name of every Thrill Seeker inscribed on a brass plate. Carl was genuinely touched.

Months later I came across an article verifying the mammoth tusk was actually quite valuable. I sent a copy to Carl to remind him it was only on loan and that perhaps it was time for him to send the relic back. He responded, "Eddie, as always, you are reading cheap magazines," and included another article that stated an even greater value.

Pranks were a part of every trip. One night, while Jeff was asleep, I emptied his backpack, placed a huge rock at the very bottom and then repacked it. Days later, Jeff remarked, "I've been eating all of my meals, but my bag doesn't seem to be getting any lighter."

Then he began to rummage through it, hoping a rearrangement would help. When he discovered what made his pack so heavy, he glared at me and said, "You dirty dog."

He held up the jagged chunk of quartz and aimed it at me. I ducked for cover behind a big boulder. Once I heard the rock hit, I figured I was safe and stood up. But I had not counted on it ricocheting off the boulder and hitting me squarely on the head, nearly knocking me out.

On another camping trip, while I was sleeping, Carl placed a tiny pile of caribou dung near my nose to wake me with its potent aroma. To get him back, I got up during the middle of the next night, and stuffed a plastic bag filled with caribou dung in his backpack. Days went by, and it became rather odoriferous. Once he discovered it, I knew he would find a way to get even. I just didn't know how.

That particular adventure to Alaska lasted ten days, during which we neither shaved nor showered. We stunk to high heaven, so on the plane ride home, I did not notice any unusual odors. Exhausted after the ten hour trip home, I dumped my backpack on the kitchen floor, hopped into the shower, fell into bed and went right to sleep. When I awoke hours later and came downstairs, I could not believe the horrible smell. What could that be? There is no way my bag could smell that bad! But it did. Carl had packaged a little of his own dung and put it in my backpack to ferment as a souvenir.

In addition to the silly pranks and the physical demands of our adventures, the Thrill Seekers also managed to have meaningful conversations. The beauty and freedom of the wilderness were relaxing and had a way of bringing us closer to our spiritual side, a side often ignored in the chase for success. One day I spoke of the guilt that I felt as a Catholic, as if my every sin was letting God down.

Carl used a stick to draw a diagram on the ground. On one side was "MAN" representing sin, on the other was "GOD" and holiness. Between the divide he placed a cross as a bridge. "Christ is the only way to God's grace, not thoughts or deeds. We're all sinners," he remarked gently. Carl then handed me a little pamphlet from his backpack. On it was written John 14:6: "Jesus said, 'I am the way, the truth and the life. No man comes to the Father, except through me." My perspective was never the same. Such a huge burden was lifted by understanding the simplicity of grace.

The Thrill Seekers' quests were about far more than just our capacity for risk, physical challenges and creative pranks. They provided a proving ground for our deep friendships. Each of us looked after the other; if someone was in a jam, others would come to his rescue. Although we continued to take memorable adventures over the years, as we married and our families grew, the trips were not as frequent nor as risky as they once were. I will always be grateful to my friend Jim, for not only did he recruit me to join a great fraternity where I forged these lifetime friendships, but he also lent me a helping hand in meeting my wife.

The Thrill Seekers in the wilderness of Alaska

Captivated

I was intrigued by the tall, sophisticated brunette who would arrive early for accounting class. She was always well dressed, poised and polite, with trusting eyes as blue and calm as the warm waters of Varadero. Although we had only exchanged greetings, I felt an immediate connection that I had never experienced before. She exuded a kind, caring and gracious personality, and I was determined to get to know her.

She was always accompanied by a male classmate. I wondered who her companion was. He stood too close for me to approach her but far enough that they did not appear to be dating. I would show up before class started, hoping to talk to her alone, but I never got the chance.

After class we would each go our separate ways, and I never saw her anywhere else on campus. The course finally ended, then came Christmas break. I had not done well and wanted to transfer to a different accounting professor but decided not to, in the hope that I might get a chance to talk to this captivating woman the next quarter. So the first day of the new session I showed up early. But I was crestfallen she was not there, and I had no clue where to find her on such a large campus.

I wondered if my fraternity brother Jim could help me. He had also been in our accounting class, and I asked him if he knew the dark-haired, pretty girl who always sat in the front row.

"I think you mean Lynn Radley. She was also in my statistics class," he explained.

"Can you help me get Lynn's phone number?" I inquired.

"I'm sure I can, she's a Chi Omega, and I know several girls in that sorority," Jim added.

"Please get it for me," I pleaded. "I want to marry her."

"Ed, you're crazy, you don't even know her!" he retorted.

"I know there's something special about her!" I exclaimed.

Ecstatic to finally talk to Lynn on the phone, she had no idea who I was. I tried to jog her memory by telling her I was the good-looking foreign guy who sat in the back of the class. But she still didn't remember me. So we talked about our mutual dislike for the accounting professor. He had the annoying habit of mumbling while facing the chalkboard as he lectured. Our conversation went on for more than two hours, and once I thought she felt comfortable with me, I asked her on a date for that coming weekend.

Lynn's sisters Cindy and Patty served as sentries as I pulled into her driveway. They peered down from the upstairs bedroom window awaiting my arrival with a date escape plan ready in case I did not pass inspection.

"Pretty nice car!" and then, "Hey, he's not bad looking," they reported to Lynn. Apparently I passed their test, and Lynn had no need to feign a sudden illness.

During our dinner at the Lookout House, a romantic restaurant in northern Kentucky, the conversation was seamless and even minor details carried a special significance. After dinner we drove back to her home, and Lynn informed me that she was not allowed to invite anyone in while her parents were traveling in Europe. So we continued to talk for hours on her backyard patio in the damp, cool early spring mist. I was shivering but I didn't want to leave the warmth of her presence, and we talked the night away until nearly daybreak.

After that long evening slipped by so quickly, I was eager to see Lynn again. We soon started dating regularly, and she discovered my intensity about work. The long hours at the job sites and the long distance across town to her home meant I was often apologizing for being late. Lynn always gracefully accepted my delays and later revealed that she vented her frustrations by playing the piano while waiting for me.

We had been dating for nearly a year when Lynn broke the shocking news that she was transferring to the University of South Carolina. Her father was closing his medical practice in Cincinnati, having accepted a position at the Veterans Administration hospital in Columbia, and she was moving there with her family. I was once again haunted by the familiar and painful feeling of separation while kissing her good-bye and fighting back the tears.

It was a struggle to maintain our long-distance relationship. We talked on the phone nearly every day and I visited Lynn as often as I could, but it seemed our time together was always too brief. The following summer, she came to visit me in Cincinnati, and we discussed how hard it was to keep having to say good-bye; our time apart seemed endless. So we went shopping for her ring and decided to get married right after Lynn finished school that coming winter.

We planned a small wedding. Since we lived in two different cities and came from two different cultures, organizing a large event would have been too complicated and stressful. Also, Lynn's father had offered her the choice of a larger wedding or a gift of cash, and after consulting with me, we chose the money.

However, we did manage to make the occasion a memorable celebration and on December 20, 1972, our immediate family joined us in Williamsburg, Virginia. Lynn's mother and father had been married there before he was shipped to Europe during World War II, and it was Mami and Papi's 28th anniversary—both a place and a date with special meaning. The short ceremony was performed at the nearby historic Williamsburg Presbyterian Church, followed by a reception dinner at the Williamsburg Inn. It was the Christmas season, and the colonial town was glowing with festive holiday decorations dusted with a blanket of freshly fallen snow—truly a winter wonderland.

I surprised Lynn with a lit Christmas tree in our hotel room decorated with a silver Wallace ornament engraved with "Our First Christmas." We stayed in Williamsburg a few days after the wedding and toured the historic buildings. In one of the quaint shops, we saw a small BRIO wooden train and tracks. Even though we had no immediate plans to start a family, I thought it would be fun to buy a gift for our first child on our honeymoon. Lynn laughed, "How do you know that we're going to have a boy?"

I confidently replied, "I just know!"

Building the American Dream

Our married life began in my small apartment with nothing more than a few pieces of furniture and an antique Chinese rug that had been in Lynn's family for generations. I was struggling to grow the small business I had purchased from Mr. Byrnes, and invested every dollar of profit back into the company. So we lived very frugally, buying only a kitchen table we found for thirteen dollars in a close-out sale at a discount store.

Unlike typical young married couples, we did not spend much time together. We rarely went out or entertained and did not take vacations, either. I was obsessed with success, often putting in twenty-hour days, sometimes not even bothering to drive home to sleep. But whenever I finally returned, I could always count on one of Lynn's delicious home-cooked meals. I think I could have eaten her chicken à la king every night of the week, it was so good.

Getting used to Lynn's delicious cooking was easy, but getting used to her love for animals was not. She had adopted the neighbor's roaming cats, and I was not thrilled. On the rare occasions I tried to get a full night's rest, Shortstop and Scruffy would pounce on the bed in the dead of the night and awaken me from a deep sleep. I would jump up, with my heart racing as I cursed the little critters. I would then toss and turn trying to get back to sleep as the business concerns of the upcoming day percolated in my mind.

Within less than a year after getting married, we were caught up in one of those ugly turns in the business cycle, and my contracting business was now going through tough times. In the spring of 1973, we lost the city contract which we had depended on for years, long before I had bought the business from Mr. Byrnes. Things were looking bleak. A newlywed, a new business owner with no contracts and no cash flow, I did not want to burden Lynn nor anyone else with my troubles. *Los Neyras no lloran.*

The pride that had been instilled in me as a child had by now penetrated to my inner core; to save face, it was better to conceal fear and camouflage vulnerability than to reveal it. I had learned that in order to survive it was imperative to compartmentalize—master the art of isolating events from their associated emotions. The Revolution had trained me well.

But I also had learned that tough times were temporary. Sure enough, within a year, this setback actually turned into a blessing. It provided the incentive for me to put together an aggressive marketing and sales plan that no longer relied primarily on one major account. By the following year the business had doubled, and the city contract had returned too. The financial difficulty had fueled my fear of failure but also detonated my determination to succeed.

By 1975, my contracting business had grown considerably, and I knew I would have a competitive advantage if we manufactured our own surfacing products. I also believed that we could use our field experience to develop superior materials, so I decided to forge ahead. The crew building the plant were very dedicated employees and worked long hours, often going home past midnight. I would stay even later to do the prep work for the following day. When my loyal crew returned early the next morning, sometimes I would still be hard at it without having realized that another night had gone by. I was so driven by adrenaline that I rarely got more than a few hours' sleep each night. Occasionally I would go home, but more often I would just lie down on the office floor.

I did attempt to take one night off to celebrate Lynn's birthday and surprised her with a new silver Mustang adorned with a bouquet of roses on the roof. We went out to dinner, but my mind was still on the men I had left behind working. Lynn sensed my preoccupation and knew that I was anxious to get back to my project. She graciously suggested I should head back to the plant as soon as we were finished with our meal. Even though I was now married, I was still Eddie-No-Home.

I never gave a thought to how Lynn must have felt—ignored, unappreciated, perhaps at times even unloved. But never once did she complain, nor even inquire when our life would get better. She seemed to take it all in stride. Ironically, her understanding and trust in me added to the pressure I already placed on myself to succeed.

Immediately after our ribbon-cutting ceremony, I began traveling extensively throughout the Midwest to sell our materials. My contracting experience was very helpful, and we became more than just a material supplier, evolving into a sales and marketing consultant to our customers. As the demand for our product grew, we established satellite plants in other regions. Business was booming, and although I did not like being away from home, I enjoyed seeing America and cherished the friends I made across the country.

I traveled constantly, driving from very early in the morning to very late at night, never hesitating to leave home for a three-hundred-mile road trip just to meet a prospect for breakfast. The days ran together, and I hardly knew which city I was in, sometimes renting a motel room only to take a shower. I would listen to the radio as I spent endless hours on the road, windows open, singing along to popular tunes to stay awake. I really identified with the lyrics of Sam Cooke's "A Change Is Gonna Come," covered by Billy Davis and The Fifth Dimension:

I was born by the river in a little tent
Oh and just like the river I've been running ever since…
It's been too hard a-livin' but I'm afraid to die.

Of course I wasn't born by a river or in a tent, but that humble imagery symbolized my eternal restlessness—never satisfied and always running to get somewhere else.

I regularly called the office for updates, especially on the day when payroll was due. Cash flow is always a challenge to any starting or growing business, and we were certainly no exception. I called Jane, my trusted assistant and payroll manager, from a customer's office in Pittsburgh on a late Thursday afternoon. She reminded me, "Paychecks are due tomorrow, and we are 'a little short.'"

"How much do we need?" I asked.

"A lot more than we have," Jane replied.

"Don't worry. I'll be driving back tonight, and tomorrow morning we'll work it out."

The next day I called a couple of past due accounts and told them that I was on my way to pick up a check, since I needed to cover my employees' pay. It was a scene that would be frequently repeated. Somehow we always made it work—but occasionally collections got a little confrontational.

A customer with a substantial overdue account would not take my phone calls at his office, so that evening after dinner I began calling him at home every hour until three in the morning, when the man finally decided to take his phone off the hook. To this day, I still wonder what took him so long. The following morning, I drove straight to his office. I introduced myself to his assistant, who by now knew my name and certainly my voice. She told me that he was not in, although I had caught a glimpse of him sitting at his desk when she had gone back to check.

"When you talk to him, tell him I will wait all day in this lobby, but I will not walk out of here without the money he owes me." I explained, "We did an honest job, and I expect to be paid."

Two hours later, he realized I had no intention of leaving. After not being intimidated by his shouting or his size during a verbal confrontation, he finally released a check, and I walked out with that week's payroll secured.

I appreciated my employees and thought of them as an extended family. They believed in me, and I knew that timely compensation for their hard work was essential to our relationship. The idea of violating that trust was humiliating. I was not about to allow a customer whose payment was past due prevent me from meeting my own payroll responsibility.

However, not all my collection adventures were successful. In one case I had driven across the state, through the night, in blizzard conditions and arrived at a debtor's house before dawn to block his driveway. Unfortunately, during the stakeout I had to make an inopportune bathroom run to a nearby motel. By the time I got back to my post, he had slipped away. I tried to follow his tracks in the fresh snow but lost sight once I got to the main road.

But these confrontations were the exception. In general, we had great relationships and open communications with our customers, and I was always cooperative when a contractor conveyed a genuine pledge to pay a bill as soon as he was able. All I required was honesty and integrity.

It seemed as if the challenges never ceased. Once I jumped from the second floor trying to catch a fleeing employee who had threatened to reveal proprietary information. Another time I was at an industry convention and would not allow a former customer to leave an elevator. He had stolen a piece of our equipment and also owed us a great deal of money for materials. I held my forearm to his throat until the police arrived.

The rush of business combat intoxicated me. I craved the risk, the pressure of meeting deadlines, the duel of wits and the empowerment of making decisions—I loved it all. I was so grateful to have my own company and stopped by a church every day on my way to work to thank God. No matter how difficult a situation seemed, I had complete faith in finding a solution. I visualized success and focused solely on that goal.

One financial ace I always kept in the back of my mind was our antique Chinese rug. Mr. Newman had collected Oriental rugs, and I knew the best dealer in town. One day I took our heirloom to Mr. Markarian to have it appraised. He offered a price that could easily cover my weekly payroll. I told him I really did not want to sell it, but that I would let him know. "That is a rare rug in great shape, and we will buy it any time you wish," he assured me.

A few weeks later things got really tight once again, and I was frightened that this might be our last week in business. I swallowed my pride and headed downtown to sell the rug to my trusted dealer. But first I had to consult Lynn.

"I have no problem parting with the rug, as long as we give my sisters and brother their fair share of the money," she explained.

I protested, "If we do that, I can't cover payroll!"

"I am sorry," she said. "But it belonged to my family, and that is only right."

I was frustrated by her uncooperative response. It was hard for me to accept she did not seem to understand the severity of my situation. But fortunately, our marriage, the business and the rug were saved when a delinquent customer came through with a payment at the last minute yet again.

The rug was then permanently taken off the emergency list. It became the centerpiece of our home's entrance, where it was much more than a beautiful accessory, but a symbol of survival and of our many years of struggle.

Treading Water

One day a competitor came by for a visit and jokingly asked the receptionist "Is there more than one Ed Neyra?"

She laughed and shook her head, "No, why do you ask?"

"Perhaps he has a double—for no matter where I go, he has already been there!"

To me, selling was a matter of statistics. The more prospects you contacted and the more often you visited them, the greater the odds of making a sale. Although I had a very focused strategic plan, it really all boiled down to persistence. It was that simple. You just had to have an unwavering determination to get up early every single morning, work a long day and drive many miles.

My pace never slowed. But periodically I became so exhausted that I would crash for a couple of days and do nothing but sleep—not even eat—waking only to go to the bathroom. It was a complete physical and mental shutdown. Afterward, it usually took me a couple of days to ramp up my adrenaline and regain my intensity.

Lynn, on the other hand, had always been a calm personality. But in trying to accommodate my hectic schedule, she found herself repeatedly run-down and exhausted. After a couple of visits to Dr. Wright, who also happened to be Lynn's godfather and a close family friend, he assessed the root of her problem: me.

Lynn had witnessed her father's orthopedic practice demanding long hours and had been supportive of what I was trying to accomplish. So I was taken by surprise when three years into our marriage she expressed that our relationship was not going well and suggested that perhaps we should seek professional counseling. I completely opposed the idea and refused to even discuss it. "People don't need to talk about their relationships," I declared. "They either make them work or they end them."

I remained obsessively focused on pursuing the American Dream and ignored all the signs of our stressed marriage. But even Mami noticed that we were going through a rough time. My mother adored Lynn and remarked pointedly, "If you and Lynn have any problems getting along, don't come crying here, for we already know who is at fault."

I didn't realize it then, but I was blinded by my myopic view of success and by my self-image as an exemplary provider. I had an insatiable need to achieve, to justify the sacrifices my mother had made in sending me away. Besides, I was the self-appointed family *don*—I felt compelled to financially help out many in my large extended clan.

In spite of my protests, Lynn and Dr. Wright collaborated on a scheme to get me to show up for a physical. Lynn, coming from a medical family, believed in preventive medicine. I, on the other hand, detested the idea of seeing a doctor for any reason. Her real purpose was to seek his input on my stubbornness as much as on my physical well-being.

After several months, I finally gave in to the idea of a checkup, even though I felt fine and had never been sick. The doctor gave me a thorough examination and found me in perfect health. But during the course of the lengthy exam, I thought that his interrogation went far beyond the physical. He wanted to know about my background, work habits and business interests. This was one nosy doctor.

Several years later, I finally learned from Lynn about the conspiracy and his ultimate advice to her: "You have two options: divorce or adapt. He is the most determined and intense young man I have ever met. I don't think he will ever change."

Although my hectic pace continued to put a strain on our relationship, life slowly began to improve financially. After six years of marriage, we finally were able to move to a bigger apartment, purchase some real furniture and begin to think about starting a family. The following year, in May of 1979, Nathan Radley Neyra arrived. Our seven-pound, nine-ounce perfect baby boy was born. It was a natural birth, and if it had been up to me to deliver, we would still be childless. But Lynn was determined to go without any medication and an hour later was walking to the bathroom unescorted. The nurse caught her, and she got a severe scolding.

We had gone through the childbirth training classes together; fortunately, fathers were now encouraged to be more involved in their child's delivery. I nearly passed out, but recovered to proudly cut the umbilical cord of my newborn son. Lynn's father had warned her beforehand that the staff might be more involved in propping me up than in delivering the baby. But Lynn was not about to let me off. God, was I glad. She always seemed to direct me on the right path, even when I resisted. This was truly the experience of a lifetime, a pivotal moment which transformed my priorities. Suddenly life was not all about work. I stopped long enough to realize how much I loved Lynn, how much I loved my baby boy and how blessed I was to have them both.

The following sunny spring day, on my way to visit Lynn and Nathan back at the hospital, "Danny's Song" by Anne Murray came on the radio. These lyrics became so powerful—I started to cry as they reminded me that indeed I was "the lucky one."

When I arrived Nathan was nursing contentedly, and life seemed to take on a new, expanded meaning. Someone else's welfare was now far more important to me than my own. Lynn and I spent the day like most proud new parents, going gaga over our newborn son. We were excited to hear that we would be allowed to take him home the following morning, Mother's Day.

Lynn's parents still lived out of town, so we decided to surprise Mami and Papi with a visit on our way home from the hospital. I anticipated my mother's reaction to seeing her first grandson. On the way, I could not help thinking about the pain she had endured in her life—the uncertainties of her marriage, the death of my brother Alfredito, the trauma of parting from Melba and me. I thought of all that she had lost and lived without. I remembered the look in her eyes the day we said good-bye at *La Pecera* in Havana over seventeen years earlier. But in Lynn's arms was a brand new baby boy who I knew would instantly eradicate all of her pain from the past. It was difficult to hold back my tears of joy, pride and gratitude. I could not wait for Mami to hold Nathan!

Sure enough, as we entered my parents' home, Mami's face lit up. She was so enraptured that for a moment she seemed to go a little crazy. "*Ay, qué bello! Mira qué grande es!* Oh, how beautiful! Look at how big he is!"

Once she was able to calm herself enough to settle on the couch, I leaned over to gently place my precious bundle in her arms, kissed her on her forehead and proudly whispered, "Happy Mother's Day!"

Living the Dream

Our life now seemed more complete. Although I continued to work long hours, I tried to cut back on traveling in order to spend time with my son. Nathan went through a rough infancy, suffering from colic, crying constantly from the pain and rarely sleeping through the night. Lynn had pratically become a zombie trying to care for him. I would often come home and lay Nathan upon my chest for a nap. I guess the warmth helped relax his constricted stomach, and both he and Lynn would get a few hours of much needed rest. Even though Nathan struggled with colic, it was so much fun to watch my baby develop into an energetic little boy, who walked at nine months and had such a delightful giggle when we would wrestle on the floor.

He was also extremely inquisitive. Less than three years after Nathan was born, Lynn became pregnant with our second child. She told him that a little brother was on the way and growing in her belly. One day, while driving him to Tumble Bees, Nathan was fascinated by Lynn's baby bump and wanted to know how this all happened. Lynn explained in toddler's terms the basics of how the father's seed fertilizes the mother's egg. Lynn was watching him in the rearview mirror and saw his concentrated expression. After a pause, Nathan then blurted out loud, "Do you have to be lying down to do that?" Lynn almost wrecked the car!

Our second son, Justin Radley Neyra, arrived in April of 1982, with a full head of hair and feet kicking. It was just as thrilling the second time around, and I proudly cut his umbilical cord with great joy. At eight pounds, three ounces, he was another long, lanky and healthy boy, just like his older brother. "This one is going to be about six foot five," predicted the doctor, as he placed Justin in Lynn's arms.

When we got him home, Nathan was so excited—he wanted to hold him, talk to him and constantly be at his side. Nathan and Justin had an inseparable bond from that very first day, although Nathan did ask if we could send Justin back after a week of hearing him cry. "No, he is ours to keep," chuckled Lynn.

Mami and Papi were always ready to spend time with their grandchildren, and Lynn and I sometimes welcomed a break. Our favorite brief escape was to drop them off with my parents on Sunday mornings while we enjoyed a peaceful brunch at a nearby restaurant.

Even though Mami still did not speak English, she thought Lynn was a great mom and was respectful of Lynn's way of caring for her sons, so she always asked questions to make sure she was doing things the way the boys were used to at home. And I was a willing translator between the two considerate mothers.

By the early 1980s my businesses were doing well and Lynn and I could now build the home of our dreams. In 1983, we learned of a lot for sale in the village of Indian Hill, a pristine Cincinnati suburb. Nearly two-thirds of the village's vast acreage of lush forest and farmland were greenbelt areas permanently protected from future development.

I fell in love with the privacy of a country setting on a five-acre lot located on a cul-de-sac. The woods were filled with wildlife, and the one-acre pond, bordered with cattails, was the home of mallards, geese and sunbathing turtles. I was enamored with the idea of living peacefully with the herd of deer that strolled by, the blue heron that fished daily in the lake and even an occasional fox or a coyote. It was not exactly Varadero Beach, but I thought it was the ideal Midwestern compromise.

Lynn, on the other hand, had serious reservations. She feared the danger of our little boys playing near a pond. As a child, she had fallen into one and had to be rescued by her older brother, Tom—who to this day jokingly reminds her that without him, she would be long gone.

We postponed our decision to purchase the property and went to Hilton Head for the month of September with our two preschool age sons. Now that I had two sons, I had developed the habit of taking vacations, although I took advantage of being on the East Coast by visiting customers and prospects in that area during the week.

While on vacation, Lynn suggested that perhaps we could fill in the pond. I appreciated her cooperative spirit, but I was not interested in pursuing that costly option. I was determined to have water within view for its calming effect on my restlessness—my own little speck of Varadero.

I was actually more concerned about the dangers of the swimming pool we were planning to build than the pond. "The pond is filled with critters, and its darkness is intimidating to a child. The edges have a gentle slope, and the water is cold—not welcoming. Besides, it will be in plain view from the house. You never let the boys leave your sight, and it won't be long before they are old enough to be past that threat anyway," I reasoned with Lynn.

Lynn relented, so while walking the shores of the Atlantic, we decided to buy the property as soon as we returned home. But it was too late—the lot had been sold while we were gone. Lynn, always the consoling, philosophical anchor, seemed to take it all in stride. "I guess it was just not meant to be," she said. I wished I could be more like her. Frustrated and disappointed, I tried to negotiate with the new owners and made them a generous offer through my friend Jeff, an attorney. But they would not budge, so I reluctantly continued my hunt for another building site.

Months later, the phone rang late at night. It was Jeff. "Do you still want to buy a lot in Indian Hill?" he asked.

"Of course," I answered emphatically, "Where is it? I would like to see it." I had been tracking every piece of land for sale, and nothing had interested me.

"You don't need to look at it, Eddie," Jeff insisted.

"What do you mean? I am not going to buy a piece of property I have not seen."

Jeff laughed. "It's the lot you wanted! The new owners have decided not to build on the site and are ready to sell the land now, but close in six months to defer capital gains tax. It's going to take you that long to design the house anyway. So if you want it, it's yours. Think about it," he concluded. "Let me know tomorrow."

"I don't need until tomorrow! My offer is still good—but tell them, not another dime."

Life is Beautiful

*b*uilding a new home can be traumatic and full of conflict for most couples But for Lynn and me, it was pleasurable. We already had stood the test of building our first home, a four-bedroom two-story colonial in Loveland, a small town on the northeast side of Cincinnati. Lynn and I had very similar ideas and also respected each other's area of expertise. As an artist, she had talent for choosing colors and adding extra interior touches, while I was experienced in construction and knowledgeable about building materials. We both enjoyed the challenges of designing a workable floor plan.

The architect, a ΣAE fraternity brother, drafted a blueprint for us. I had always been interested in architecture and became very involved in the design of our traditional red brick Georgian home, which had a formal decor with the privacy of divided rooms—along with an adjoining kitchen and family room where we could build a fire and all hang out together. We also added all the amenities for our active lifestyle: lighted tennis courts, a heated swimming pool, a hot tub and a pool house in the middle of it all, fully equipped for family fun.

As the general contractor, I was usually at the homesite before dawn, preparing and reviewing the daily to-do list. A few hours later, I would head to my office at the manufacturing plant, returning to the building site every afternoon to inspect the progress; occasionally I would even stay there all day to help.

Nathan was five and Justin was two when we began building in September 1984. Romping around the site, they would climb on the construction equipment and soon knew each by name. Nathan carried his own tool belt and claimed he was a carpenter. They used to pretend they were construction workers, often "borrowing" tools and getting scolded. But it never made any difference—the next day they would do it all over again.

Justin was my bulldozer buddy, riding with me as I cleared land and shaped the yard. He would fall asleep, secure in the crook of my arm, but as soon as I turned off the diesel engine and the noise and vibration ceased, Justin would start howling.

For the most part, the construction went according to plan. However, the first winter snowstorm dumped eight inches of snow on the second floor before the house was under roof. Lynn and I spent an entire Sunday afternoon shoveling snow off the subflooring so it would not warp. As progress continued, I set my sights on celebrating the next Thanksgiving in our new home, even though the house would not be completely finished.

We had scheduled moving day for Tuesday, two days prior to the big feast, but it was a miserable, rainy fall day. The movers arrived, and Lynn and I headed to our new home with both of our cars packed. But by late afternoon, we were still waiting for the truck. I had to track down the moving company owner at home to find out what was going on.

He explained that the moving crew parked the truck loaded with our furniture back at the warehouse because it had been a long day due to the rain delays.

"It's going to be even longer, because I expect everything delivered today as we originally agreed." I was determined to stay on schedule.

"Are you sure?" he asked. "It will be very late by the time the crew makes it back to your house."

"I don't care if takes all night. I am having Thanksgiving dinner in my new home. Send the truck!" I demanded.

The accommodating owner rounded up his men, and they finally arrived late that night. The rain had only gotten worse—it was pouring. Everything coming into the house had to be covered with plastic. The movers could hardly see in the dark, and the wood floors were getting soaked. We struggled until three in the morning to unload all the furniture.

The following day Lynn and I proceeded to put the room together, and she began cooking for the big feast.

Unfortunately, my parents could not join us, since they had moved to Miami. However, Lynn's parents, who had now moved back to Cincinnati after her father had retired, joined us for an intimate and memorable Thanksgiving celebration. I had a lot to be thankful for.

But it would take an additional six months to finish the rest of the interior, including the wood trim. The most time-consuming part of the project was the handcrafted walnut panels for the library—a peaceful, elegant space with a fireplace and large windows framing a clear view of the pond, strategically designed to be my sanctuary. The living room was used to store lumber, and the family room was the woodworking shop. Our conversations competed with the high-pitched grinding of the power saw, and occasionally our meals were peppered with a little dust. But it was all worth it.

When our home was finally completed during the summer of 1986, I had a housewarming get-together including Lynn's parents, Melba, Lalita and also the Bells and Mrs. Allen. By now Eleanor Bell required a wheelchair, and I gladly built a temporary ramp into the house so she could join us. I wished that Mr. Newman and Mr. Bass could have seen our beautiful home, but both had died a few years earlier. I proudly raised an American flag in the front yard and dedicated the new flagpole to Mr. Newman, with a brass memorial plaque at its base. I was so grateful for what they had all done for me.

I felt so blessed, and it seemed I had the perfect house, the perfect family. Nathan and Justin now had plenty of space to burn their endless energy. The boys and I fished in the pond and spent hours in the pool, and Lynn's parents would join us to play baseball in the side yard.

Our grounds were so private that I was able to take outdoor showers, so delightfully back-to-nature and reminiscent of the beach at Varadero. The boys and I even took to relieving ourselves outside. "A dozen bathrooms in this house and the three of you are out there peeing like puppies," Lynn remarked one day, shaking her head.

"You ought to try it," I suggested.

"No, thanks," she laughed.

Often on the weekends, I would get up early with our two energetic boys and take them out to do something adventurous while Lynn caught up on her much-needed sleep. After a hearty breakfast at our local diner, we would tromp through the woods to our favorite creek to skip rocks on the shallow water. I loved being with my sons and always made sure we did fun things together. On cold mornings we would visit the fire station to check out the shiny red trucks and all the rescue gear, or the police station where the officers allowed us to sit behind bars after taking a sobriety test.

As the boys grew, every season was crowded with sports—hockey, baseball, basketball, football, soccer, swimming, wrestling, skiing, tennis. It did not matter which sport, Lynn and I never missed an event. Over the years, we were also fortunate to be able to take memorable vacations together. Nathan earned his scuba diving certification in Hawaii where he awakened at six in the morning to swim with sea turtles, coming out of the frigid water with purple lips, shivering in his wetsuit. Since Justin was still too young, Nathan wanted me to join him in the underwater training, but there was no way I would swim in the cold Pacific. A few years later, Justin and I were certified in the warm Caribbean waters in Cayman, and he was quite proud that his score was higher than mine on the written test.

Since my parents now lived in Florida, they would come north to stay with us for a couple of weeks in the summer to spend time with their grandchildren. It was heartwarming to see Mami and Papi communicate with the boys in Spanglish. I was not always sure that they understood each other, but you could certainly feel the love between them. Mami and Papi would sit in the shade next to the pool to watch the boys swim and play "Shark and Minnows" for hours. The boys would take their grandparents for a ride in the golf cart around the grounds to show them all their secret hiding places. Mami was petrified by their most dangerous stunt—climbing on the roof of the pool house, pretending they were scaling a mountain.

But Nathan's and Justin's most mischievous prank was to steal Papi's cigarettes so he would stop smoking. They would take the pack and hold it under running water to drown his smokes. Papi would find the soggy cigarettes and just laugh.

Life indeed seemed beautiful.

My parents with Lynn, our sons and me at our home in Indian Hill

Tear Down the Wall

Even though I spent time with my family, I still had an insatiable desire for success. Life never seemed to move fast enough. In addition to owning the contracting and manufacturing companies, my restlessness, curiosity and ambition drove me to buy many different enterprises, ranging from advertising to eyewear to real estate development. I always believed I could push farther and do more; collecting and accumulating seemed to be how I established my sense of worth.

The travel business was an industry I knew little about, other than my frequent road trips, but that did not stop me from buying a large travel agency. The company was well staffed and had operated successfully for nearly half a century, so there wasn't much needed beyond a touch of strategic planning and common sense.

The agency's slogan was "Managing travel everywhere under the sun," which fueled Lynn's and my desire to see other parts of the world. We were fortunate that Lynn's parents enjoyed looking after Nathan and Justin, and we felt very comfortable leaving a retired doctor and a nurse in charge of our children. As agency owners, we received exceptional service and were always assigned deluxe rooms, the best tables in restaurants and cars chauffeured by the most gracious and knowledgeable guides.

Except in London, where we had a young guide who simply would not stop talking. He barraged Lynn and me with a constant monologue about British history, the royal family, the museums and the importance of every landmark. He continued on and on with endless details, including what color dress the queen wore to a certain ball and why—never even allowing us a chance to absorb his previous factoid.

I did not know how to stop his chatter without hurting his feelings. Finally my annoyance rose to anger, and I blurted out, "Steven, when it comes to history, I think Henry Ford said it best."

"Oh, really? How is that?" he wondered.

"History is more or less bunk," I sharply quoted.

Needless to say, the young man was shaken and became much more subdued throughout the rest of our tour. Ironically, I would later uncover my family's own history and understand just how riveting that journey can be. My rude and arrogant response was merely a sign of my irritation and ignorance.

Our most memorable travel adventure, however, was to witness the fall of the Berlin Wall in November 1989. We were returning to the United States from the Soviet Union on a flight from Leningrad via Frankfurt, Germany. The day before our departure, we learned that the Wall was coming down and that the whole world was watching. I contacted the agency, and they arranged a detour from Frankfurt to West Berlin. In a mad rush, we boarded our flight for a rendezvous with history.

But before we could depart the Soviet Union, I had to get through Customs. In my suitcase, layered between my clothing, were two dozen unframed oil paintings I had purchased in St. Petersburg and Moscow. Our tour guide cautioned me that I could never get them out of the country, so after filling out my departure papers, I decided not to declare the art. I was excited to daringly test the accuracy of the Russian scanning machine, and I breezed right through and smuggled the canvasses right out under the nose of the Communist government. So much for their engineering—even as a boy in Cuba I never had thought much of it.

Wilhelm, our English-speaking German guide and driver, was at the airport in West Berlin to welcome us.

"Please take us someplace where we can buy a hammer and a chisel," I instructed.

He responded with a befuddled look and a thick German accent. "It's past midnight, sir, and there is no place open. There is neither a single hammer nor chisel to be found anywhere in the country. Everyone has been chipping away at the Wall, since it is coming down in the morning."

"We have a flight in just a few hours, Wilhelm, and I am not going home without a piece of this Wall," I stated firmly. "Let's go to the center of the gathering by the Brandenburg Gates."

Wilhelm clearly wanted to be a proper host but already appeared unnerved. "That will be difficult. Every news organization in the world has a transmitting trailer parked nearby and the streets are full of military equipment and personnel."

"I lived through a revolution and have dodged a few bullets, Wilhelm. I can certainly make my way through the crowd," I boasted.

As we approached the area, I could not believe the sea of humanity, shoulder to shoulder and shuffling like snails. We drove as close as we could, parked the car and began walking and weaving among the unyielding mob.

It was like a scene from a movie with a cast of tens of thousands. Cameras were everywhere and high-voltage flood lights lit up the night sky. Dignitaries were being interviewed, everything televised for the world to see. People had climbed atop the Wall to display the German flag, joyously anticipating a nation united once again. They chipped away the west side of the concrete wall to take home souvenirs, while guards with loaded guns stood in total control of the east side, but there were no crowds there and nothing to celebrate except the end of a regime that failed. The police on both sides seemed equally tense, concerned they might be rendered powerless by the tremendous throngs of people awaiting the collapse of the divisive Wall.

I could not stop thinking about the term "Iron Curtain." Although merely a metaphor, it had such a chilling, eternal sound—cold, immobile and impenetrable. Cuba, unlike Berlin, had never been divided by any manmade structure. There was nothing to tear down; only the endless beautiful blue ocean surrounded us. There was nothing to remove and represent a change, nothing on which to vent our anger. Taking down this Wall would be therapeutic. Conclusive. Victorious. I was determined to be a part of it.

"Wilhelm, we have to find tools." I needed him to translate my urgent request. "Please ask that man with the red hat if he wants to sell his when he is finished."

The man responded with a firm no. "He had a friend bring them from Italy, and he has to give them back," Wilhelm explained.

I persisted, "I am sure that in the midst of all these people frantically pounding on the concrete, someone will sell us a hammer and chisel."

Poor Wilhelm. He kept trying, but no one wanted to part with their tools. Everyone was laboring intently to break loose even a tiny piece. I scanned the area for a nice set—one with a big hammer, more like a small sledge, because I could see that the German-engineered, steel-reinforced divider of humanity was going to be almost impossible to penetrate. I spotted another prospect and signaled Wilhelm to translate my request. But the answer was the same.

"*Nein.* These tools are not for sale."

"Wilhelm, please inform the gentleman that I have traveled thousands of miles to take home a piece of history."

The man kept working, but he didn't say no. That was encouraging.

"I will wait," I told him.

By now I could tell that my friendly persistence was having an effect. I pulled out my Deutschmarks and peeled bills from my palm and placed them in his. Laughing, I kept repeating the gesture until the man's smile widened. That's how I knew when to stop. To seal the deal, I placed one more bill on his hand, and then said, "*Danke schoen,* Thank you," as I took possession of the tools.

I immediately started hammering away. I pounded on different areas, hoping to find a tender spot that would shatter easily, but no luck. After a couple hours, I had finally chiseled free several pieces. Lynn stockpiled and guarded our treasure while scanning the wall for graffiti—she thought the colors made a more artistic and desirable keepsake.

Worn out, we carried our historic relics to store in the trunk of the car. As we turned a corner, there was a vendor, selling nothing other than pieces of the Berlin Wall, just like souvenirs at a theme park.

"I wished we had spotted him a few hours ago!" I groaned.

Lynn consoled me, "But his doesn't have any graffiti."

Chipping away at the Berlin Wall

Behind the Iron Curtain

I wondered what it would be like to stand on the east side of the Berlin Wall. Would it look, smell, feel any different? For some strange reason, I wanted to confront the confinements of Communism that I had fled so many years before, but this time with the comparative safety of being able to return to freedom at will. I felt that exhilarating rush of risk that always drove me forward, but it was tempered by anxieties from the past.

Lynn, as usual, was unperturbed. But then, how could she know? I don't think anyone born in the United States could imagine the fear, insecurity and powerlessness that surrounded your life when you lived under constant government surveillance. I had been half-heartedly hoping that she would nix the idea of crossing over, so I would have someone else to blame for missing the experience of a lifetime. I was certainly not about to reveal my own trepidation.

The tall wall was merely a foot thick but separated two distinctly different ideologies that were worlds apart. One was free, the other was not. One was colorful and crowded, the other dark and desolate. One displayed the glitter of mass merchandising, the other lived under the gloom of despair and disrepair. I understood those contradictions all too well.

"Wilhelm, how can we get over there?" I inquired.

His eyes widened. "When?"

"Now!" I exclaimed, "Where is the border checkpoint?"

"Nearby—but things are very unstable," Wilhelm explained. "There have been shootings. Besides, it's in the middle of the night, and there is nothing going on except for plenty of apprehensive, armed guards ready for confrontation."

"Show me the way," I insisted.

Wilhelm was willing to escort us to Checkpoint Charlie, but he was not about to cross the border himself. "I will wait for you right here," pointing to the spot where we stood. Then, almost as an afterthought, he added, "Don't get into any trouble."

We strolled up to the immigration booth. Beyond the post, we could see straight ahead into a dark alley. The street lights had been switched off, or perhaps the light bulbs had burned out. There were no civilians anywhere, no one except for the gun-toting guards who would be in control for only just a few more hours. How ironic their last assignment was protecting the border from a lone American couple.

There was no line, no wait. Staring at us was a stone-faced immigration attendant bitterly savoring her final night of power. I pulled out the only Deutschmark from my pocket, snapping it as if to make sure there were no more, but it tore in half. I handed her the pieces, but she glared at me and refused to accept my money. Since I knew that her Cinderella clock was about to strike, I boldly asked, "Do you have any Scotch tape?"

Radiating hostility, she stared first at me and then at Lynn. I gestured that I was sorry and emptied my pockets to show that I was out of German cash. I offered her U.S. dollars, but she shook her head and said, "*Nein gut!*"

I realized that the longer I stalled, the greater our chances of being allowed through. She had already examined our passports and seemed to be warming up to the idea of letting us in, probably thinking, "Oh, what the heck. It's the last night." Grudgingly, the Communist comrade finally decided to wave us along.

Entering East Berlin was like walking into a sinister ghost town from an abandoned movie set. We wanted to explore, but there was not much to see, only rows of rundown buildings between dark, narrow alleys and an occasional military guard running surveillance from a desolate street corner. We were surprised to find a Chinese restaurant, with a burned-out neon sign surreally sputtering in the darkness.

It did not take much time before we felt we had been there long enough. As we headed back, I decided to put in my pocket a small piece of the granite pavers that were piled up blocking the road. It was my last chance to take home a chunk of both the East and the West, although I was secretly terrified at the possibility of being searched in some back alley. But like so many of my fears, it never materialized.

Souvenirs in pocket, we walked across Checkpoint Charlie one last time. Wilhelm had been waiting patiently, and he drove us back to the hotel where we arrived with just enough time to shower and then head to the airport to catch our pre-dawn flight.

My carry-on bag was filled with chunks of concrete and the strap dug deeply into my shoulder. As we approached security, the agent strained to place it on the counter and asked me what was in the bag.

I proudly stated, "Pieces of the Berlin Wall."

"Sir, you can't take those with you," she informed me.

"I was not aware," I apologized. "Would you like a piece?"

"Oh, no, sir, we cannot accept gifts from passengers." But I could see a glimmer of compassion in her eyes.

"I understand," as I dropped a sample into the lower pocket of her blue smock.

"Thank you, have a good flight," she smiled, as she let me through.

I displayed the pieces of the Wall, along with the hammer and the chisel, in my library. They served as emblems of two Communist revolutions. One I was privileged to view in its death throes as an observer, and from which I had carried home these mementoes. The other I endured firsthand, and its scars were still lodged deeply in my soul.

Only in America

I had become a U.S. citizen in 1977, but it had been an emotional decision. Although I loved my adopted country and was proud to become an American, it was difficult to reconcile the guilt of officially abandoning my native land. I took my responsibility as an American citizen very seriously. I pledged my loyalty to a country I did not take for granted—living in America was such a privilege and a blessing. Only in America could anyone do what I had done.

Any disrespect shown toward our great nation always incensed me. Unfortunately, years later I witnessed this at one of my son's sporting events at a rival school. During the national anthem, several classmates had to be reprimanded for talking and acting up. I was upset by that incident, but I also realized that the national anthem was not even played at our home games.

I approached the school administration about the situation, and they only offered objections: "We don't have a working sound system. We don't have a flag by the football field." Frustrated by their apathetic reaction, I decided to take matters into my own hands. I had the PA system repaired. And in addition to a new flagpole, I had created a small memorial in my mother's honor for everything she had done to get me to America. Park benches flanked the flagpole, and beautiful landscaping surrounded it. At its base was a poem I had written cast in a bronze plaque:

Our America

America is her people, the love between you and me
The home of the brave and the land of the free.

Where courage knows no boundaries to protect and defend
And neighbors have compassion for family and friend.

America is her land, on Earth the most beautiful place
Her mountains and plains all blessed with such grace.

America is liberty, where you have the freedom to choose,
Whether you sing or dance, whether you tie, win or lose.

America the people, the land, so gracious and free.
Thank God for creating it, for you and me.

And here we proudly salute the brave women and men
Who serve to preserve this magnificent land.

America, your message of freedom rings loud and clear,
To you, America, we stand, we honor, we cheer!

Once everything was completed, a ceremony was held at halftime during the last football game of Nathan's senior year. Justin was also on the varsity team as a freshman, and it would be the last game they would play together.

We always had enjoyed spending the crisp fall Friday nights supporting the team, but this evening was even more exciting. Nathan played like a man possessed. He was hitting, blocking and tackling like never before. After the game, as we walked across the field arm in arm, I thanked him for all the great memories. But I also confessed, "I'm glad that it's over. Before every game, I said a prayer for you and your brother's safety."

The last football game Justin and Nathan played together

I thought about how at every game, Nathan would acknowledge my presence in a special way. I would wear his bright orange parka so he could always spot me in the stands. Right before kickoff, he would raise his arm and point at me and I would mirror his gesture. One time, a parent sitting next to me incredulously asked me if my son had just motioned to me after he had made a particularly good play. I nodded. "My son barely talks to me, much less sends signals during a game," he remarked. "You are one lucky dad."

But this kind of closeness was nothing unusual with my sons. The previous week, I had returned from a business trip overseas and had made special arrangements to be at the game on time. I ended up arriving early and during the pre-game warm-up, Justin broke away from his team on the field to welcome me home. I was surprised to receive a big hug and a kiss on the 50-yard line right in front of his teammates as well as the opponents.

Fortunate in so many ways, I had a wonderful family, a beautiful home and everything materially that I had ever wished for. Yet unknowingly, my deepest fears lurked just beneath the surface—only my constant denial kept them at bay.

God has unconventional ways of getting our attention. Like the warning of an oncoming train, it begins with a subtle, distant sound. Something soft, easy to ignore. Then comes a whistle. And finally, a roar, but by then we are immobilized by the oncoming headlights. Although we have been forewarned, we have chosen to disregard every signal along the way.

Pride Goeth Before a Fall

*C*ars had fascinated me since childhood, and as an adult I acquired an extensive collection. I owned a vehicle for every occasion and a fourteen-car garage to house them all. My obsession embraced many cultures, both in art as well as in machinery. In addition to the appreciation of the world's best engineering, it was also gratifying to see an international display of hood ornaments behind every garage door. I thought I was on top of the world.

Oddly, I never considered vanity plates. Like bumper stickers and dealer emblems, monograms and designer logos, they revealed far too much—as if the cars themselves were not already sending a clear message.

Our grounds manager, Fred, kept every vehicle in pristine condition. "I don't know how you keep track of all the stuff in your life," he would tell me, waving his arm. "You're always busy. I have driven your cars more than you. Slow down and take time to enjoy them!"

Unfortunately, that was a luxury I could not afford. Another dilemma with owning all these cars was deciding which one to drive. I will never forget one incident at the airport. I had just returned from an extended business trip, and I could not remember where I had parked. I walked around the huge multi-level parking garage, up and down the stairs, wandering through the aisles, on a bitterly cold winter day.

A security vehicle approached me and the guard asked, "Sir, can I help you find your car?"

I hesitated for a moment, irritated by my own helplessness, annoyed that I could have stayed in sunny Florida for yet another day and proudly reluctant to accept his offer. But I had had enough of walking and hauling my luggage in the bone-chilling wind.

"Yes, thank you. You came just at the right time. I have been looking for my car for quite a while," I ruefully admitted.

"We know," he laughed. "My supervisor spotted you on the surveillance camera. He told me you have searched every level in the garage. What kind of car are we looking for?" he asked.

I was silent. I could not remember which car I had driven.

"What color is it?" the guard continued without waiting for the answer to his first question. By then I was feeling like a complete fool. What could I say? I was stalling, frantically groping for my keys for a clue, but the keys were stored in my briefcase—which I had stowed in the bed of his pickup truck.

"Don't worry about the keys," he said, trying to be helpful. "We have to find the car first."

"Could you please stop for a moment? I need to call my wife to let her know I am running very late, and my phone is in the back," I explained.

I got out, grabbed my briefcase, unzipped the small compartment for the keys and also took out my cell phone. Then I got back into the truck. "It's a black Mercedes sedan."

"There's one!" he shouted. "Are those your tags?"

I had no clue what my tag numbers were. Fred had ordered them, along with a hundred other company trucks, trailers and cars. Maybe vanity plates were a good idea, after all. Something like "LOST 1" or "I 4 GOT." Spanish would be easy to spot, with "*MIO*" (mine) or "*AQUÍ*" (here). But I would probably forget those, too.

In addition to my occasional memory lapses, accumulation and indulgence were soaring out of control, as I collected cars, companies, art and property. I also overindulged my sons in a genuine effort to be a better provider than my father had been. I showed my love with a toxic generosity. I lavished my two teenagers with new cars, tropical vacations and plenty of spending money, even though Lynn continued to share with me her apprehension about the consequences of providing the boys with such an affluent lifestyle.

Although Lynn had repeatedly expressed her concerns and tried to set limits and establish rules, I failed to enforce appropriate boundaries and undermined her disciplinary efforts, which Nathan and Justin frequently took advantage of. I was unable to say "no" to them.

My dream life was now turning into a nightmare. My sons were behaving irresponsibly, developing a disturbing sense of entitlement;

and Lynn and I were in constant conflict over our different approaches to parenting, which put even more pressure on our already strained marriage. In addition, Mami had been diagnosed with Alzheimer's and my manufacturing business had lost its largest account.

As I tried to balance all of these conflicting demands, I was pursuing expanding our company's product line into Central and South America and flew there regularly to visit prospects. One day in Mexico City, while waiting for my appointment, I noticed that my vision was blurred. But since I had a bad head cold, I dismissed it. Unexpectedly, my meeting was canceled, and I rushed to catch the next plane home. During the flight I tried to read and found it very difficult. My eyes were extremely irritated. I covered my left eye with an open palm. My right eye was weak, but that was nothing new; I had never been blessed with great vision. I then switched to test my left eye and found that not only could I not read, I could not see. I could only detect peripheral images.

Driving home, the road signs looked distorted, and I could barely see the lane markings. It had been one of those twenty-hour days, so I figured that my eyes were just tired—or perhaps my sinus infection had put pressure on my optic nerve. After a night's rest, nothing had changed. Lynn insisted that I see a doctor, but I refused, hoping I would get better as my sinus inflammation subsided. After a few days, my condition had not improved, and I finally scheduled an appointment with an eye specialist.

"You have a hole in your macula," the ophthalmologist told me, "and you are one of the youngest cases I have ever treated. If you had been here six months ago, I would have sent you home, and gradually you would have gone completely blind. However, there is a new procedure which is effective with this condition."

I asked the doctor if my vision would be restored to normal if I opted for this procedure. I had just recently finished race car training, and my first thought was that my career was over before it had even started. I had won my first race, and my instructor congratulated me, "Ed, you drive like a Doberman with a grenade in its mouth." That pretty well summed up my whole life—an adrenaline junkie.

The doctor's sober words snapped me back to reality. "We may be able to close the hole, but your vision will remain blurry and your depth perception will be impaired. Also, over time you most likely will develop a cataract from the trauma of the surgery. At any rate, we need to operate as soon as possible."

My racing days were over for sure. "When?" I asked.

"Hopefully I can schedule your surgery for next week," he offered.

"I can't do that. I have planned a family vacation to Hawaii for spring break. Will the cabin pressure during such a long flight affect my eye?"

"We really don't know for sure, but I recommend you don't go," the doctor cautioned.

He explained what was involved with the procedure. "We will insert a gas bubble to separate the retina from the macula, allowing the hole to heal. For thirty days after this surgery, you will have to stay at home in a dark room, face down, to ensure the bubble remains in the center of the eye until it dissipates."

"I am not canceling our trip. Schedule the surgery immediately after we get back," I directed.

I dimly realized that something was not right, and my priorities were out of order. Why was I risking my sight for a family vacation? But in spite of my instinctual self-preservation warnings, I forged ahead with our scheduled trip.

Once we returned, I had the operation immediately. As I recovered and lay face down sequestered in the dark for thirty days, the proverb "Pride goeth before a fall" echoed in my mind.

I had become concerned about how I had spent my life and the direction it was headed. Despite my material prosperity, I knew I was not happy. I was extremely restless and had no idea why or what to do about it. I tried to retreat into my usual defenses of compartmentalization and denial, but that was a lot harder to accomplish alone in the dark. Eddie-No-Home was now confined to his room, unable to run.

Facing the Fear

Perhaps I was experiencing a midlife meltdown? I felt compelled to examine my past, but my childhood had long been buried. To excavate the burial site would require going back to my roots, to Cuban soil. Although my eye had healed fine, I made myself increasingly miserable by agonizing over returning to my homeland.

I was uncomfortable discussing the subject with Lynn. My conflicts regarding my heritage were a mixture of both pride and denial, and it was nothing new to her. She was aware that back in college, I had overturned a display table filled with propaganda from the Venceremos Brigade, an American socialist group sympathetic to Fidel Castro's Revolution, that was recruiting U.C. students to cut sugarcane in Cuba. Manipulating young people's idealism to help a diabolical dictator was repulsive to me. Fortunately, my friends had hauled me away before the campus police arrived on the scene.

About a year after my surgery, Lynn and her siblings gathered at our home for an Easter celebration. Since most of them had traveled from out of town, they decided to drive over to their old neighborhood on the west side of Cincinnati where they had all grown up. As I watched them depart I had felt disconnected, sad and alone. When they returned, Lynn described how much fun they had.

"I wish I could visit my old neighborhood," I sighed.

"You can," she said gently.

One night a few months later, Lynn had invited my friend Jeff for dinner, which surprised me, since Jeff and I always arranged our own get-togethers.

As we enjoyed the first glass of wine, I sensed there had been some extensive orchestration. With planner in hand, Lynn announced, "Jeff and I are going to Cuba. You can come along if you like. We're available on...." as she rattled off three different dates, and added, "If these are not good for you, then give us an alternative."

I tried to use my busy schedule as an excuse, but that did not work. Next I attempted to cite the complexities of making travel arrangements to Cuba. But these two accomplices were persistent and determined to get me back to my homeland.

"What am I supposed to tell my parents?" I finally asked.

"You're forty-five years old, Ed!" Jeff retorted. "I think you can handle it."

For most Cubans living in the United States, the prospect of going back to the island was an issue guaranteed to provoke a heated response. I had promised my parents that I would never return, not even for a visit, as long as the Castro government was still in power. They warned me that it was too dangerous, and I had agreed out of loyalty.

So I had to talk to my parents, and soon. If Mami or Papi died before I confronted the issue, I felt it would be a greater betrayal than if I had just gone without their blessing while they were still alive. I could hardly believe the anxiety building inside me whenever I thought about telling them I was planning to visit Cuba. I decided to seek their approval on my next visit.

As my parents grew older, I traveled to Miami regularly to check up on them. They had moved there in the early 1980s after Papi had suffered several heart attacks and had recovered from quadruple bypass surgery, and they were now living in a home I had bought for them.

Life in Miami had been bittersweet for Mami and Papi. Even though they were apart from their beloved grandchildren, they were able to reestablish a sense of community with our extended family there. I was fortunate that my cousins who once had slept with me on the sun porch and teased me about *el Norte* were now lovingly and willingly helping me with my parents. My cousin Julio had become a lawyer and vigilantly looked after all their financial and legal matters. Cousin Jorge, a renowned cardiologist, cared for my father with great love and affection and helped both my parents with their medical needs.

On this trip, I was on a mission to win their approval, so after going out for dinner we returned home to talk in the living room. Mami was in the early stages of Alzheimer's and had difficulty following any lengthy conversation, but Papi's mind was still razor-sharp and so was his resentment of Castro's Communist regime. I finally mustered the courage to tell him that I was thinking about visiting Cuba. I wanted him and Mami to understand my decision. As a strong supporter of the embargo, he filled me with the usual horror stories about those who went, ran into trouble and never came back—stories usually told in the third person without any corroboration. But he finally accepted my pending trip and was happy to know that I was going to financially help our family left there.

"When you go, please tell the family that we are always thinking of them, and give my nieces and nephews a hug for me. Be careful," he added, "and call us as soon as you get back." He then asked if Lynn was going with me.

"Of course. My friend Jeff is also going," I replied.

I did not tell him she was actually the catalyst for the trip—he might have held it against her, regardless of how wonderful he thought Lynn was. Although he was never thrilled with the idea, he had an easier time accepting it knowing that my wife and a close friend would be going with me.

Once I got home I told Lynn I had felt like a teenager without a driver's license, asking his father if he could borrow the car for a cross-country road trip. No longer hiding behind a curtain of misplaced loyalty, I was now dealing directly with my own fears. I would lay awake at night, sometimes blaming Lynn and Jeff for cornering me, always ambushed by questions. What would Cuba be like? How would I feel? Did I truly want to resurrect all of those buried emotions? My mood seemed to sway back and forth almost daily from exuberant anticipation to paranoid anxiety.

Snapshots of armed guards, military trucks and tanks flashed in my mind. Being under a totalitarian government where even its own citizens had no rights, no protection, no due process, no control—and could be detained or interrogated at will—was frightening. My family had made a big sacrifice and taken a great risk to get me out—and I wanted to walk back in? Just thinking about going through Immigration triggered panic. I was counting on Lynn and Jeff as security blankets, protection against being marooned in my homeland, which was now a foreign country to me.

As our plan moved forward, I kept trying to build in safety measures. One trusted Cuban friend who already had gone back mentioned that he had hired a driver to pick him up at the airport. "I don't like to drive in Cuba," he explained. "I don't know the area that well. Besides, if there is an accident, I do not want to be the one behind the wheel." He recommended Bebo, a retired army colonel who was well connected in Havana.

Due to my apprehension, I also insisted that we take only carry-on luggage to avoid waiting for our bags once we landed and to get through Immigration and Customs as quickly as possible.

The morning of our departure, I was excited but quiet and reflective. I was grateful for the past thirty-four years of my life in America and was now looking forward to seeing my homeland. I tried to retrieve the sights, sounds and smells I had left behind and wondered if the image of the beach I had branded in my heart decades ago had tarnished with time. I found myself gulping back my emotions—knowing that eventually they would erupt.

¡Bienvenidos!

*W*hen I heard the captain say, "¡Bienvenidos! *Welcome to Havana, José Martí International Airport,*" I felt a lump in my throat. As the passengers applauded the landing and then chatted happily, I turned inward, just as I had at the end of my departing flight in 1962. Lynn asked me if I was okay. I could not speak, and my lips quivered as I choked back the tears.

Lynn and Jeff breezed through Immigration, but for some reason I was taken aside. The agent called his supervisor on the telephone. Together they reviewed my papers, gave me The Stare, and then held an animated discussion inside the booth where I could not hear them. Although I did not flinch, I was almost paralyzed by worry. I wondered if they were posturing to extract a bribe. I had heard of people tucking a twenty-dollar bill inside their passports; however, the risk of being wrong could be perilous.

Finally, after a half-hour delay, they allowed me through. We sailed through Customs, and now all we needed to do was find Bebo, our driver. I had no clue whom to look for. It was the middle of the night, and the airport was deserted. Our flight had been delayed five hours, and I seriously doubted he would have waited that long for someone he did not even know.

Much to my surprise and relief, a man approached and asked, "*¿Es usted Eduardo Neyra?*"

"*Sí*, Bebo. Thank you for waiting for us!"

We checked into the *Hotel Nacional*, Cuba's finest old hotel, a large and impressive colonial structure crowned by two towers and built on a bluff with a magnificent view of the Caribbean Sea. We awoke the next morning and walked around the extensive and beautiful hotel grounds. In the elaborately tiled lobby, a woman was hand-rolling cigars and selling them for two dollars apiece. The Hallway of Stars, above the pool and patio bar, featured hundreds of framed autographed photos of famous patrons including kings and queens, professional athletes, mafiosos and movie stars from its decadent heyday. We had our pictures taken while standing over the large Cuban map embossed on the terrazzo patio floor, overlooking *El Malecón*, Havana's renowned seaside boulevard that connected Old Havana to Miramar, the newer part of the city.

As we waited for Bebo in front of the hotel to begin our tour of Havana, we met Hank Aaron and a CNN sports reporter while waiting for a taxi. Jeff and I began a conversation with the home-run king and his companion. They told us they were producing a segment on Cuban baseball players through Aaron's eyes.

Jeff asked, "I hear a lot about the talented baseball players on the island. Are they really as good as they claim?"

"Absolutely," the reporter answered. "There are many who could go straight into the Major Leagues."

He said two brothers, one nicknamed *El Duque*—Orlando Fernández—and his half-brother, Livan Hernández, could pitch in the majors today. Baseball fans know the rest is history—after fleeing Cuba, each helped his team win the World Series, Livan for the Marlins and *El Duque* for the Yankees.

As we drove around Havana, it was difficult to appreciate the grand colonial architecture, for most buildings were in desperate need of repair. Jeff remarked, "The only fresh paint in this city is the Socialist slogans slathered on the walls."

The slogan painted on the wall reads: "The most beautiful word is homeland." But look beyond the wall. This is Cuba.

Bebo said that the country had experienced very difficult times since the fall of the Soviet Union. The Special Period, it was called. Most people had trouble finding enough food to eat—even cats on the street were disappearing to become someone's next meal. The country was in deep economic distress.

Lynn had read some travel guides and suggested we try a restaurant called *El Tocororo*. Bebo had never heard of it. We had a little fun, joking that my American wife might be leading us to some great Cuban food. The restaurant was named after Cuba's national bird, which was featured on a colorful stained glass panel amid a festive, tropical atmosphere.

The waiter informed us there were no menus—they could fix anything we wanted, cooked any way we liked. We never saw a price list. We each requested a different dish—and they were all prepared to perfection. But it was also expensive, an outrageous amount in Cuban terms. While eating we watched businessmen and government officials looking over their shoulders before whispering their private conversations. It was obvious that the Special Period did not affect everyone equally.

That afternoon Bebo took us to Hemingway's Marina, a twenty-minute drive across Havana past the plush colonial mansions that now housed corporate headquarters, embassies and residences for high-ranking officials. At the marina we counted eighteen yachts; we were surprised to see that twelve flew American flags. We also visited the marina grocery store. It carried everything from Pringles to Crest to Coca-Cola.

What embargo? I thought.

During the past day, swift winds from the north had been blowing in, and

Cuba was reporting an all-time low temperature, so I found myself scrambling unsuccessfully to find Lynn something warm to wear. As we hurried from shop to shop, she teased me, "Oh, no, it never gets cold in Cuba!" Luckily, that was our last day in the city, and we were on our way to the beach.

The next morning we headed for Varadero. Along the way, Lynn was struck by the vibrant colors of the countryside, and Jeff could not believe the immense size of the royal palms.

Unfortunately, I had come to the conclusion that Bebo had not been a good idea after all. He talked nonstop and I just could not keep up in translating his compulsive monologues. The two-hour ride to Varadero seemed more like two days.

Bebo had become an obnoxious diversion and prevented me from sharing my own impressions of Cuba with Lynn and Jeff. But perhaps suppressing my feelings was what I subconsciously desired. Lynn was understanding, and she never complained about Bebo's constant chattering. She knew that I was emotionally exhausted and was very supportive.

Once there, we had a hard time getting a hotel room. But with Bebo's persuasive maneuvering and a few dollars for incentive, we were finally able to find accommodations—even though we had to stay in a different place each night. The Imperial, the hotel that had belonged to my aunt and uncle, which was now called *Los Delfines*, had no vacancies. I had deliberately not made reservations; I was just not ready to deal with the sentiment of staying at my old summer place. Once we were settled in, I let Bebo know that I would like to spend some time alone with Lynn and Jeff and asked him to come back the following day to take us to Cárdenas to visit my family.

I was excited to walk around and share stories of my many neighborhood pranks. We visited the park where I used to play, the movie theater and *Santa Elvira*, the church that I attended. Visiting these places brought back wonderful memories of my childhood friends and all the fun things we did together.

The next day, we had lunch at *Los Delfines* on the outdoor patio facing the ocean, right in front of the stone wall where as a child I had enjoyed watching the sunsets and the surf. After we ate, Lynn reclined on my childhood lookout post to enjoy the warm, clear day. Admiring the view, she turned to me and affirmed, "After twenty-five years of hearing about Varadero, I now know what you meant. This is the most beautiful beach I have ever seen!"

Suddenly I felt overwhelmed by this surreal experience. My wife, the mother of my two wonderful sons, was relaxing on the very wall where as a child I had sat for hours, wracked with uncertainty about my impending move to the United States. My eyes were flooding, but fortunately the tears were hidden behind my sunglasses.

Una Reunión Cubana

*b*ebo returned that afternoon to drive us to Cárdenas. I could tell we had arrived in my hometown when I saw the huge concrete sculpture of a crab, proudly displayed at the entrance to the city. Although Cárdenas was decaying, it had one distinction that would remain forever: *Ciudad Cangrejo*, Crab City—famous for its large, delicious land crabs. I could still remember Abuela's great crab stew, the best east of Havana.

Driving through my hometown was depressing; the side streets were full of potholes and the buildings were crumbling. Piles of excavated dirt remained in the middle of the road from abandoned repairs. In some areas, there was even exposed raw sewage. What a sad epilogue for a city with such a colorful history. Cárdenas was also known as *Ciudad Bandera*, Flag City, in formal recognition of the site where the Cuban flag was first flown.

All this proud history had seemingly been forgotten, evidenced by the damaged and decaying infrastructure. Yet in spite of all the changes,

I recognized many landmarks, including the last school I had attended up until the Bay of Pigs invasion. As we walked through the courtyard, the principal spotted us and ordered us to leave. Jeff teased me, "Ed, you are the only guy I know who has been kicked out of the same school twice."

We then set off to surprise Tía Elvira. We knocked on her door, but no one responded. A neighbor appeared. I asked her if this was Elvira Neyra's house. The neighbor answered evasively, then shrugged.

Still certain I was in the right place, I knocked again. I explained to Lynn and Jeff that the neighbor did not know us so she was protecting my aunt. Finally, Tía Elvira opened the door. She stared for a moment and then yelled, "*¡Eduardo! ¡Mi sobrino!* I can't believe that it is you! It's been so many years."

After a long embrace in her doorway, she guided me inside with her arms still tightly wrapped around my waist. I introduced her to Jeff and Lynn. "*¡Muy bonita!*" she proclaimed to Lynn.

Tía Elvira immediately enlisted everyone's help to put together an impromptu celebration. Her daughter Elvirita began to coordinate the refreshments, sending her son Omarito on his bike to pick up various items. Elvirita then dispatched a friendly neighbor to fetch her brothers, Jorge and Guillermo, as well as their families.

It was not long before we had a full house. The excitement of this reunion filled my heart and soul. We sat in their living room, engaged in a rapid dialogue, trying to fill in the blanks after more than three decades apart.

"Tell me all about Melba!" Elvirita insisted. Elvirita and Melba were close in age and had not seen each other since Melba's fifteenth birthday party in 1961.

The joyful reunion with the Neyra family in Cárdenas

I joked that it was not surprising that studious Melba had earned several degrees, which had helped her to become very successful in business. She had married a wonderful man named Barry who became like a brother to me. They had a daughter named Tina who was even prettier than Melba, and I was her proud godfather.

Because of Barry's frequent job promotions, they had lived in many different cities across the United States, and I had visited them whenever possible. While they were living in Memphis, Tennessee, Barry had been diagnosed with brain cancer, a drawn-out illness that had left him partially paralyzed after three unsuccessful neurological surgeries. I used to visit as often as I could to help Melba and Barry during his decimating illness. I would bring old records and we would sing along to the tunes that had once played on the radio while we were on a double date. But the aggressive tumor responded to neither treatment nor surgery, and Barry tragically died when he was only forty-four years old in 1987. Elvirita acknowledged that she had heard of Melba's tragedy.

I continued to tell them that several years after Barry passed away, Melba remarried a terrific guy named Brian. In fact, they had the reception at our home. Then my cousin Lalita continued our little family tradition and also had her wedding celebration there when she and Rich exchanged vows in September of 1994. Lalita had asked me to give her away, and I proudly stood in for Tío Ramón. That following spring, I was honored that Tina had also chosen me to escort her down the aisle in her large, traditional Southern wedding in Memphis. She looked so beautiful; I thought of Barry with every step we took and wished he could have seen her that day. "Even though I never had daughters, I managed to give three women away!" I boasted.

As I wrapped up the family update, I became distracted as I glanced around the room. I could see the home was in desperate need of repairs. Large cement patches on the masonry wall were still exposed. Water stains from the leaky roof dotted the wood furniture. The tile floor was cracked. Clearly, food and money were in short supply—and here we were, eating ham and cheese with crackers, drinking soft drinks and beer. I felt so guilty that I could hardly swallow.

My cousin Elvirita kept touching me, holding my hand. "I can't believe you are actually here," she would repeat lovingly.

She pulled me aside to explain that the toilet did not work, but there was a bucket full of water nearby to make it flush. I was hoping that we would not have to use the bathroom in order to protect her pride. They were all so hospitable, so loving, with such a welcoming spirit.

I began to feel distant, triggered by my own guilt. How could I have waited so long to return? I had been so blessed; why had I not been there all along to help? Until now I had always supported the embargo, yet here I was, eating their food, fully aware of the hardships of rationing.

Suddenly, I found myself emotionally drowning once more, unable to express myself. I had to end the visit. I abruptly asked Bebo to allow me a few minutes alone with my family. He joined Jeff and my nephews outside where they were enjoying the night sky, stars ablaze in the darkness.

Lynn and I had brought separate envelopes with money for Tía Evira, Elvirita, Jorge and Guillermo. I thanked everyone for a very memorable day and for their gift—a folder containing old photographs of my parents. In parting, Elvirita said, "It was so good to see you. I thought you had forgotten us."

"No, I would never forget my family. You will see me again," I promised.

As we drove away, I was inundated with emotions—joy, love, anger and grief—and vowed to never forget this moment. To prevent an outburst of tears, I bit my tongue so hard I tasted blood.

Soon after we pulled away, I realized that I had forgotten the photographs. I could not bear to go back, but I had to; this time, only I went inside. Unannounced, I entered the room to find my relatives kneeling on the tile floor. They were carefully dividing the bag of toothpaste, razors, soap and other toiletries we had brought them into neat piles like newly found treasure. Overwhelmed, I gathered up the folder and quickly left Tía Elvira's home.

A blackout had darkened the streets, yet bicycles were everywhere and nearly impossible to see. I was glad that Bebo was driving. He tried to console me as I sat in silence, "*¿Es duro, no?* It's hard, isn't it?"

Bebo explained that the food and drinks we had been served were probably the entire block's ration for the month. He had apparently picked up on how Elvirita choreographed acquiring the food. Omarito and Jorge had to barter with neighbors and that is why it had taken several attempts.

When he dropped us off at the hotel, Bebo asked if we wanted to see other parts of the island during our final two days. Having seen enough of Havana's deteriorated buildings, we opted to head west to see the countryside the following day. We drove to *El Valle de Viñales*, a two-hour trip into the province of *Pinar del Río*, an area well known for growing the tobacco for Cuba's world-famous cigars.

The attraction was not the tobacco farms, but the enormous rocky cliffs, known as *mogotes*, shaped like giant fists of hard limestone with steep, vertical sides surrounded by the flat, fertile fields. We also visited the nearby caves, *Cuevas del Indio*, before heading back toward Havana.

I found myself withdrawing, trying to deal with my past, turning over in my mind how much the country had changed. How much I had changed. Cuba was worn and torn—and so was my spirit. I was ready to return to Cincinnati.

On that last afternoon, while Lynn was getting ready for dinner, I went downstairs to the lounge. It was early, and the only other people in the room were the two bartenders. Striking up a conversation with them, I was careful about what I said, not wanting to offend nor challenge their political or philosophical views. It felt strange to have to work to fit in with the locals in my own country. The stilt-walking stunt had come full circle.

Ironically, the music playing in the background was American. I suppose they wanted to make the tourists feel safe and welcome, but to my ear, the golden-oldie song served as a strange soundtrack to my identity adventure. Feeling neither *turista* nor local, I aired my disappointment that they were not playing Cuban music, even though I knew American songs were played all over the world. I told them about my trip to China years earlier, stopping in a foul-smelling, four-hundred-year-old roadside bathroom pit on the way to the Great Wall. Upon entering, Stevie Wonder serenaded me with "My Cheri Amour."

They laughed, then asked, "What's it like to live in the United States?"

"It is wonderful, but very different. It is a fast-paced, consumer-driven society with lots of opportunities, but it is easy to allow your life to become consumed by work. You are defined by what you do," I explained.

"Is it true that most Cuban refugees in the United States are millionaires?"

"No," I laughed and added, "but many have prospered."

Lastly they wanted to know how I felt about living in the United States now that I had been back to Cuba. I struggled to verbalize what I had experienced in the past few days and finally answered by quoting a line from the Eagles' "Lyin' Eyes" song: "Every form of refuge has its price."

My journey to Cuba had become more than just a nostalgic sightseeing tour through the old neighborhood. I was uncovering places within me that were still too frightening to visit. So I hastily screwed the lid back on this storage jar of fermenting insights and put on my game face to meet Lynn and Jeff for dinner.

The next day, Bebo picked us up and we headed for the airport. I had warned him that I was apprehensive about going though Immigration; the fear of being unable to leave resurrected many unpleasant memories. Under no circumstances did I want to cut it close. Bebo respected my request, and we arrived in plenty of time. He helped us with our luggage and made sure that we were safely on our way. I gave him a hug and handed him a letter of gratitude that Lynn, Jeff and I had written, along with some money to help him and his family.

At Immigration, Lynn went ahead of me. The agent gregariously announced that it was his birthday.

"Which birthday?" I inquired.

"Thirty-one," he answered. "Here, take a drink of my birthday rum."

"Okay." I sipped from the nearly empty glass. "There's not enough," I said. "We need to toast you. I'll be right back."

I walked over to the duty-free store, purchased a bottle of rum, returned to the booth and declared, "Now we can really celebrate!"

The young man opened the bottle, and we shared several toasts to his birthday. Lynn and Jeff sat waiting patiently at the gate, just watching our little party. Only in Cuba, I thought. Finally, he had to leave for his break. He hugged me good-bye and thanked me. As he walked away with what was left of his bottle he yelled, "Come back soon, brother!"

What a powerful lesson. What had terrified me for decades had evaporated within moments—through the simple act of connecting with another human being. Relief washed over me. It felt as if I had scaled an insurmountable wall and landed safely on the other side.

When we arrived back in the United States, I actually wanted to kneel down and kiss the soil like a returning soldier. Instead, I turned and kissed my wife in gratitude for her having escorted me on such a remarkable journey. She had taken me much further than she could ever know, far beyond the island of Cuba.

With Lynn, overlooking the Havana harbor

Resolver

resolver means to resolve, but in Cuba resolver *has become synonymous with* survival and is ingrained in daily conversation:

"*¿Cómo estás?* How are you?"

"*Aquí, resolviendo.* Here, getting by."

Life in Cuba is a struggle. *No es facil,* it's not easy, is the common refrain. Everyday items that we take for granted like food, fuel, medicine and clothing can be difficult to obtain. The simplest errand can become an arduous challenge.

Part of the problem is the low standard of living. The average Cuban worker earns only about eight U.S. dollars per month. A doctor might make as much as seventeen, and not surprisingly in a totalitarian state, a policeman at least thirty.

Scarcity is another accomplice in the daily struggle to survive. The Communist government issues *la libreta*, ration booklets, which allow citizens to purchase their meager allocation of basic goods at a government store. But the shelves at these subsidized *bodegas* are often empty. On a lucky day, you might be able to buy a bread roll, not a loaf; or an egg, not a carton. Dozens, pounds or gallons of any food are simply not available to the average citizen. In fact, milk is only distributed to children under age seven and the elderly with serious medical conditions. And just twice a year, each person is rationed only a half pound of meat, chicken or fish—whichever is available.

When you cannot find what you need at the government store, which is usually the case, a more expensive option is *El Mercado*, the market store—licensed by the government in a co-op arrangement with the vendor, somewhat like an outdoor farmer's market. Usually there is a better and wider assortment of goods; however, the prices are drastically higher—often twenty times as much. There is also the "dollar store," set up primarily for tourists and owned by the government, where you can buy just about anything you can imagine, provided that you have U.S. dollars. Of course, all of these constraining conditions—rationing, high prices and currency restrictions—create an ideal breeding ground for the thriving black market.

Fishing is a very risky food source. A license is required, but they are only available to tourists and for commercial fishing. The average citizen cannot get one, unless he has a connection.

Cuba has great fishing spots, and one of the best is Varadero. Early one morning, Lynn and I were walking on the beach when we saw two round objects out at sea slowly moving towards us. They were difficult to identify at such a great distance.

Finally, as they made their way closer, we realized it was two men in separate inner tubes paddling to shore. They had come from so far out that I was interested to know what they had been up to. These two *pescadores* had been fishing, and each was towing a stringer full of beautiful large red snapper that glinted in the sunlight. It reminded me of my boyhood days, fishing off the pier near the yacht club at the other end of the beach.

By now it was nearly eight in the morning, and as they deflated their vessels and neatly tied them into compact bundles they could easily carry, I asked them how long they had been fishing. The more forward fellow answered, "*Desde la seis*. Since six."

I was so happy for them—they had this big catch to share with their families, or to sell or even barter for other items they might need. I congratulated them, "Wow, that is a lot of fish for just a couple of hours." Tired and wet, the two men looked at me and shook their heads. "*No, amigo*. Since six o'clock last night," one sighed.

The persistent *pescadores* had been submerged in the salty sea, straddling the makeshift canvas seats in their inner tubes, powered only by their fins, for nearly fourteen hours—all night. After working at their jobs all day. Then risking arrest or confiscation of their unlawful catch while having to hitchhike home. That is *resolver*.

Most Cubans do not own cars. Those fortunate enough to own one drive old clunkers from the forties and fifties, also know as *almendrones*, or giant almonds, for the distinctive curved, bulky shape of these vintage vehicles. Parts are hard to find and most often "imported" by visiting relatives from abroad. Some are homemade—amazing testaments to ingenuity—imagine a car powered by an engine rebuilt with handmade piston rings from the windings of an old grandfather clock. The time and craftsmanship required to hand-file the coiled metal to such precision is impressive. Some of these banged up "beauties" have been given facelifts with lots of Bondo and a paintbrush finish—although the tires and rims rarely match. Many have been modified with diesel engines, since gasoline is rationed and extremely expensive.

Even Cubans who own cars walk or use their bicycles unless traveling a long distance. It is not unusual to see an entire family, three or four people, on one bike. Theft is common, and bikers must keep an eye on their wheels, for tires are expensive and hard to find.

Transportation in smaller cities like Cárdenas is more primitive. Passengers ride horse-and-buggy taxis, entering the boxcart from the rear-center steps and sitting on wooden benches that line both sides, or often standing when crowded.

In Havana, late-model European cars such as Mercedes, Volvos and Peugeots provide taxi service for hotel guests—a ride that only tourists can afford. By U.S. standards, the fare is quite a bargain; you can go anywhere in Havana for less than ten dollars. The meters are always visible, and there is no quibbling or price gouging. Tips are greatly appreciated. Occasionally, I will tell a driver, "You don't need to run the meter for me. I know how much it costs to get there." We both know what that means—the driver gets to appropriate more of the cash for himself. A cab ride in Havana can be very educational, as it is not uncommon for the driver to have a degree in medicine or engineering. Unfortunately, driving a taxi is more lucrative in Cuba than any highly skilled profession.

Locals use vintage U.S. cars as unlicensed taxis. Many drivers moonlight illegally, dodging the law to transport carloads of *Habaneros*, Havana residents, across town in these old jalopies for about forty cents per person.

Mass transportation is available on the *camello*, the camel, essentially a semi-truck with a hump-shaped trailer and large windows but no air conditioning. The sweltering riders packed like sardines need to keep a tight grip on their wallets, as pickpockets are plentiful. They must also be nimble getting off, for *camellos* sometimes have poor brakes or worn-out clutches and cannot always come to a complete stop.

Hitchhiking is the only affordable means of getting around for many Cubans. At every intersection, whether in the city or at a highway ramp in the countryside, large groups of people cluster looking for rides, often waiting for hours under *un sol qué raja las piedras*, the rock-splitting sun. When an empty flatbed pulls over, dozens rush to the truck, and the men help the women and children climb up. I often help stranded hitchhikers myself, especially women with children. It is difficult to limit who gets in, because so many are soliciting lifts. However, in my experience, all the riders have been extremely polite and very grateful, with no heckling from those left behind.

One day, Lynn and I picked up a mother with her little boy. He must have been about five years old and was quite a character. He stood on the hump in the back holding on to our bucket seats. He kept wanting to move to the front.

"*¿Cómo te llamas?*" I asked.

"*Me llamo Robertico*," he responded. "Can you please put the radio on?" he politely requested. "Thank you. Louder please!"

Robertico then started dancing to the music and felt comfortable enough to ask me if he could drive. I jokingly inquired if he had a license.

Robertico quickly exclaimed, "Of course not!"

He looked dismayed so I suggested he come up to the front and help me steer—and if he wanted, he could also shift the gears. Robertico was elated to accept my offer and looked quite proud of himself as he sat on my lap and "drove." We soon dropped them off at their home, and as we were leaving I told him, "Make sure you check your pockets before you wash your shorts!" Robertico looked puzzled. I wish I could have seen the expression on his face when he discovered the folded hundred dollar bill I had slipped in there.

Another day, on my way to Havana from Varadero, just outside the city limits of the resort, I stopped for two young hitchhikers. Once the young ladies settled in the back seat, I offered them bottled water from the cooler I always kept stocked in the car. It was almost noon, and the sun already had cracked the earth.

"¿A dónde van?" I asked.

"*Universidad de la Habana, Señor*," one replied.

At this point they were about eighty-five miles from their school and had already traveled twenty-five miles since early that morning. I wondered what time their classes began.

"At two in the afternoon," one responded. These determined students were attending the university three days a week, and just getting there was a full day's work.

Not everybody is trying to get somewhere within Cuba; some are trying to get out altogether. There are thousands of stories about creative escapes involving inner tubes, wooden rafts or floating bathtubs. But the most amazing instance of Cuban ingenuity and determination I have ever heard of was the 1951 Chevy truck mounted on oil drums and fitted with a propeller. The vessel was just forty miles from freedom when it was confiscated by the U.S. Coast Guard. The amphibious truck was sunk, and the "truckonauts" were shipped back to Cuba. Less than a year later they attempted to flee in a modified 1959 fin-tailed Buick but were intercepted once again. They finally reached the United States via Central America in a treacherous two-thousand-mile journey on foot. A triumph of *resolver*.

Getting perspective on Cuban life and understanding the great risks taken is a challenge for anyone accustomed to living in a country with such abundance as the United States. For over thirty years, the Soviet Union had subsidized Cuba, which according to some estimates grew to a whopping $6 billion per year. The Soviet collapse in 1991 sent the Cuban economy into a tailspin. In the five years that followed, known as *El Período Especial*, Cubans were asked to help rebuild their faltering country by getting by with even less. Cuba's GNP dropped by 35 percent virtually overnight—a devastating blow that made daily life even more difficult. To put this precipitous decline in perspective, the GNP in the United States dropped 23 percent during the Great Depression.

To stimulate the economy, Cuba legalized the use of U.S. currency in 1993 and demanded that all tourists pay with U.S. dollars—while still retaining the Cuban *peso* for domestic commerce. In other words, Cuba became a country with two currencies. Once Castro legalized the dollar, Cuban-Americans could help their families by sending them money, and U.S. family assistance grew into the No. 1 lifeline bolstering Cuba's economy. According to a 2000 U.N. study, it was estimated that nearly $750 million was sent annually to the island from relatives abroad, mainly from the United States. It is also believed, however, that up to an additional undocumented $100 million was received in cash, clothing, personal care products and medicine from visiting relatives and friends.

By the late nineties, the Cuban economy managed to recover to almost where it had been before *El Período Especial* due to this infusion of U.S. dollars as well as increased tourism. The United States is the fourth-largest visitor to Cuba, behind Spain, Canada and Italy. Half of the quarter-million American visitors are just like me—Cuban-born American citizens who are allowed to apply for a special license from the U.S. Treasury Department to go back once a year to visit family. However, in 2004 the Bush administration tightened restrictions on travel and family assistance, so in retaliation, Castro switched Cuba's primary foreign currency from the dollar to the euro.

Jobs in the tourist industry are coveted, although the salaries are no better than in other professions. The great benefit is receiving tourists' tips in dollars. Also, it is not unusual at the day's end to see hotel and restaurant employees walking home with care packages of food for their families.

Once while visiting a large hotel I heard a story that, like so many in Cuba, is both comic and sad. The hotel restaurant opened early for an elaborate breakfast buffet, and the manager routinely inspected this huge display of food before serving. One morning he noticed that the large bread basket was nearly empty. Immediately he gathered all of his employees, "I understand and empathize with your situations, but I have a responsibility, and so do you. In ten minutes, I will make my 'final' inspection, and I need to see all the rolls back in the bread basket!" When the manager returned, the basket was full, and he thanked everyone for their cooperation.

Although the resiliency of the Cuban people can be observed daily in many ways, nothing is sadder to witness than the sex trade. Prostitution is prevalent, particularly in Havana and other tourist spots. Though severely punished by ten years in jail and a fine of ten thousand *pesos, jineteras* solicit customers on crowded streets and in nightclubs.

Their clients also pay a heavy price. A tourist found guilty can be jailed for ten years and fined ten thousand dollars. But since Cuba prides itself on protecting tourism, uniformed police are stationed on almost every street corner. All hotel lobbies have guards on duty around the clock to make sure no locals are allowed in, and visitors are shielded from con artists and prostitutes.

Beautiful and often well-educated, young *jineteras* sell their bodies to earn astronomically more than they could at legitimate jobs. A *jinetera* can earn one hundred dollars per night. Even if she only works three or four nights each week, that is enough to make her wealthy in a country where doctors and engineers earn less than four hundred dollars a year.

Once I was approached while walking on *El Malecón* by a woman younger than my own sons—perhaps eighteen or so. She volunteered her price: one hundred dollars.

My silence surprised her.

"*Por toda la noche*," she advertised. "For the whole night."

"*No. Gracias*," I sadly shook my head.

She continued to press on, and I asked her why she was doing this. She answered it was the only way as a single mother she could feed her baby boy.

It made me wonder how far I would go in terms of caring for my loved ones. Where would I draw the line if ever placed in so desperate a situation? God only knows.

As I questioned her in Spanish, she became concerned that I might be an undercover police officer. Then I handed her a hundred-dollar bill.

"Go home," I instructed.

She stared down at the palm of her hand nearly in shock, looked up at me and said, "*¿Está usted jugando*? Are you kidding?"

"No," I said. "Please go home and hug your son."

I knew that my assistance was only temporary, and she would soon be back soliciting on the streets. Unfortunately, that too is *resolver*.

Absolution

"*You've got to do something about that man,*" Mami demanded during one of my visits to their home in Miami.

"What man?" I gently questioned her.

"The one who is living here. He runs around in his underwear. I was not raised around that kind of behavior, and I don't intend to tolerate it now. He must go. You have to kick him out."

Mami had been struggling with forgetfulness for years. Sadly, her mind had deteriorated to the point that she no longer recognized her own husband. I turned to Papi: "You'd better behave yourself or you could be sleeping in *el patio*." We both chuckled.

The Alzheimer's Association had taught us about the disease and coached us on how to care for Mami after she had been diagnosed in the early stages of Alzheimer's a few years before. We learned that she had lost all sense of logic, so there would be no benefit in trying to explain anything because she could no longer process a thought or retain any information. The best thing to do, we were told, was to avoid confrontations by diverting her attention.

Mami had always been an exceptional cook, mixing ingredients from memory with no written recipes, but now would get confused halfway through the preparation. She frequently left the stove turned on, once resulting in a small fire. Papi and I discussed that the best solution was to go out for dinner. It was going to be tough since he had been spoiled by Mami's tasty, homemade dishes.

Each day brought a new challenge. Mami would occasionally escape to wander the streets of Miami while Papi was napping or in the bathroom. Once he called me in Cincinnati, in a panic since she was missing. My father would frantically search, only to find her disoriented, meandering down a side street, or at the grocery store a few blocks away, mumbling about shopping for food. Papi had to maintain constant vigilance to protect Mami and finally had a door latch installed high out of her reach.

Time passed and this dreadful disease seized more of Mami's mind and continued to gain greater control of her life. She became more distant and disconnected. One evening while driving my parents back home after dinner, Mami demanded to know why we were not home yet. At this point, we had to yield to an oncoming train. The traffic barriers began to lower, the lights were flashing and the warning bells were blaring. We could vividly see the cargo blitzing by, hear the sound of the steel wheels against the rails and feel the thunderous vibration of their weight.

Mami wanted to know why we had stopped. I talked to her about the train, commenting on its speed and pretending to be amazed at how much it could transport—all to ease her anxiety. But Mami refused to hear any excuses. She emphatically declared that the train had nothing to do with our delay, and that I needed to get the car moving. I tried to explain that I could not go anywhere, for there was still another car in front of us. That made no sense to her either. It was heartbreaking not to be able to reach her.

Once Mami was in the advanced stages of the disease, she became completely unaware of her environment. I had set them up in relative comfort in a modest home in a Miami suburb and flew down to see them at least once a month. Papi was doing his best to take care of Mami, but I thought it was time to hire someone to help. There was enough room in their home, but Papi still insisted on shouldering the burden himself.

Many times during my visits, Mami would awaken in the morning and not remember that I had spent the night. She would enter the bathroom while I was shaving and stand close to me the entire time. I could see the look of fear in her eyes, as if she was not quite sure who I was. She would make small talk to veil her confusion—and repeat her complaint about the strange, ill-mannered man walking around her house. I learned to distract her by suggesting we go to the kitchen to get a glass of water.

Over time, Mami became more and more irascible. Occasionally she would get angry enough with Papi to hit him with her purse. There was something comical and even a bit satisfying about seeing this docile, loving person who had always put his needs before hers suddenly turning into a bit of a shrew.

My visits were often scheduled to coincide with Mami's doctor's appointments. One day while in the waiting room, Papi commented that

Mami was deteriorating fast. "She can no longer shower, dress herself or know when to use the bathroom. She doesn't even know day from night."

Papi then started to laugh and told me that Mami had gotten aggravated with him a couple of nights earlier and punched him in the chest. As he simulated her feisty motion, his face wore an expression of fondness and affection that I had never witnessed before.

"¿*Qué le hiciste*? What had you done to her?" I grinned. Then I couldn't help adding, "Maybe Mami should have roughed you up fifty years ago. You might have behaved better!"

Papi looked at me and smiled. Then his face turned serious again and in another moment became a mask of near despair. "She is a great woman, but she is very ill."

Melba and I suggested finding someone to help look after Mami. But Papi was not yet ready. He expressed his gratitude for how much Melba and I had helped, and he did not wish to add to the expense. I knew better than to argue when his pride was involved. I also knew that he was very protective of their privacy.

"Let me know if you change your mind," I repeated.

Although the disintegration of my mother's mind was painful to witness, the transformation of my father's self-absorbed behavior was inspiring. In the final years of their life together, Papi cared for Mami like an extremely dedicated nurse. He lovingly fed her, groomed her and washed her soiled linen—all without a word of complaint. How could this be the same man I had overheard in Cuba threatening to leave his wife? Somehow that emotional imprint was now rendered insignificant. Papi had managed to completely redeem himself in my eyes.

Months went by and the situation grew more complicated. Mami's mental and physical condition continued to decline, and then Papi was diagnosed with prostate cancer. I was shocked. Even though my father was in his late seventies, he appeared to be in perfect health—energetic, muscular and mentally sharp. Melba and I confronted him with the grim reality of possibly having to be hospitalized, and then Mami would have no one to look after her.

On my next visit Papi revealed to me that his cancer had actually spread, but he had not wanted to add to our burden. "You should never have kept that information from us!" I insisted.

Papi pleaded, "My son, please don't criticize me." He then broke down and cried.

I felt sympathetic but also sad and confused. None of this was making any sense; my own father had become like a stranger to me. An entire lifetime of *"los Neyras no lloran,"* the creed he had instilled in me, was swiftly swept away by the bursting dam.

"Are you okay?" I asked him.

"Yes," he replied, pulling a hanky from his pocket to wipe the tears that were still running down his face.

I was astonished to see how devoted he had become to Mami, how much he had mellowed and how sentimental he had become. Everything I thought I knew about Papi had turned upside down. The better I got to know him, the more I was touched by his tender heart and the more I loved him for who he really was.

We were soon blessed to find relatives to look after my parents. Daniel was my mother's nephew, the son of her deceased eldest half-brother Julio.

His wife Eva had been a nurse's aide in Cuba. They had recently arrived in Miami, both in need of jobs and a place to live. It was an ideal match.

Eva cared lovingly for my mother, did the housework and was also a terrific cook. Daniel drove my father to the doctor and helped with the grocery shopping and other errands. During my visits, Eva would prepare feasts of Cuban cuisine that were better than any restaurant on *La Calle Ocho*, in Miami's Little Havana district. I would return home several pounds heavier and raving to Lynn about her cooking.

Mami and Papi were both deteriorating to the point that Lynn and I felt we should pay them a family visit, bringing along the grandsons they so adored, even if Mami might not recognize Nathan and Justin. Once school was out for the summer, we were on our way to Miami.

Papi excitedly made plans for a big meal at their home. He loved to see his grandsons eating authentic Cuban food, and his grandsons loved to oblige. I knew how emotional this gathering would be; it would very likely be the last time Mami and Papi would see our boys, who were now sixteen and thirteen years old. The entire family, all three generations, settled in the living room, and I sat next to my mother holding her hand.

But Mami's eyes were glazed. "Who are you?" she wondered, perplexed that I was rubbing her arm.

"Eduardo, your son. And these are your grandsons, Nathan and Justin."

"Please don't tease me. You are not Eduardito. Eduardito is at school. I need to start dinner so it's ready when he gets home," Mami would argue in her confused state.

It was difficult to make any conversation at all. Lynn asked her questions and kept a dialogue going, even though there was zero comprehension on Mami's part. The two of them chatted away in different languages, neither grasping a single word, but with their affectionate bond unmistakable and unbroken.

Then, suddenly, it was as if Mami had awakened from a long sleep. She recognized Lynn and broke into a wide smile, her eyes shining, and joyfully exclaimed her name: "Leeennn!" A mere flicker of energy, like a shooting star—bright, swift and fleeting. In an instant she returned to her shrouded, private world. It was the first expression of joy I had seen on my mother's face in years. I knew it was a moment I would cherish forever, and I was so grateful that Lynn had made my mother smile one last time.

Less than two weeks after we returned home to Cincinnati, Daniel called, requesting that I fly back to Miami. "Your father is getting weaker and has been losing weight. He wants to see you."

I immediately returned and found Papi depressed and very concerned about Mami. He said he was okay, but that he had lost much of his appetite. I continued to probe, certain that I was not getting the entire story.

"*Papi, dime que está pasando.*"

He hesitated. "An X-ray has detected a small spot on my lung—*muy pequeña*," he insisted as he held his thumb and forefinger close together in front of his face and squinted his eyes. "They are going to do additional tests and let me know what my options are."

I stared at him, not sure if Papi was trying to ease my concerns or his own. But there was one thing I knew for certain, based on how much he had smoked all of his life, there was definitely plenty to worry about. He had been a chain smoker of several packs each day, in addition to his daily cigars. As a child I remember seeing dozens of cigarette butts by his bedside during the course of a single night. I had even witnessed brief interruptions of his snoring sleep as he awoke to take puffs from his cigar, which he held lit, even as he dozed off. I could not believe he had never caused a fire. Occasionally Mami, tired of standing guard and wanting to get some rest herself, demanded that Papi put out the stogie.

"*Nunca fumes, por favor.* Don't ever smoke, please," Papi would say to me. And I never did, except for an occasional cigar as a male-bonding thing with my Thrill Seeker buddies. Unfortunately, Nathan's and Justin's pranks of wetting Papi's cigarettes had not worked and he was trying to quit far too late.

Papi was very restless during my two-day visit—but that was nothing new. He was constantly seeking reasons to make runs to the store. He never made a list; he just bought whatever he thought he needed, and then would return shortly thereafter to purchase anything he had forgotten, even if he did not need it that day, or even that week. Papi had a fixation about stockpiling non-perishable food items as well as toiletries. His pantry and limited closet space were always filled to the brim. He hoarded enough soap, deodorant and toilet paper to last a decade.

Another of Papi's pastimes was to look after his car. I had given him a brand-new Buick as a birthday gift a couple of years earlier, and he made a career of having it washed and changing the oil. He never drove far, but he always kept the tank topped off. "You never know when the oil companies might run out of gas," he insisted. I guess he was still haunted by all those years of rationing in Cuba.

Mami was to the point that she could no longer be taken out to dinner.

She could barely walk, nor handle eating utensils. She had also forgotten how to chew and was mostly fed liquid supplements and puréed food. So now we just stayed at home.

In the evenings Papi and I sat and talked in the living room. He proceeded to reveal his concern about his illness and worried who would take care of Mami if something happened to him. I thought it sounded a bit pessimistic for someone who had worked so hard to convince me that the spot on his lung was *muy pequeña*.

But he had also confessed to holding out on me again. He had known not only about his prostate cancer but also his lung for quite a while. Finally he told me that it might already have spread to the bone. I could tell he was worried, although he tried to make light of it.

"Don't keep any secrets next time, or I'll call the doctor myself!" I warned.

"Son, I promise you I will tell you everything."

It was time for me to leave and as usual, Papi escorted me to my car for one last good-bye hug. This also gave us a chance to discuss anything else regarding Mami. Even though she could not understand our conversation, he was always considerate to not say anything she could overhear regarding either her illness or his.

Papi told me to give Nathan and Justin a hug and a kiss for him when I got back home. "Take care of my grandsons," he said, but he paused as if he had something more on his mind. "*La familia es todo*," he said. "Family is everything. Don't make the mistakes I made." Then he added, "You are fortunate to have such a wonderful wife."

"You, too, have a wonderful wife," I reminded him.

"Yes, that is true," he readily acknowledged.

Papi raised his eyes to look into mine and admitted, "But I was not always faithful to her. When you are young, you make mistakes and do things you later regret." He then asked for my forgiveness and told me he was sorry for any pain he had caused. "When one grows old, you realize the only thing that really matters is the family," he said softly.

My father had chosen an odd time to unburden himself. Traffic whizzed by and the garbage man squeezed between us to collect the trash. Although I had to hurry to catch my plane, I suddenly stood still while life's busy background noises faded to mute. I was stunned as I absorbed the impact of his confession. My nearly eighty-year-old father was seeking absolution from his only living son after a lifetime of carrying this guilt and shame.

"What happened, happened," I reassured him. "I love you, and I am really proud of the way you have looked after Mami." I could see in his eyes that my approval meant a great deal.

For the first time in my life, I realized just how much his life had reflected my own. It was like looking into a mirror. His honesty inspired me, penetrated my armor. So I had to be honest with him in return.

"I, too, have made the same mistake, Papi."

He sighed. "Well, my son, don't wait a lifetime like me. Guilt is corrosive." As we kissed and hugged good-bye, he continued, "It is your responsibility to go home and make it right. You have too much to lose."

Redemption

Papi was soon scheduled for an operation to remove his left lung. The surgery was supposed to take several hours—but within forty-five minutes, Melba and I were called in for a consultation. "This is not good news," she deduced. Unfortunately, she was right.

The surgeon apologized, "The cancer was so extensive and interwoven throughout his chest cavity that it would have been impossible to remove. I had to just sew him back up. I am sorry."

"How much longer does he have?" I asked resignedly.

"We really never know—but I would say anywhere between a week and a month. Six weeks at the most," the doctor reluctantly offered.

"Is there any treatment?" Melba wondered.

"Not really. Only pain management," he explained.

Papi assumed that the operation had gone well and perceived that the variety of medications prescribed was a sign that something proactive was being done. Once he got home, Papi made a slight recovery before he took a turn for the worse. His medication had become toxic and he began to hallucinate, acting confused and paranoid. He even walked around the house nude, claiming that people were trying to break in and that bugs were crawling on the walls. Papi wanted to keep a gun or a kitchen knife nearby for protection, but Eva and Daniel were afraid he might seriously injure himself or someone else.

The following week, we had to put Papi in an assisted-living facility. But his paranoia quickly escalated into aggressive behavior. The state agency stepped in and determined that he needed to be institutionalized, and he was transferred immediately. That night as I drove from Cincinnati to Columbus to meet a customer for dinner, I received a call from the evening nurse attending to Papi.

"Your father has become very difficult and is demanding that we let him go home now. We are concerned that his aggression is a danger to himself and others. We need your permission to restrain him," she explained.

"What are you talking about? A straitjacket?" I exclaimed.

"We find it necessary to tie his arms so that he is safe to be around. We need your consent," she answered calmly.

"Do we have to really do this? I mean, I know my father can be feisty, but I have never seen him do anything violent. He may just be trying to get his way, " I pleaded.

"We cannot afford to take the chance. He has been evaluated by a psychiatrist, and his behavior has been described as dangerous," the nurse elucidated.

I could never have imagined being put in this position, having to approve my father's restraint. He had the same restless temperament I did, and the thought of him being tied up was agonizing. But I also could not take the chance of someone else being hurt.

"How much time do I have? What do I need to do?" I asked.

"Sir, I need your authorization now," she replied.

"You mean, right this minute?" I felt so pressured.

"Yes, I am turning on a tape recorder so that we have a record of your consent. It is required by the state," she instructed.

As soon as I hung up the phone I began to sob, and I cried all the way to Columbus. What must Papi be feeling right now? I felt I had totally betrayed my father's trust in me and hoped the nurses would not reveal that his son had authorized a straitjacket. What if some frustrated caregiver handled Papi more roughly than was necessary? How would I ever know?

When I arrived at the restaurant, I must have looked pretty distraught. Fortunately the customer was a great friend, and I was able to tell him about the difficult decision I had to make during my drive. It was nearly midnight when I began the trip back home, and I called the nurse in Florida to find out how Papi was doing.

"He is okay," she assured me. "We have given your father sedatives, and he is calm now."

"Do you still have him restrained?" I inquired.

"Yes, sir, but he is asleep. Tomorrow the doctors will review his medications, and once we know he has settled down, we will set him free."

I was thankful for her gentle reassurance and began to feel some sense of relief.

Melba and I immediately flew down to see him. By then he was stable—his medication had been changed, which lessened his anxiety and eliminated his aggression. He kept telling us how good we both looked and complimented Melba on her hair and jewelry. We knew he was trying to con us into letting him go home, but that was out of our control—the state required that he pass a psychiatric evaluation before they would release him. Soon his behavior improved and he was able join Mami at home. However, that proved to be too much for Eva and Daniel, and we had to transfer Papi back to a small, private elder-care home.

As Melba and I continued our frequent visits, his overall health was deteriorating rapidly. Papi complained each time about how much he missed Mami, and he was deeply concerned about her well-being. He cried and pleaded, "After fifty-five years of marriage, I don't want to die without us being together."

Mami was also clearly in the final stage. She was sleeping most of the day, no longer eating and barely drinking fluids. She was living in a tomb. Since Melba and I knew they both had so little time left, we discussed the situation with Eva and Daniel, who agreed it was best that Papi now return home.

Soon after, on March 11, 1997, while on a business trip to Colorado, I received a telephone call from Lynn in the middle of the night. She rarely called when I traveled, so I feared it was an emergency.

"What is the bad news?" I immediately asked.

"I am sorry, Ed," she informed me in a broken voice. "Your mother has passed away."

We talked for a little while—Lynn wanted to make sure I was okay. But there was something very serene about Mami's passing. Earlier that evening I had had a premonition that Mami was gone and felt her loving good-bye before falling asleep. Somehow I was prepared for Lynn's telephone call.

After we hung up, I had a good cry, but every time I thought of Mami, I thought not of sadness but of her bright smile, her calming personality and unconditional love, which had wrapped and sheltered me since birth.

"Good-bye, Mami," I said aloud. "*Te quiero, adiós.*"

I had to find the quickest way home, ducking out of a group tour of NORAD (North American Aerospace Defense Command) in Colorado Springs that had taken months to organize and arrange for security clearance. My parents had agreed that Cincinnati would be their final resting place, so after my mother's body was embalmed, it was flown there and we had a simple gravesite service.

Although I was relieved that Mami's long struggle had finally ended, I was not prepared for the rush of emotions while flying home with her remains in the storage compartment of the plane. It was incomprehensible to think of Mami as mere cargo. I kept agonizing about how cold, dark and lonely she must be. As I was flooded with grief, it was difficult to accept that Mami was gone forever. I mentally viewed an endless loop of images of her beautiful face and loving smile. As I reminisced about our lives together and her courage and devotion, I found myself remembering things that now made me chuckle, like when she gave me my only spanking for tripping Melba by jerking a string from my hiding place under the bed.

Once Mami was buried I returned to Miami to visit Papi, who had been too ill to make the trip for her funeral. When I arrived he was relieved to see me but looked worn and beaten and not fully aware of what was happening because of his heavy medication. Even though Melba already had visited him a few days earlier and explained everything, he wanted to hear about Mami's funeral service again. I think he needed affirmation that his commitment to her had been fulfilled. "Papi, we have buried Mami in Cincinnati. Your grandsons were right at her side during the burial prayers. She is now at peace and in a much better place," I consoled him.

"Yes, I know. She was my best friend. A lifetime together. Over fifty-five years married." As he began to cry, he added, "She suffered a lot. What I had to do is over." I could hear the pride in his voice and could sense that he finally felt redeemed. Papi wanted to be reassured that his final resting place was next to hers.

"I am glad, because I don't have much time left," Papi prophetically pronounced with a sigh of relief.

Exactly two weeks later he passed away.

In the end he, too, had demonstrated unconditional love. Papi had held onto his very life so that he could care for Mami. A man given six weeks at most to live had survived over a year—and then abruptly departed once she was gone and he felt his duty was done.

I never returned to their home in Florida. I gave Daniel and Eva Papi's car, all the furniture and appliances and offered to let them stay in the house until it was sold. I only requested that they send me the personal items that had sentimental value.

Even though my parents' passing was not unexpected, losing both at once thrust me face to face with the painful finality of death. It forced me to begin evaluating my own life and accept my own mortality. I missed them tremendously. They had sacrificed so much for Melba and me—our success had become their American Dream. The depth of their dedication to their children and each other awed me, and I realized I had much to learn about love and commitment.

What's Happening, Ed?

*A*fter my parents' deaths, Papi's advice about making my own life right echoed in my mind and made my heart uneasy. He had buried his feelings of guilt and shame for most of his life, and I wanted to wisely invest the insight he had shared with me, determined to not make that same mistake. I knew I needed to accept responsibility for my hurtful and reckless behavior, and I confessed my infidelity to Lynn. It inevitably drove a wedge into our already strained marriage of over twenty-five years. As we tried to work through the difficulties of salvaging our relationship, one of Lynn's unwavering demands was that I tell my two sons, who were now seventeen and twenty, what I had done. In her wisdom, she knew that in order to rebuild trust within our family, there could be no secrets.

"You're not the person I thought I knew," Lynn confronted me. Although she was supportive, my strong-willed wife insisted on a separation: "You need professional help to figure this out."

Jerry was a psychiatrist with both credentials and experience, combined with a great reputation. He had been highly recommended by a good friend and more resembled a retired NFL lineman than someone who would ask, "How does that make you feel?" I had decided to give Jerry three visits, and then he would be out—sort of like baseball. Three actually seemed like a generous allowance, a convincing number. I wondered what in the world would I need to work on that would take any longer than that?

Psychology had always been of great interest to me. In college I was intrigued by the classes, especially the human behavior course which required reading *Man the Manipulator*, by Everett Shostrom. Various personalities were identified along with the techniques each used to get what they wanted. We were all manipulators at heart; some people exploded, some cried, others withdrew. Whatever approach got the desired results was the tactic we ultimately adopted.

It was an easy game to play, and I was defiant, proud of my accomplishments and my instinct for survival. As a successful, self-made multi-millionaire, I thought counseling was a waste of time and money. I did not need a shrink telling me how to run my life. But deep down in my hardened heart, I knew my boundless ambition had fueled not only my success but also had fanned the flames of pride and arrogance, damaging what mattered most to me.

I was used to being in charge, but suddenly it seemed that my life was out of control. My wife was deeply hurt and my sons were understandably angry. In addition, my businesses were hemorrhaging red ink. The reality was my life was coming unglued. Guilt and shame had now drained my drive, and I felt alienated and alone, disconnected from my family. I was numb.

As I walked through the door into Jerry's office that first afternoon, I heard his raspy, commanding voice issue a greeting that would become all too familiar: "What's happening, Ed?"

He explained his direct, sometimes confrontational approach. That was fine with me. Pen in hand, Jerry asked question after question, jotting down my answers without ever looking up or making eye contact. How rude, I thought. About midway through our first one-hour session, I had had enough.

"Are you ever going to look at me, or are you just going to stare down at your damn notebook?"

He looked up in disbelief, then smiled and answered patiently. "I need to write down this information as efficiently as possible. Once I have my database, then we will engage in a dialogue."

When I saw the strength in his eyes, I knew he could be trusted. I liked his no-nonsense attitude right away and my instincts told me I was in good hands. Maybe it was the fact that he turned out to be the son of immigrants himself and seemed to know far more than just the gymnastics of therapy.

Jerry reviewed several psychological tests I had taken, including the Myers-Briggs, which identifies personality differences. I was classified as an "ENTP," which includes individuals who are innovators and entrepreneurs; visionaries looking toward the next horizon, always pushing the edge of the envelope. But the ENTP tendency to experiment recklessly could destroy the work of a lifetime, both in careers and relationships. On another test, the Millon Index of Personality Styles, there was a characteristic on the graph that spiked like Mount Everest. I was a narcissist. But, I thought defensively, these things are not always accurate.

Jerry also verified through another screening that I had Attention Deficit Disorder. At least I was in esteemed company, right alongside Einstein, JFK and Rockefeller. Apparently about one-third of all males have ADD, ranging from mild to severe. Jerry sketched a diagram illustrating how the connectors in the brain that transmitted information did not quite line up, but he confirmed the odd contradiction: The same mind that could be sidetracked by the slightest interruption was also capable of an obsessive focus, a tunnel vision that made it impossible to rest until the task at hand was completed.

I discussed with Jerry the rush I experienced whenever I did anything exciting or dangerous. We discussed *Men's Secret Wars* by Patrick A. Means, which explained addiction to one's own body chemistry, in my case, adrenaline. It served as a shield against feeling anger, rejection, fear or resentment. That "fix" was, in fact, a form of self-medication—just like taking drugs, abusing alcohol or even overeating—and a diversion from confronting issues. It was far easier to seek out conflicts that created fresh "surges" than to examine what really lay beneath them.

As our sessions progressed, Jerry and I discussed *The Wisdom of the Enneagram*, a fascinating summary of thousands of years of universal wisdom. The enneagram is a geometric diagram that maps out nine fundamental human personality types and their complex interrelationships. Each type has extraordinary gifts and predictable pitfalls.

Of course, I rushed to find which type characterized me—or rather, which one best described what I wanted it to be. But I found that there was no such thing as best. In fact, the very characteristics perceived as strengths could disintegrate into weaknesses. Conversely, with work, your weaknesses could be integrated into strengths. It was a matter of emotional maturity. Reviewing the characteristics of each personality type often resulted at first in denial—sometimes even anger, Jerry explained. Excessive defiance was an obvious sign of the need for closer self-evaluation.

After accepting both its positive and its negative attributes, I was finally able to pinpoint myself as "The Achiever," someone who relies on superior performances to feel accepted and worthwhile. It was true. I had always strived to be the best at whatever I did, with a competitiveness that bordered on obsession. Pride and arrogance usually laid the groundwork for my actions, and I did whatever it took to achieve my goals. I had often been asked to what I attributed my business success and had always credited my focus, drive and persistence. However, after deeper analysis during these sparring sessions with Jerry, the real reason became painfully clear. It was fear—fear of failure, emptiness and worthlessness.

I had been so determined to become the ideal family provider, beloved father, praised husband, respected businessman and consummate deal-maker that by blindly pursuing success, I had literally lost myself. Maintaining this illusion had required severing the connections to my true feelings. What a Pyrrhic victory! I thought I had covered every angle, only to find out that I had drained my own heart and soul to fill my insatiable need for praise.

The Grave

*a*s I continued to work with Jerry, I longed to go back to Cuba and learn more about my family as well as myself. This time, I was ready to confront the one family member whom I had never been able to talk to: I wanted to pay my respects to Alfredito, the older brother I had never known.

Alfredito's life had been difficult from his very first breath. He was born with jaundice and then contracted hepatitis, so his first two years were spent fighting for survival at Havana's children's hospital. When I was older, I heard stories about my mother's legs swelling during her pregnancy with me, from sleeping on a bench inside Alfredito's hospital room. But she refused to leave his side.

As an infant, I was cared for by my grandmother and my aunts. Abuela, Tía Elena, Tía Gisela and Tía Gladys looked after me as well as Melba, who was then four. It was not until Alfredito died that Mami was home regularly. I cannot begin to imagine the depths of her emotional and physical exhaustion—grieving the death of one child while trying to nurture a newborn. But Mami never spoke a single word about her loss. Never.

I was confused by the connection I had always felt with my deceased brother. Even though I had made great friends throughout my life, a brother was someone exceedingly special, and I had fantasized how wonderful it would have been to share experiences with him.

I had always admired the closeness that existed between my father and my uncle. They were supportive, inseparable. They were the youngest and the only brothers to be elected city councilmen in Cárdenas during the same term. My uncle, like my father, had two sons and a daughter. I was so envious of my male cousins' relationship that as an adolescent I prayed that someday I, too, would have two sons.

Those prayers had been answered and my sons had developed a great friendship. As young boys, they would even invite each other to stay overnight in their rooms. On the rare occasions when they had a tiff, a sadness would swell inside me until their quarrel passed. I would think, if I still had my brother, I would never allow small things to come between us. But Nathan and Justin always made up by bedtime and would then invite each other to "stay over" once more.

The one drawback to their close relationship was in trying to discipline them. As teenagers, they would often cover for each other, never squealing. No matter how hard Lynn and I tried, it was impossible to pry information. Justin's history teacher approached me at his grade school graduation and remarked, "I have taught for twenty-five years and have seen many siblings come and go. But I have never seen brothers who look after each other more than your two sons." What a gratifying compliment.

Jerry's counseling helped me sort through all these powerful feelings, heal the scars from my past and reprioritize my life. It took a long time to make any real progress since I was never one to let my guard down easily. But with Jerry's guidance, I slowly gave in to the process and began to experience understanding and relief I had never imagined possible.

Lynn and I began to rebuild our relationship after being separated for several months, going through extensive counseling as a couple as well as individually. Lynn suggested we could best work on our marriage if we lived together again so she allowed me to move back home. Fortunately, she was also willing to return to Cuba with me even after all the heartache I had caused her.

After Lynn and I arrived in Varadero and had lunch by the beach, we drove the ten-mile stretch of the *autopista* to Cárdenas. Not a speck of white could be seen in the brilliant blue Caribbean sky, and the extreme heat radiating from the pavement created a shimmering mirage. I had vivid memories of traveling this highway as a child, long before it was paved. I would beg Tía Gladys to drive fast, and she usually caved in to my need for speed. I wanted to see the big cloud of dust churned up from the gravel surface as we roared down the road.

The walled-in cemetery where Alfredito was buried lay right beyond the infamous crab sculpture. Across the street from the entrance, I saw a house that sat back from the road with a sign advertising *flores* for sale. Lynn stayed in the car and I walked down the worn path, admiring the neat rows in the garden where the flowers had been cultivated.

A young boy who appeared to be about ten years old saw me coming and ran into the house, but his gait seemed a bit awkward. Once I got closer to the house, the boy's mother approached me with a smile as she dried her hands on her apron and asked if she could be of help.

"I would like to buy some flowers for my brother's grave."

She motioned toward the flowers on the ground stored in old, rusted food cans filled halfway with water. They were beautiful in color, but drooping from the intense heat of the relentless tropical sun.

She asked, "*¿Qué color prefieres?*" I pointed to the multi-colored bunch. The woman directed her son to roll them in some wet newspaper, explaining how this would help the flowers stay moist. When the boy brought me the wrapped bouquet, I recognized the features of Down syndrome. Suddenly I began to tear up.

The woman noticed my compassionate reaction and assured me with a smile, "We are okay. Thank you for your purchase." I asked her how much I owed.

"*Un peso*," she responded. A single Cuban dollar. I smiled and gave her a much larger bill.

"*Señor, esto es mucho,*" she objected, "this is way too much."

"*Señora*, it's for you and your son. Have a nice day!"

Now we were both in tears. I looked at the boy and his mother, and we experienced what I will cherish as an eye-to-eye hug.

The cemetery's colonial-style façade was painted white with bright canary yellow trim and surrounded by huge, hundred-year-old laurel trees.

A gated arch, flanked by symmetrical towers, funneled four lanes into one. An administrative office sat on the left, just beyond the gate where we had to stop and register.

I saw a small, elderly man hunched over, sweeping the curb. As I approached him, he put down his broom, welcomed me with a smile and asked how he could help.

"*Señor*, I have come to visit my brother's grave. It has been fifty years since he died, and I have been waiting all of my life to pay him a visit."

He placed his hand on my shoulder, steering me gently toward the shade of the majestic trees and asked, "Where are you from?"

"I was born right here in Cárdenas," I responded.

The caretaker looked doubtful and wanted to know my brother's name.

"Alfredito Neyra," I replied.

He appeared puzzled and softly repeated the name several times, as if trying to recollect. "What is *your* name?" he further inquired.

"Eduardo Neyra."

With a glimmer of recognition the wizened old man then asked me, "Do you know José Alfredo Neyra?"

"That was my father," I acknowledged.

His weathered face broke into a wide grin, "Where is he? How is Neyra doing?"

I sadly informed him, "He passed away not too long ago."

"*Lo siento*," he said. "I am sorry." Then he pointed to the sidewalk. "Your father built that walkway for the people of Cárdenas so that they could go to the cemetery to pay respects to their loved ones on Sundays after church without getting their shoes dirty." Five feet wide, this long stretch of concrete ran over a mile all the way to town. The man seemed to grow taller with pride as he straightened his back, placing his hand on his chest while proclaiming, "I poured and finished the concrete."

The old man's fondness for my father established an immediate bond between us. He beamed with joy, yet in his sunken eyes, stress and malnutrition showed. His face was worn and weather-beaten from the years of unprotected exposure to the extreme sun.

He clasped my hand and said, "*Yo te llevo*. I will take you, Neyra. I know where your brother's grave is."

Sabanilla, as he was called, had been the cemetery's caretaker for nearly forty years. "I know where everyone is buried. I clean their graves, sweep the streets and make the repairs."

I motioned for him to follow me to the car where Lynn had been waiting. He checked us in at the gate office with the director, who was also the security guard. As we drove toward Alfredito's grave, emotions washed over me. The sense of being transported back in time was so profound that I actually welcomed the distraction of Sabanilla's ongoing monologue.

He was clearly proud of having been the caretaker for so long. "I know the name of everyone who has been buried here," he boasted again. He apologized for the condition of some of the graves but reminded us that they were very old. Others had been damaged by storms. Also, many family members had fled the country, leaving no one to help maintain them.

"*Aquí estás*," he said suddenly, pointing out Alfredito's grave.

I thanked him and gave him a hug as he said, "Please let me know if you need anything else. I will walk back to the gatehouse."

Graves in Cárdenas were above ground, because of the high water table. The remains were placed in mausoleum-like structures, often alongside other family members. Our family's tomb was decorated with a small, sky blue memorial dome resting on several pillars with a silver angel perched on top. The surface of the tomb had a sealed lid that was flanked by handrails on each side. When I gripped the rail to kneel down to say a prayer, it fell off. I could not help laughing, although the sorry state of this structure was depressing.

I scanned the stone markers trying to locate Alfredito's and read the names of several other family members laid to rest there. I saw Abuelo Matanzero and Tío Cheo, but I began to grow a little impatient looking for Alfredito, wondering if we were indeed in the right place. Irritation served as a temporary mask for everything else I was feeling.

Finally, I looked behind the pillars and found his white marble plaque among the others. I could not read it, so I pulled it out. There was a small cross on the left bottom corner, signifying his death and the date, June 5, 1950. The inscription read: "In eternal glory, Alfredito. Your parents and your brother will never forget you."

Your parents… and your brother.

My floodgates burst as I leaned against the structure and sobbed for my brother and for the friendship we had missed. I was so glad to have Lynn at my side. We held hands and said a prayer, and I told her how blessed and grateful I was to have her and my two sons. We tried to photograph the stone, but the glare from the sun was too bright. Lynn creatively suggested we make a rubbing instead, so she went back to the car for paper and a pencil.

We took a few pictures of the grave and then went to look for Sabanilla, whom we found pruning shrubs at the entrance. I asked if there was anything we could do for him.

"Are you going into town?" he asked. "Perhaps you could give me a ride."

During the drive, Sabanilla told me other enlightening stories about my father and how committed he had been to the people of Cárdenas. I had often wondered how Papi, an ethical man, had managed to work with Batista's corrupt regime. Sabanilla repeated the philosophy Papi had shared with him over forty years ago, *"Con estos bueyes, hay que arar.* With these bulls, we have to plow." This colorful metaphor explained how he worked within the flawed system in order to help the people. Although it was long ago, and the Revolution had completely changed the political landscape, Papi was still remembered and admired for his active support of the community.

Sabanilla thanked me for the ride and beseeched me to visit his home on my next trip. I thanked him for the offer, gave him some money to enjoy a fine meal with his family and promised that I would come back. I realized that my visit to Alfredito's grave had raised more questions than it had answered.

The only photo of Alfredito, the brother I never knew

Desperado

"What's happening, Ed?"

"Jerry, there is something that has been haunting me. I have always felt this puzzling bond between my deceased brother and me, even though I never got a chance to know him. I went to Cuba to visit his grave, trying to figure it out, but I have not yet made much progress. In spite of their deaths, I still feel a strong connection binding my brother, my mother and me."

I had recently been given the only known picture of Alfredito by my uncle Beni, my mother's youngest brother who had just come back from a visit to Cuba. I finally had a photo of Alfredito and could see that his legs had never developed enough muscle for him to walk. He looked so frail, sitting next to his first birthday cake. I could not look at him without tearing up. What was this all about?

Jerry explained, "Among the three of you there is a much closer tie than you realize. Your mother was pregnant with you while Alfredito was dying. You have told me she slept at the hospital practically every night while you were in utero. So every moment of anxiety she endured, you also experienced. The body chemicals she released under stress, you received. So in essence, the three of you lived through that loss together—not to mention her grieving process after his death. You felt it all."

"Just think about it. After you were born, you did not spend much time with your mother. She was with your brother at a hospital in another city. Those first few months of bonding between a mother and child are crucial. In your case it never happened, and you are still grieving. It is good that you have learned to accept and embrace that loss. This is the first step in allowing yourself to let it go."

Jerry further explained, "In addition to the first six months of life, the year preceding adolescence is just as critical in a person's psychological development. You were separated from your mother during both of these essential phases. The trauma or spiritual wounding caused by the separation can definitely have lifelong effects."

Jerry continued, "The greatest fallout from a traumatic separation is the inability to establish intimacy. Intimacy is the ability to entrust your feelings and your most private thoughts to someone else. Intimacy is the passageway to the heart, and without it you cannot give or receive love."

Discomfort was setting in. Equally as painful was realizing the high price that I had paid for my own avoidance of the truth. I could no longer deny that the separation from my mother had indeed shut down my heart; the glass at *La Pecera* had become a permanent barrier. I recalled my silent vow to never again allow myself to feel that vulnerable, and as the years went by I developed an impenetrable armor. The more I loved someone, the more I needed them, the more essential the shield became. I was a rock, an island. Simon and Garfunkel had that one right.

After these intense sessions, I was often emotionally drained and could not return to work, so I would go straight home and share with Lynn what I had learned. She was very supportive as we worked hard to rebuild our relationship. Some weekends we would spend at a nearby state park in a cabin, and the rustic retreat was always rejuvenating.

On our drive back home, we turned on the radio and the Eagles' smooth harmonies serenaded us with "Desperado." "Every time I hear that one, I feel as if I could cry," I told Lynn.

"Why?" she asked.

"My mother used to call me '*desperado*.' I find it ironic that the lyrics seem to mirror my life. I have even romanticized that she somehow understood that, and her maternal message from heaven is the final line."

Lynn nodded as we listened to Don Henley soulfully deliver the painful parting advice, "You better let somebody love you before it's too late…"

*A*MISTAD

Ever since my parents had died, my curiosity about Cuba and my family history became an insatiable hunger. When I walked the streets of Havana, I would wonder which of my ancestors had strolled down these same squares of pavement. I felt as if I were picking up pieces of the past, one by one, and putting together some long-dispersed puzzle. Although I knew my relatives would be willing to help me, most had long since left Cuba. I did not know how or where to search for the records, or if indeed they had not already been destroyed, but I sensed I was destined to learn far more.

On a previous flight, I had sat next to Greg, an American who was enamored with Cuba. He knew a lot about Havana in particular and gave me a long list of great restaurants, quaint hotels and other places of interest in the historic city.

On this trip back to Cuba, while I was wrestling my carry-on luggage into the storage compartment, I was surprised to hear a familiar voice greeting me by name. "Hello, Ed!" I looked down, and there was Greg, once again seated next to me.

"I can't believe this," he exclaimed. "This is incredible! I've been thinking about you, wanting to call you for over a year, but I didn't know how to reach you."

"Yes, I also wanted to thank you for that great list of restaurants you gave me," I replied. "*La Cocina de Lilliam* had turned out to be my favorite. Their pork was almost as good as my mother's." Lilliam's was a *paladar*, a state-licensed restaurant operated in a private home restricted to seating no more than ten people. But as usual, someone must have been paid off, because this *paladar* was much larger; we could sit outside in the expansive, plant-filled courtyard and enjoy the tropical evening breeze.

It was pleasant to have someone to talk to since the flight into Cuba was always so emotional for me. We discussed our mutual interest in art, particularly oil paintings. Greg raved about the art museums in Havana and some of the fine galleries he had visited.

The historic section of Old Havana was not laid out in a symmetrical grid; narrow one-way streets were angled like spokes in a wheel all leading to its hub, the Capitol building. Also, some shops were on the second floor of buildings and not well marked, so I paid close attention to Greg's directions.

One of his favorite artists was Ernesto Villanueva, a successful Cuban painter in his early thirties who already had exhibited his work throughout Europe and even in the United States. "I am going to his house directly from the airport," Greg told me. "My friend Luis is picking me up. Why don't you come along?"

By now we had landed, and I noticed that in the distraction of our conversation I felt strangely calm about being on Cuban soil once again.

Luis drove us to Ernesto's studio and we gratefully accepted the refreshments his wife, Marielmy, offered, while we admired his artwork. We talked for hours; it was fascinating to hear Ernesto's interpretations of his own contemporary paintings.

That night I joined Greg and Luis for a delicious Cuban meal at *Las Fontanas*, Greg's favorite *paladar*. During the Creole feast, our conversation never stopped. We were having a wonderful time sharing our life experiences, and our newfound friendships were growing roots to last a lifetime.

The next day, as I was wandering around the streets of Old Havana, I realized I was passing Ernesto's house so I decided to stop by and say hello. Marielmy welcomed me inside. In Ernesto's upstairs studio he recounted the story of how his career had begun. "I was studying both art and engineering when a tourist insisted on purchasing a class project, a charcoal study of shadows. I had a difficult time explaining to my professor that I had sold my assignment. He reluctantly gave me an extension to create another one." But from that point on, tourists continued to admire and buy his work.

We talked for hours. Marielmy, a medical doctor by profession and a gracious hostess, joined in the conversation. A great fondness and connection seemed to be developing quickly among the three of us. I shared with Ernesto how much I loved walking around Havana without any destination in mind. Although it was rundown, I found the old city exotic and addictive. I called it my "Latin fix."

He asked me, "How does it feel to live outside your country of birth?

I have traveled considerably, but I always feel a void until I return home."

Marielmy added, "His artwork seems to have darker tones when he paints outside of Cuba."

After a moment of thought I answered, "It reminds me of a Neil Diamond lyric, 'L.A.'s fine, but it ain't home. New York's home, but it ain't mine no more.' Although there has always been a part of me that wonders what if I had stayed in Cuba, I feel extremely fortunate to live in the United States and appreciate the tremendous sacrifice my parents made."

I proceeded to tell them my story of leaving the country as a Pedro Pan when I was just eleven years old and how much I enjoyed coming back to visit my family in Cárdenas and especially Varadero, which I planned to see the following day.

Marielmy laughed, "My father was born in Cárdenas. Everyone who comes from there proudly boasts it is the center of the universe."

"I can take you there tomorrow since I have a free day," Ernesto offered. "It will be fun!"

We took our time during the next day's coastal drive, with a stop along the way for Ernesto to savor a cup of strong Cuban coffee while I conversed with the locals. As we drove, Ernesto talked about the most beautiful beach home he had ever seen and how eager he was to show it to me.

As we approached the tollbooth nearing Varadero, I mentioned that I should stop by *Los Delfines* hotel, since they were holding a room for me just for the day. I gave Ernesto directions—but as we drove down the boulevard I abruptly begged him to stop. I had recognized a fellow sitting on a porch as someone I had known as a child. Ernesto was dumbstruck.

"You can't tell me that you recognize that guy from forty years ago! *¡Tú estás loco!*"

"Yes, Ernesto," I admitted, laughing. "But I know that man. I can feel it. Please, let's go back!" I pleaded.

As we pulled up to the curb, I called out the window, "Chino!" The man turned his head, rose and started toward me. We met at the gate of his front yard. He still looked puzzled, until I said, "Eduardo! Melba! Lalita!" He then immediately knew who I was. We hugged each other and wept.

We sat on his porch for a little while and chatted about old times. Chino was a few years older than I was and had owned a motorcycle. Whenever he was cruising by, he would let me grab onto his shoulder while I was riding my bike, pulling me up and down the streets of Varadero. Chino's real name was Víctor, but since he was of Chinese descent, as children we called him Chino. In the Cuban culture, it was considered a term of endearment, not an ethnic slur.

Chino, like his deceased father, worked as a photographer at the local tourist spot. He invited us to meet him that evening at the floor show of the Varadero International Hotel and promised us a great table. However, I told him that we were only in for the day and would be leaving before nightfall.

Ernesto was still in awe as we moved on. But as we approached the hotel, he said suddenly, "*¿Cómo lo sabes?* How did you know?"

I did not understand what he was talking about. "What do you mean?"

"This is the beautiful home I was telling you about!" he exclaimed incredulously.

"Well, this is my summer place where I lived until I left for the United States!" I explained, laughing at the coincidence.

Most of the employees knew this was my former home; on a previous trip I had even given the manager a collection of fifty-year-old photographs of the hotel in its earlier days—so I now stayed in my childhood room at no charge. They also went out of their way to set up a private table on a second-floor balcony so that I could enjoy dinners while watching the sunset. My hotel ID card read, "*Huésped de Honor.* Guest of Honor." This gesture seemed sweetly sentimental and more than a bit ironic, considering all that had happened.

Some of the hotel staff had been friends of my family long ago. I had come to realize that they were no more responsible for our losses than I was for theirs. The Revolution had changed everything, and we were all victims of one man's obsession for absolute power and complete control. They had been trapped, unable to leave, and were now just trying to survive.

Ernesto and I enjoyed a few drinks while spending the beautiful afternoon at the beach, lolling in the ocean. From the water, I gazed back toward the hotel and felt that familiar fondness and pride. I shared with Ernesto stories of the endless summer I had spent as a child with my friends in these shallow, calm waters.

As we walked out of the ocean, Ernesto asked if I wanted to meet a friend of his. Ricardo Garcia, known as Kiko, was an elderly genealogy buff who had lived in Varadero all his life and knew everyone. When we arrived at his home the gate was closed, and the front door was locked. But that did not stop Ernesto. "Kiko!" he yelled. No response. Ernesto yelled once more.

Still nothing. Just as we turned to walk away, the front door opened. We had awakened Kiko from his daily *siesta*, but he invited us inside anyway.

After introducing us, Ernesto told Kiko that I was born in Cárdenas and had also lived in Varadero. But he wanted to know more—my name, my birth date and my parents' and grandparents' names. Then he asked me, "What do you know about your family?"

"Not much. I have been gone for nearly forty years, and my parents both recently died."

"Did they ever tell you anything about your ancestry?" Kiko inquired.

"No, *señor*. It is something that no one ever talked about. I only know that my father's parents came from prominent families."

Kiko peered at me. "I know who you are."

His statement intrigued me. If he only knew how many sessions with Jerry I had invested in pursuing that very issue. Kiko's confident declaration made me realize that who I am was not just about me. There was a family history, and this revelation energized me. I was elated, sure that I was about to learn something significant. But when I requested that he tell me more, he declined.

"I need to review some documents, so I don't want to discuss this just yet." He added, "And besides, you're not going to believe me!"

My curiosity was on fire, but Kiko refused to say another word. "You will just have to wait," he insisted.

That evening, Ernesto and I had a great meal at *El Bodegón*, a restaurant down the street from *Los Delfines*. It was a beautiful limestone building with bright red trim matching its Spanish tile roof. The Caribbean breeze wafting through the arches of the wraparound porch where we were dining brought back memories of the old neighborhood.

"Fifty years earlier, *El Bodegón* had been a Presbyterian church," I began, as I reminisced about one of my childhood capers. "We sneaked out in the middle of a Saturday night, or rather a very early Sunday morning, to carry the wooden pews outside, lining them up in neat rows with a center aisle, on a side street, so the service would be held in the sunshine."

After a good laugh, Ernesto suggested that we should head back to Havana. He did not like to drive late at night because it was the time of the year when large land crabs were crawling everywhere. He explained they could be difficult to dodge and their pincers could puncture the tires. As he predicted, the crabs were all over the road, but we managed to reach Havana without a flat.

Greg, Luis, Ernesto, Marielmy and I met the next day for lunch at *El Floridita*, a well-known Cuban restaurant where Ernest Hemingway used to enjoy his daiquiris. In fact, the *Papa Doble*, which had double the proportion of rum, was named after the renowned American writer. In the late 1930s, he lived at the *Ambos Mundos* hotel, which was within walking distance of his watering hole.

Luis joked, "I don't know why they call this 'Hemingway's Bar,' because every bar in Old Havana is Hemingway's bar. He got drunk everywhere!" and we all had a hearty laugh.

It was wonderful to have such good friends in Cuba, and I raised my glass in a toast to *amistad*, friendship. As we tipped our glasses, *Trío Taicuba* was singing the theme song of *El Floridita*, "The Cradle of the Daiquiri." Ernesto bought me their CD and wrote on the cover, "Who am I? Too American to be Cuban and too Cuban to be anything else." He ordered another round of drinks and on my napkin added, "For a friend who for now is finally at home." My eyes flooded. Marielmy noticed but looked down so as not to embarrass me. She was weeping, too.

This was my last night in Cuba, and Ernesto and Marielmy surprised me with a front row table at *El Gato Tuerto*, The One-Eyed Cat, an upscale jazz club. One of the performers was César Portillo de la Luz, who was nearly eighty years old and on stage only briefly. I was stunned when Ernesto requested he sing one of my favorite Cuban boleros, "*Contigo en la Distancia*, With You in the Distance." My mother used to sing these lyrics, and I could almost hear her voice while César, who had first recorded his composition back in 1952, performed it live. At the end of the sentimental melody, I hugged Ernesto and Marielmy good-bye after we drank our final toast to amistad.

Centering

"What's happening, Ed?"

"Jerry, before my last trip to Cuba, Lynn and I drove Nathan to the airport for a flight overseas. As soon as we got there, my blood pressure soared and my personality changed. I was giving instructions as to what lines Nathan should be waiting in and when he should board the plane—even though I knew he was an experienced traveler capable of making his own decisions. I recognized my controlling behavior but I was actually feeling agitated, hyperactive—out of control. This was not the first time I had felt this way at an airport."

"Looking back, I realized that I also had a habit of barely making my scheduled flights. I routinely cut my driving time to the airport so tight or stayed so busy on the phone that I often nearly missed the plane. On one occasion while traveling with Lynn, she jokingly kissed me good-bye and then boarded while I was still chatting on a pay phone with my office. I had to sprint to the closed cabin and then pound on the door to be allowed in."

"So you always have been looking for ways to sabotage your separation?" Jerry suggested.

"I never really thought about it that way. Recently, I had a far more jolting encounter. Lynn had called me at the office to let me know that relatives who had been staying in Cincinnati after fleeing Cuba had abruptly decided to move to Miami. If we wanted to say good-bye, we would have to hurry and meet them at the bus station since they were leaving in less than two hours. When we got there, I felt as sad as if they were leaving forever. I'm not sure why. At one point I had not seen them for thirty-four years. Besides, I knew I could fly to Miami to visit them any time."

"On the way home, I felt chest pains but I didn't want to alarm anyone. Lynn warned me that I was driving carelessly and unusually fast. The closer I got to our house, the more severe the agony became. I was convinced that I was having a heart attack. Once we reached home, our sons bailed out of the back seat, but Lynn and I sat in the car for a moment. Only then did I let her know what I was experiencing. Finally, I went inside to lie down and after awhile the pain subsided."

"The very next morning Melba was coming to town on business. After picking her up at the airport, the chest pains returned during our drive home so Melba and I headed directly to the hospital to see Dean, my college buddy and cardiologist. He supervised a chest MRI and found nothing abnormal. He asked me if I was experiencing any unusual stress. I told him no, but I was certainly beginning to see a pattern."

Jerry reminded me that a strong reaction was a red flag signaling a deeper problem within the subconscious. He suggested that perhaps I was suffering from separation anxiety, originally triggered by the trauma at *La Pecera*. My vow to never, ever feel vulnerable again had only repressed my pain, not eliminated it. Over the years, this damage deepened and ultimately manifested itself as outbursts of anxiety whenever I encountered an impending separation from anyone I felt close to.

I was utterly amazed. Despite my emotional responses when landing in Havana, I had deceived myself into thinking I had not been affected by having fled Cuba as a child. I was tough. I was a Neyra. *Los Neyras no lloran.*

Jerry explained that emotions did not cause problems, but suppressing them did. For example, anger was a perfectly acceptable feeling if honestly voiced; it led to a healthy assertiveness. But pushed down long enough, the suppressed anger could lead to anxiety and even severe depression.

He added that anger wielded as a weapon to control people and situations was actually a defense mechanism to hide hurt. In reality, all destructive behavior masked fear. The fundamental question was: What am I afraid of?

Doing the hard work of learning these lessons was not easy, especially the idea of letting go. Jerry asked me to name something that I owned. I chose my car.

"Can you give it away?" Jerry demanded.

"Of course. I can give away anything that's mine," I replied defensively.

He then asked me to choose something that did not belong to me. "The couch I am sitting on," I jokingly responded.

"You get my point," he continued. "You cannot give away anything that you do not own. You had been taught to ignore, avoid and suppress feelings, hoping that they would eventually disappear. But you cannot heal a pain until you first acknowledge and confront its source. It is the only way to achieve inner peace."

Smell of Home

i was really excited about my next trip to Cuba, since Nathan would be visiting my homeland with me for the first time. I had imagined for years how special it would be for our oldest son to meet his relatives there, share the Cuban culture and humor and enjoy delicious meals in the lively restaurants surrounded by Latin music. I wanted to show him all of my beloved landmarks and have him experience the sights, sounds and smells that were such an essential part of my identity.

Arriving in Havana, I was eager to tell him all I knew about the buildings and monuments on the way to our hotel, the *Santa Isabel*. Long ago, it had been the palace of a Spanish noble family and was located right in the heart of Old Havana. The ornately patterned tiled terrace of our third-floor suite overlooking the *Plaza de Armas* beckoned us to enjoy the commanding view of the colonial Governor's Palace.

Nathan, an adventurous traveler, was ready to roam the streets as soon as we unpacked our suitcases. Strolling through Havana with Nathan gave me a feeling of joy and pride beyond words. We headed to the Museum of the Revolution, the former Presidential Palace where Batista had narrowly escaped an assassination attempt in 1957. Nathan was amazed to see the spray of bullet holes that still scarred the grandiose marble staircase from this failed coup d'état. I shuddered as I thought of the bullets that whizzed over my head on that dreadful spring day in Cárdenas when Batista's forces terrorized the funeral procession of José Antonio Echevarría, one of the slain plotters.

We stopped for lunch at one of Ernest Hemingway's hangouts, *La Bodeguita del Medio*. The internationally known dive was located down a narrow back alley and had a relaxed, laid-back atmosphere. The walls were covered with sixty years of photographs, graffiti and travelers' signatures— an extensive global display of messages and good wishes in many colors and languages. *La Bodeguita* was also world-renowned for inventing the *mojito*, a rum and lime spritzer whose unique flavor came from the *yerbabuena* herb, a cousin of spearmint.

We enjoyed *mojitos* and great Cuban food in the small, crowded courtyard while being serenaded by Marianita and her guitarist René, my favorite duo in all of Havana. Before the Revolution, Marianita had hosted a successful television show, but like all Cubans, her life had changed abrubtly after Castro assumed complete control of the island. He had confiscated all broadcast media and strictly censored the airwaves with programs whose performers were hand-picked by his regime.

My relationship with Marianita had begun on a previous trip. On that first visit to the restaurant I had requested, "*A Mi Manera*, My Way," the famous Frank Sinatra tune. Marianita regretfully informed me that she had neither the music nor the lyrics. The following year, I had brought her a cassette with the Spanish version, and by now she had perfected it.

After a few *mojitos*, I would often borrow Marianita's maracas, and with my off-key vocals, enthusiastically join her in a duet of "*A Mi Manera*." After our performance, I hugged Marianita. As I held her in my arms, I noticed the crucifix she was wearing. "Thank Him," I said, "for He blessed you with the beautiful voice that we can all enjoy."

"*Es verdad,*" she said with a glow of joy in her eyes. "It is true. For the rest of my life, every time I sing this song, I will think of you." It was a proud moment, made even more meaningful by having Nathan along to share it with me.

As we inhaled the sights and sounds of Old Havana, Nathan commented on the distinctive scent of the colonial city. He described it as an intoxicating mixture of tobacco, spices and salt from the sea perfectly blended by the warm breeze. "It's like walking through a gigantic tropical humidor, Dad." To me, it had always smelled like home.

I wanted Nathan to have a memorable gift from our trip, something that he would enjoy for the rest of his life. We wandered through an open-air market near the Havana Cathedral Square dedicated to booths filled with arts and crafts from local vendors and we browsed in the galleries that lined the streets. An art enthusiast, Nathan finally spotted a piece that fascinated him, an unusually clever and creative surrealist oil painting. When viewing up close, the image appeared to be an open-armed angelic figure; but upon standing farther back, the "angel" was transformed into a bull's head with horns and a nose ring.

He also found a folk art crucifix to add to his collection back home. This one was made of wood and metal with a child's face at the center of the cross. The intriguing part was the piece of Coca-Cola can wrapped around the top that read, "*siempre*" (always), from the old Coke slogan.

Nathan was thoroughly enjoying the Cuban people and their sense of humor. In an alley near the cathedral, he got quite a kick out of a tiny, elderly gypsy woman dressed in bright red with a large matching hair bow, flashing gold earrings and several strands of multicolored pearls. Her big smile gripped a huge cigar, just like the ones she was selling for four dollars apiece. As we approached her, she called out, "*¿Cómo estás, mi amor?* How are you, my love?" We laughed, amused by her jovial gesture. Nathan stopped to buy a cigar and had his picture taken with her, puffing away on the hand-rolled *tabaco*.

This colorful character pointed to her dangling earrings, asking Nathan if he liked them.

"*Sí, mucho,*" he answered with a grin.

"*Mi amor me los trajo,*" she told him. "My love brought them to me."

Wondering who could possibly court this wrinkled, weather-beaten dynamo, Nathan asked innocently, "*¿Quién es?*"

"*Tu papá!*" she exclaimed, cackling with glee.

On an earlier trip I had asked if there was anything I could bring her from the States, and she had requested the very earrings she was now wearing.

Nathan wanted to see as much of Havana as possible, and we spent the afternoon touring historic buildings, art museums and monuments. He often commented about the fabulous architecture among the ruins, casualties from the colonial era that just could not survive the subsequent neglect and the effects of severe storms.

Our last stop was *El Capitolio*, an extravagant replica of the U.S. Capitol building, now home to the Ministry of Science, Technology and Environment. You could tour the former government chambers, and Nathan and I were able to sit where his relatives, Alejandro Neyra and his cousin, Santiago, had once served in the Senate and the House of Representatives before the days of Batista's dictatorship.

Nathan was astonished by the opulence of the building's architecture as well as *La India*, the famous Statue of the Republic, a noble Indian woman cast in bronze and gilded in 22-carat gold. One of the tallest indoor statues in the world at almost sixty feet, she dominated the grand three-hundred-foot-high domed entrance.

Sightseeing on foot for hours had made us very hungry. Havana was full of good restaurants, and Nathan loved Cuban food. As a child he enjoyed eating my mother's home cooking, so he grew up accustomed to the seasoning and had a real hankering for it.

That evening we went to the suburb of Miramar to eat at *El Aljibe*, a bustling, thatched-roof, open-air restaurant that served the best chicken on the island. Before roasting, it was marinated in a pungent, tangy blend of sour orange and lemon juices, accented with garlic and spices—and then served with delicious pan-fried sweet plantains and black beans over steaming white rice. *El Aljibe* also had an extensive list of international wines, so Nathan, our family *vino* connoisseur, made a great selection.

We savored the delicious dinner and then taxied to Old Havana for one last walk around Cathedral Square in an effort to help digest the abundant feast before bedtime. Back in our room, Nathan commented on the mélange of music that we could still dimly hear from the nearby restaurants. "Dad, there is always music in the background, like in a movie. I really like that."

I added, "If you leave your windows open, the music carried by the warm night breeze will lull you to sleep."

The next morning Nathan and I were energetically awakened by the sound of the street vendors' homemade carts hauling their merchandise to set up booths for the day. The incessant clickety-clack of the steel wheels on the cobblestone pavement created a rhythmic reminder, "It's time to get up! It's time to get up!" I eagerly awakened, excited to know that the day had finally come for me to take my firstborn son to visit my beloved boyhood summer place in Varadero.

Full Circle

during our scenic oceanside drive, Nathan noticed the many oil wells that punctured the landscape, their diesel engines spewing puffs of dark carbon clouds into the clear, early morning sky. I explained that there were large petroleum deposits along the coastline between Havana and Varadero. Nathan was dismayed. "What a shame to industrialize this beautiful seashore," he lamented. I found it interesting that I had traveled that road many times before and had never focused on the oil rigs pumping away.

Before we reached Varadero, I took a detour toward the tiny town of Cantel. I wanted to show Nathan the country setting where I had eaten perfectly ripened tropical fruit plucked right from the tree. Where mangos had the delicious, sweet flavor that I still longed for. But most importantly, I wanted him to know the family secret that had been entrusted to me.

We stopped at the country villa where Tío Ramón had buried American dollars stuffed in old jars and capped pipes. Since U.S. currency had been forbidden after the Revolution, but could not be taken out of Cuba, Tío Ramón had frantically buried what was left of the family's savings in the fertile farmland as he planted new guava trees in his fruit orchard. During this physically arduous and stressful subterfuge, Tío Ramón was struck by his fatal heart attack. It was Mami who had found him slumped over the utility sink outside the back door with the water still running to wash his earth-stained hands.

The current resident allowed us to take a nostalgic tour and followed behind as we walked through the rooms. It was eerie to recognize some of the furniture my family had left behind, and the large mirror in the dining room, now speckled and cracked, was still anchored to the same spot on the back wall.

I then led Nathan through the kitchen and out the back door to view the expansive grounds. I whispered instructions to him so he could perhaps someday recover the buried treasure in the overgrown orchard now strewn with rusted, broken farm equipment. We momentarily considered a wild scheme to return that night to dig in the dark, but quickly discarded that idea as way too dangerous. Then the woman who lived in the home subtly interrupted, "Just so you know, I understand English." I abruptly changed the direction of our coded conversation and thanked the candid owner for letting us into her home before we went on our way.

As we continued on our drive to Varadero, I somberly shared with Nathan the story I had pieced together from different relatives about the traumatic times my family had endured after the Imperial Hotel had been seized. Mami, Papi and Tía Gladys had never spoken of these hardships.

Exiled in Cantel in rural isolation and cut off from communication with their children in the United States, they had lived in limbo for two years while waiting to flee to Venezuela.

In spite of their language barrier, Nathan had always had a loving relationship with Mami and Papi, but now as he learned more about their past, he had a deeper understanding of their struggle and a greater appreciation for their tenacity.

Nathan was a history buff and a voracious reader—he knew all about the techniques the *Fidelistas* had masterfully executed to wage this revolution that had destroyed my family's way of life. He explained how guerrillas relied on a friendly population to provide supplies and intelligence. Fidel, his brother Raúl and Che Guevara had been able to rally the *campesinos,* peasants, for this support. Guerrillas also preferred to operate in regions providing plenty of cover and concealment, especially heavily forested and remote mountainous areas like the Sierra Maestra.

Once in power, the *Fidelistas* built a solid base of grass roots support. They engaged the poor *campesinos* in the countryside as well as the oppressed urban working class by giving them a sense of citizenship. Castro's new regime quickly organized networks of neighborhood "committees" across the island, which were basically cells of civilian informants swept up in revolutionary zeal, each keeping a watchful eye on their neighbors. With the help of these vigilant snitches, any opposition was quickly and ruthlessly rooted out.

I found it interesting that Nathan knew the strategic details of how the Revolution had succeeded—a Revolution that I wanted to forget, or perhaps pretend had never happened at all. Nathan's analysis resurrected old fears and frustrations with the way our lives had been forever changed, but I was determined to apply the lessons I had learned from Jerry to not let the past spoil the present. There was so much about my life in Varadero that I wanted Nathan to see. I was looking forward to sharing with him the same room where I had slept as a child.

Before we entered *Los Delfines*, I went next door to buy chocolates, which I always brought as a gift for the hotel employees and which had become a tradition. I was affectionately greeted as *El Señor de Los Bombones,* Mr. Bonbon. I then introduced my tall, handsome son to the hotel employees and basked in their compliments. Nathan graciously thanked them for such a warm welcome in his very best Spanish, "I am so happy to finally see Varadero! My father has talked about this beach since I was a little boy."

Walking through the courtyard to our room, Nathan was impressed by the sturdy architecture and how the large blocks of limestone had been precisely cut and carefully placed to create the graceful arches that highlighted the red-tiled courtyard. Being at my summer place with Nathan brought back many fond memories. For a moment I was whisked away, recalling the carefree days of playing games of hide-and-seek behind these very columns that supported the series of arches.

Standing upon the terrace, Nathan was mesmerized by the clear, vibrant blue water and the natural beauty of the seashore that I had once called my backyard. As I stood close to my son marveling at the ocean, I had to fight back bittersweet tears—tears of sadness for my stolen childhood, mixed with tears of joy for being able to now experience together its everlasting beauty. Beneath these emotions, there was also a sense of pride and defiance—both the wave-battered beach and I had survived.

Before we settled into the seaside splendor of Varadero, we headed to a family reunion in Cárdenas. Driving through the disintegrating city, Nathan was surprised by the decay, in spite of hearing stories and seeing many photos from my previous trips. He was dismayed by the neglect of the beautiful buildings. Bricks that had once formed an impressive façade were now heaps of rubble. Ornate tiled roofs that had soared high, now sadly sagged—no match for the tropical rains. Even though Nathan was a seasoned traveler and had viewed squalor like this in other countries, a crumbling Cárdenas carried an emotional significance. He was uncharacteristically somber as we viewed the devastation of my hometown, and I believe it awakened in him a deeper appreciation for what I had lived through.

Tía Elvira and her daughter Elvirita were anxiously waiting to meet and hug my son. After a long embrace, Tía Elvira could not take her eyes off Nathan, and she softly repeated loving endearments. I could tell Nathan was aghast at the condition of their home, but he was far too polite to allow his almost imperceptible reaction to show.

When Tía Elvira finally finished complimenting Nathan, Elvirita eagerly offered stories about my childhood and Nathan was all too willing to listen.

"Your father was kicked out of two schools by fifth grade. He even relieved himself during class right at his desk on the classroom floor!"

"What was Papi's reaction?" Nathan wondered.

I replied, "While meeting with the principal, I told my side of the story. I had requested permission to use the bathroom several times but was not allowed. 'Why not?' my father had asked. Evidently, the teacher did not think I really had to go. To which my father responded, 'I would have wet the floor, too.'"

Nathan met Elvirita's son Omarito, and they decided to cruise around town in his 1953 Nash. I was elated that Nathan could experience this brief taste of life in Cuba with his cousin. Nathan put his charming, sputtering Spanish to good use, sharing the stories of his childhood in the United States. Omarito told Nathan his own tales of growing up in Cárdenas. It seemed to strengthen a bond that had been instant. It was undeniable that they came from the same gene pool. Omarito told Nathan he wanted to sell his car and buy a motorcycle, a Harley-Davidson. "That's what the girls like," he said. Two cousins from two completely different cultures with so much in common.

While they were gone, I told Elvirita about our stop in Cantel. I described how I had almost revealed the location of the buried treasure to the current resident. Elvirita laughed, "I forgot to tell you the last time you were here. It was on the news a couple of years ago. The money in Cantel was discovered."

Our visit seemed to merge two worlds into one, at least for this short time. Nathan and I were having fun, but it had gone much too fast. I wished I could have stopped the clock and savored that day forever—but it was now time to return to Varadero. As we pulled away, Nathan solemnly said, "Even though I know we made them really happy today with our visit,

I feel so badly for them, I wish we could do more." I reminded him we had to accept the political limitations of their situation, and we needed to stay focused on what we *could* do, which was to help them financially. These family reunions always ended with the sobering reminder that their lives were so controlled.

Back in our room I told Nathan for the first time about my ordeal of having left Cuba as a child of eleven, the anxiety at *La Pecera*, the pain of the separation from my parents. "I didn't fully appreciate their courage until you were that same age, and I tried to imagine shipping you off alone to a foreign country. Could I have done it? Probably not. The torment and worry would have been indescribable."

As we drifted off to sleep at my summer place, I realized life had come full circle. On this memorable night, as I listened to the gentle waves of the ocean, I whispered to Nathan the closing to the bedtime prayer I used to say when he was a little boy, "Jesus loves you, and you can be anything you want to be. Just be your best self."

Proud Past

before Nathan and I had left for Cuba, Marielmy had called me to say that my genealogical sleuth was ready to talk. So the next day after breakfast, Nathan stayed behind at the hotel to study for final exams while I headed to Kiko's house. He was waiting for me in his rocking chair, wearing his customary "uniform:" white shirt, white shorts, white socks and white gym shoes. Kiko had lived in this same masonry beach home for most of his life; as a widower who lived alone, he always welcomed company.

After we greeted each other with a heartfelt hug, I was too excited to sit down. But Kiko gently guided me toward his rocker and walked across the cluttered room to turn on a fan and direct it toward me. He inquired about my family, my health and the details of my trip, but I was anxious to get past this courteous and customary exchange which in Cuba was required to begin every polite conversation. To ask immediately about the results of his research would have been insufferably rude, so I tried to hide my impatience. Kiko then offered me a beer. I declined, but he went ahead and brought one anyway—another typical Cuban hospitality gesture.

"*Te va hacer falta,*" he said. "You are going to need it."

I sipped politely, trying to keep my composure with my eyes fixed on the mound of papers at Kiko's side. He pulled his chair closer to me and placed the palm of his hand on top of the thick stack. "I have your information here," he instructed me. "I am going to give it to you in chronological order." I stifled the impulse to grab the entire pile to my chest and dart out the door like a thief. I knew I had to let Kiko savor the moment.

The first thing he handed me was my birth certificate, something that I already possessed. Then he showed me several successive certificates. Because of their ages, not all could be found at civil offices; many had come from church records. All had been certified with seals, stamps and signatures. Every birth certificate listed three generations: the newborn, the parents and the grandparents, thereby providing a trail to generations past.

"They are all here," he nodded. "You can find any person's name and their records if you know where to look." Then he proceeded to tell me that I was a Sotolongo. "Do you know who they are?"

"*Sí*, it was my Abuela Amélia's maiden name. They were a prominent family. That's all I know."

"Well," he said, "there is a lot more."

He continued to work through his pile, and with each paper I learned something new. My great-grandfather and my great-grandmother had been cousins—a common practice in colonial days to protect both power and wealth. Amélia Sotolongo Limendoux had married Alejandro Abascal

Sotolongo. I was amazed to hear that the Sotolongos were one of the founding families of Cuba.

"It was the noble family from which all noble families branched," Kiko told me. "The noblest of the nobles. The Sotolongos were descendants of Juan who had come to Cuba in the early 1500s."

Juan? I had no idea whom he was talking about. By now I was somewhat embarrassed at how little I knew so I just kept listening, protecting my ego by pretending that I had a better grip on Cuban history. I would definitely need to find out who Juan was.

Kiko showed me the detailed family tree that he had drawn himself. "This is not well done. It can be done better by a professional." I had hoped to hear about perhaps three or four generations—and here Kiko was ready to take me back five hundred years. I was proud, yet shocked and bewildered.

Then Kiko told me about a rare book, the Bible of Cuban genealogy, written by El Conde de San Juan de Jaruco, which could trace my ancestors all the way back to Spain. Kiko gave me a transcript of my family's succession that he had copied by hand from an archive copy.

He then handed me a hardbound book, *La Historia de Cárdenas* by Carlos Helberg, where all mentions of the Neyras and the Sotolongos and their active involvement in the development and governing of the city had been underlined. Diego de Sotolongo had secured Cárdenas in its entirety as a land grant. My hometown had apparently once belonged to my ancestors! Not only that, the Sotolongos also had owned many large tracts of land throughout Cuba. They were, in fact, founders of several cities besides Cárdenas, including both Havana and Trinidad, one of the oldest cities in Cuba.

Kiko suggested, "When you return to Havana, you must visit Señor Eusebio Leal, the city historian. His office is at the museum in the old governor's mansion at *La Plaza de Armas*. Tell him that you are a Sotolongo and interested in more information about your family. Also, did you know that your grandmother's home and birthplace was at what is now the *Hostal Valencia* in Old Havana?"

I knew exactly where the beautiful old building was, but had never dreamed it had once belonged to my family. It took me a moment to gain my composure and be able to speak. "I could never thank you enough for all you have done," I told Kiko.

"You don't owe me anything. It all belongs to you. I can tell by the joy in your eyes how much it means. Do you know what day this is?" Kiko asked.

Still stunned, I shook my head. I was not sure what he was leading up to.

"Today is your father's birthday. This is his gift to you. He knows what you have been looking for."

I choked up. In the excitement of the trip I had totally forgotten.

Kiko's brilliant mind had a tremendous capacity for memorizing historical details. He had also traveled to several different municipalities and churches to gather all of these documents—not easy without a car. He had gone through so much trouble for me.

"How did you know I would want all of this?" I wondered.

"I felt it the first time I met you. I could tell by your reaction to our conversation."

As Kiko handed over all of the papers, the drawing and the book, he abruptly asked me, "Have you ever read *The Celestine Prophecy*?" After I confessed that I had not, he advised, "When you get home, read it and you will know why."

That evening, Kiko, Nathan and I had dinner together. I was relieved to have Nathan join us because my mind was still spinning. He was able to keep the conversation going with Kiko, while I kept drifting back to all I had learned earlier that day.

After dropping Kiko back at home, Nathan and I packed our bags and drove back to Havana. It was already dark and I was concerned about the land crabs overtaking the road and giving us a flat with their huge pincers.

Nathan made fun of me for exaggerating the danger of the infamous crustaceans. "Oh, Dad, you're bragging about how large Cuban crabs are!"

We were only ten minutes outside the city limits, when BUMP! We hit a crab. Nathan had been resting his eyes, but he opened them abruptly when the car swerved, looking alarmed. The swath of our headlights illuminated swarms of lumbering creatures scuttling across the lanes and Nathan realized I was not telling a tall tale. I teased back, "Nathan, it looks like you will have to eat crab instead of crow!"

Back in Havana, we were ready for bed when suddenly the telephone rang with a dinner invitation. Richard, who had introduced himself to us at the airport while we were all waiting for our luggage, was insisting Nathan and I meet him at *El Aljibe*. By now it was nearly midnight, but these late-night Latin feasts were not uncommon in Cuba. Before I could turn him down, Nathan interjected, "This is our last night here. Let's go."

When we arrived, Richard was already there hosting dinner, and he rose to graciously introduce Nathan and me to the large group. To my surprise, he seated me at the head of the long table right next to Alejandro Castro, one of Fidel's eight sons. I was dumbstruck and annoyed that I had allowed my son and myself to be put in such a compromising position by someone I hardly knew. But after we drank a little wine and told a few jokes, I reconciled the irony of a *Pedro Pan* refugee breaking bread with the son of *El Comandante*.

Amid the din of the friendly conversations, I became a bit paranoid and contemplated the consequences of having a Castro at the table. As the wine continued to flow, it loosened my inhibitions. I suddenly grabbed Alejandro by the back of his head, clutched his ponytail and pulled him closer to me, speaking directly into his ear.

"That's my son," I proudly claimed and pointed to Nathan, who was sitting on the other side of me. "I want him to be able to make it back to America. Are any flying bullets looking for you? Is my son safe here?"

I'm not certain just what had come over me. In spite of all my sessions with Jerry, the child within me was sometimes still dodging gunfire and hearing his mother screaming his name in panic and desperation. But now I was the parent. It was as if I had switched places with my mother, and all of those protective instincts swelled in a wave and enveloped me.

"You don't need to worry about security," Alejandro assured me. He responded with a hearty laugh and called down to Richard at the other end of the table, "I'm glad you invited this character to join us! He's got *cojones!*"

It was nearly two in the morning when Alejandro adamantly insisted, "You have to come party with us!" We finally agreed and accompanied them to a local jazz club.

An hour and a half later, Nathan and I said our good-byes to the group, in spite of Alejandro imploring us to keep the party going by heading to breakfast at his home afterward. As Alejandro grabbed me for a good-bye hug, I stiffened as I brushed against the concealed gun clipped at his waist hidden under his loose tropical shirt.

Nathan and I were more than ready to head back to the hotel for the night. But we were really wound up from all the sugar in the rum, so I asked Nathan if he wanted to walk over to see his great-grandmother's home even though it was almost four in the morning.

"Sure, let's light up a couple of cigars for the road," Nathan suggested.

The streets were deserted except for the police on their vigilant patrol. The music from the sidewalk cafes had ceased long ago, and the only sound we heard was the rhythmic pattern of our own footsteps echoing on the rough cobblestones.

As we stood outside the *Hostal Valéncia* and the smoke from our Partagás cigars slowly wafted away in the balmy late-night breeze, Nathan looked at me and confided, "Dad, this trip has been incredible. It has been great for me to meet my Cuban relatives and see all the places I have heard you reminisce about. Thank you for bringing me to Cuba!"

"Nathan, this trip has meant the world to me. Thanks for coming, son. I love you."

Historic Havana

Our last day in Havana began with a hearty breakfast and a double shot of Cuban coffee to jolt us awake. Following Kiko's recommendation, our first stop was the historian's office at the *Palacio de los Capitanes Generales* museum. We asked to see Señor Leal, but his assistant informed us he was in a meeting. He was not only Havana's historian but was also in charge of all restoration projects in the colonial area—as many as four hundred at one time.

"Perhaps I can help you," his assistant suggested. I told her that I had been directed to Señor Leal, who could perhaps help me verify and expand on what I had discovered about my ancestors.

She asked, "What is the family name, Señor Neyra?"

"Sotolongo," I replied.

Within minutes, she returned to let us know he would take a break to see us right away. Señor Leal's office, it turned out, was not at the museum.

His assistant escorted us down the narrow, alley-like streets of Old Havana to an administrative building several blocks away. Señor Leal greeted us with open arms. "I will always make time for a Sotolongo!"

"*Muchas gracias*," I said, genuinely touched. I told him that I was doing research on my ancestors and wanted to hear all that he could tell me in the time he had available.

Señor Leal laughed. "It would take hours to tell you the role the Sotolongo family played in the history of Cuba!"

He began by telling me that the country had been founded by eleven noble families who had been given land grants in the early 1500s. The Sotolongos were indeed at the top of this hierarchy of noble families. Some of the other families included Roxas, Pedroso and Calvo de la Puerta; these families often intermarried in order to expand their power and prestige. He also informed me that the names Soto, De Soto and Sotolongo were all the same family. The name had evolved as they grew in power and wealth. *Soto* meant "grove" or "forest," in reference to the vast amount of land they owned. As they amassed more and more, they added *longo*, which meant "large."

Listening to Señor Leal, I was filled with a tremendous sense of pride. I wanted to know so much more, but I was also aware of his time constraint. He mentioned several books where I could find a lot of family information, including *El Conde de San Juan de Jaruco*, the same book from which Kiko had obtained information.

I asked Señor Leal about my grandmother's house, the *Hostal Valéncia*. He confirmed that it had been the Sotolongo family home and then encouraged me to take a tour and introduce myself to the manager, Ana

Mildred Vidal. I thanked him for restoring the *Hostal Valéncia* and saving an essential piece of my family's history. He mentioned that there were many Sotolongo properties, not just in Havana but throughout the island.

"I'm sorry," he interjected, "but I must now return to my meeting."

Needless to say, I left Señor Leal's office with an enormous sense of belonging. Even better was that my son had shared this experience with me. I told Nathan, "I am glad you are my witness, otherwise it might be difficult convincing the rest of our family what we have just learned."

After a quick lunch, we decided to go back to the *Hostal Valéncia* and just walk around. All the while, I kept replaying in my mind my conversation with Señor Leal. I realized that unlike Kiko, he had made no mention of anyone by the name of Juan, and I was annoyed that I had forgotten to ask.

As we approached the hotel, there was a large tour group at the entrance and I listened in to the historical account of the home being given by their guide. She made reference to the *marqués*, a Spanish title of nobility. As the crowd moved on, I briefly pulled the guide aside to make sure that I had heard her correctly. She repeated very politely that this indeed had been the home of *Marqués* Sotolongo and went on to rejoin her group. That title attached to my family name was new to me. I remained standing in front of the large home in complete amazement.

We entered the building, and I gazed around, contemplating what it might have been like living there. This majestic mansion was painted a golden yellow. Its vaulted, paneled ceilings and arched doorways were accented by massive wooden beams and a stone floor. We proceeded to order drinks at the bar and then sat at a table to soak in the historical ambiance in the plant-filled, open-roofed courtyard.

I was surprised to see Señor Leal walk through the large entrance, and he greeted us briefly as he passed by. Within a couple of minutes, he returned to our table with the hotel manager, Ana Mildred.

"He is a Sotolongo. Please give him a private tour of his home!"

"This is quite a coincidence," she laughed, "since Señor Leal does not stop by here on a regular schedule."

Ana Mildred was well educated and extremely knowledgeable about the family history. As we walked around, I learned more about the Sotolongos' past and how they had lived. This large rustic mansion had been one of the earliest noble homes built in Cuba. The *patrónes*, masters, had lived upstairs, and the downstairs was used as servants' quarters and a warehouse for the vast stock of belongings they had brought from Spain. In order to maintain their affluent Old World lifestyle, most items had to be imported to the New World by boat.

Ana Mildred took us to the second-floor connector. She explained that we were now entering a second home, a different hotel, *Hostal El Comendador*. "As the Sotolongo family grew, they bought the adjacent property so the two mansions could be connected." We walked through the narrow passage that had been cut through thick masonry, leading to a beautiful glass-enclosed reading room that faced the courtyard beyond the graceful archway.

On the way back to the *Hostal Valéncia*, she told me that the new lobby display would include a photo of my great-great-grandfather after the picture was restored. She also confirmed that María Josefa Sotolongo had been made a *marquesa* in 1872.

"I appreciate what you have done to preserve the Sotolongo history, and I would love to stay here next time," I told her.

"I manage both hotels, so just let me know and I will reserve one of your ancestors' bedrooms for you," she offered.

Ana Mildred then suggested additional resources where I could learn more about my family. "You should go back to *el Palacio de los Capitanes Generales* museum and look for several Sotolongo heirlooms, including the china and a portrait of the *marquesa*. Many other personal items, including family photos, are stored there. Also, there is a priest who is very knowledgeable about history and specifically the Sotolongo family. Father Elpidio López stops by here once in a while. I will get his telephone number for you the next time I see him."

The tour of my grandmother's home had come to an end, and I could not find enough words to thank Ana Mildred. It was getting late; Nathan and I had a plane to catch, so I gave Ana Mildred a hug good-bye and promised to see her again when I returned to Cuba.

Our trip had become more than I dreamed it could be. How appropriate that after touring all of Havana, the last treasure we discovered was my grandmother's house. What a terrific way to end this remarkable journey with Nathan. I was elated. I looked at Nathan and said, "My son, you have now seen Cuba. Let's go home!"

Emotional Contract

"*What's happening, Ed?*"

I did not know where to begin. Taking my son Nathan to Cuba had aroused many buried emotions that I would examine in my continuing sessions with Jerry. But I was not always quite sure what I was supposed to do with these new insights that were challenging my two old and trusted servants, denial and deceit. The gap between who I was and who I had always pretended to be was now exposed. The jig was up, and the feeling of vulnerability was devastating. I was looking inside a dark room full of demons, unsure whether I wanted to turn on the lights or just continue to grope in the darkness.

But sometimes Jerry illuminated my dark room with a beam so bright that it was blinding. He had a way of getting me riled up by rubbing my nose in the stink of reality to let the aroma awaken my subconscious. Therapy was like that—unpredictable, invigorating and exhausting, all at the same time. And then one day, Jerry almost annihilated me by pushing my saintly mother off her pedestal, questioning her integrity.

"Bullshit!" Jerry scoffed.

"What?" For a moment I was taken aback.

"You heard me, Ed. Absolute bullshit," Jerry insisted.

"I've told you how it happened," I said defensively. "I distinctly remember the look of despair in my mother's eyes and the exact spot where we stood. I am not making any of this up."

Jerry countered, "Maybe it's the truth as you knew it at the time. But that doesn't mean much, given the circumstances."

I shook my head. How could anyone challenge me about something I recalled so vividly? "Tell me what you mean," I asked in frustration.

Jerry sighed, "How old were you when you left Cuba?"

"Eleven," I answered, wondering what he was leading to.

"And you think it was your own decision to leave alone without your parents?" Jerry confronted me.

"Yes." One morning at the summer place, before meeting my friends at the beach, my mother came into my room. She looked serious, although I could not recall having done anything mischievous. Mami was not given to yelling or spanking, but she had a laser-like stare that could slice steel.

"*Mi hijo*, I need to talk to you." Then she hesitated.

"*Sí, dime, Mami*," I responded. Having already heard my father's threat to leave her, I thought maybe she was about to announce a divorce. But I realized my parents were far too traditional for that. As far as I knew, there had never been a Neyra divorce, not anywhere. Besides, Papi lived a macho Latin life where he did as he pleased. Why would he want to change anything?

"The schools are closed," Mami said calmly. "I want to know if you would like to go to school in the United States."

What was she thinking? I did not want to go to school at all, not anywhere. I didn't even attend the tutored English classes that Tía Gladys had arranged. They took too much time away from the beach. Why would I want to go to America? "I thought school was going to reopen next semester," I ventured.

"Yes, maybe. But we are concerned about indoctrination." Mami gently explained that Castro's government was reorganizing public education by retraining teachers and rewriting textbooks. The private schools were closed forever.

"What do you think I should do?" I asked.

"Once you have made your decision, I will give you my opinion. You don't have to answer right now, but we do need to know soon." Then she pulled me into her arms for a long, warm embrace. "*Ay, mi hijito!*" she exclaimed. Mami had always given me such loving hugs; somehow I felt relieved of this pressing matter. It couldn't possibly be as serious as it had sounded.

"Where will we live? Who will look after us?" I wondered.

"*Los Americanos*, Mr. Newman and Mr. Bass in Cincinnati," Mami explained.

I had never heard of Cincinnati and had no clue where it was. I am not so sure Mami did either. But there was one thing we both knew for certain:

It was far away. As I leaned close against my mother's chest, I took a mental journey of galactic proportions in one deep breath, from the warmth of her bosom to the cold of *el Norte*.

"Have Melba and Lalita made a decision?" I wanted to know. Without them, I knew my answer would be fast and firm—and I could move on to join my beach buddies for the day.

"Yes, they are both going. That is the only way we could ever allow you to go," Mami confirmed emphatically.

It was not what I wanted to hear. My competitive and adventurous spirit was instantly ignited. I was not about to let the girls explore a new world without me. I was injected with courage and decisiveness and can still feel the adrenaline rush of that precise moment. The excitement of the possibilities, the adventure of the unknown and the empowerment that came from making an adult decision were all so stimulating that even before my mother released me, I had a reply. It all seemed so easy while still wrapped safely in her arms.

"*Mami, yo también voy*. I too will go."

Her benign expression assured me that I had given the right answer. She told me that I had made a good decision, kissed me a dozen times in rapid succession in our customary parting ritual and then walked out of the room with no apparent sign of emotion. But just outside the door, she turned and looked at me. For a moment there was a strange, wounded look in her eyes. How odd, I thought.

Mami, yo también voy. Four words I will never forget. Four words that still haunted me forty years later—and had led me to precisely where I was sitting right now.

"Bullshit, Ed!" Jerry exclaimed. "No eleven-year-old child makes that kind of decision. You did not decide to come to the United States, you were sent—and that is a completely different thing. Your mother made you believe you made a choice, but in reality, she manipulated you. What do you think would have happened if you had said, 'I want to stay here in Cuba. I don't want to go.'?" Jerry challenged.

I thought for a moment. "I don't know. I suppose my mother and my Aunt Gladys would have tried to convince me that leaving was in my best interest."

"And how did you feel about your mother?" Jerry prodded.

"I adored her. I would have done anything to please her."

"Yes, of course. You had an emotional contract. You agreed to behave in a certain way, as long as you received the desired payoff. You pretended to choose, even though the decision had obviously already been made. Your payoff for the 'proper' answer was your mother's everlasting love and approval."

Jerry explained why it was difficult for me to deal with the abandonment aspect. "It would have been easier if your mother had been a wretch. But the fact that she was such a loving, unselfish person only meant that you could never think of her as abandoning; it would have been too great a betrayal. Abandonment is not about circumstances, it is about the empty feeling of being left behind."

Of all the lessons that my counselor guided me through, acknowledging Mami's manipulation was the most difficult to accept. I'd been duped, all right—but for the most loving and selfless of reasons. I found myself more awed than ever at her strength and nobility. She had convinced me that leaving had been my idea so that I would not feel powerless. Mami had accompanied Melba and me to *La Pecera*, said good-bye to us through a partition and shouldered the entire burden of grief in order to spare me. Somehow Mami had still found the strength to keep her composure long enough to reassure me one last time that she loved me, rather than sink to her knees in desperation.

What happened once I boarded that plane and was out of her sight, I can only imagine. Not a single word was ever spoken about it. How I longed to have her back for one moment, place my hand against hers once again, this time in humility and gratitude rather than self-absorption, and tell her that I now understood the magnitude of her courage and the enormous sacrifice she had made.

A Royal Palm Welcome

*E*very time I returned from Cuba, I always gave Melba and Lalita an update from my trip. My glowing reports intrigued them, and I was hoping their apprehensions about returning were beginning to subside. I was eager to be their tour guide—not just because I now knew my way around the streets of Havana—but more importantly because Jerry had opened my eyes to the emotional significance of our escape. I felt a certain sense of pride, for they had looked after me when we first came to the United States, and now I wanted to reciprocate by escorting them back to Cuba nearly forty years after our traumatic departure from *La Pecera*.

We finally selected a date for our trip. The necessary paperwork was completed, and after several weeks we were clear for take-off. The excitement was building, but during our discussions, I began to notice that Lalita rarely sounded positive or excited about our journey back. I was getting concerned that maybe she was not really ready to go.

"Why don't you ask her?" Lynn suggested.

A few days before our scheduled departure I called Lalita. I wanted to make sure she did not feel obligated, and that my enthusiasm had not influenced her decision to go. Her reaction was one of instant relief.

"Ed, I have prayed about this trip and have finally realized I am not emotionally ready—just thinking about it makes my heart flutter." She thanked me profusely for doing all of the preparation work, for my willingness to escort her as a gift and for my openness in discussing the issue, but she had come to the conclusion that the time was not right for her.

"Melba and I are still going as planned, but I hope that someday the three of us can return to Cuba together," I consoled her.

Melba and I met in Miami the night before our departure, having arranged to meet our cousin Julio, Uncle Toto's son, and his wife, Gloria, for dinner. Julio also had invited another couple to join us at Coconut Grove, a large outdoor urban mall with countless shops and restaurants. Despite the noisy crowd, we attempted to have a civil conversation regarding traveling to Cuba—a divisive topic for many families of Cuban heritage.

Julio had become an articulate attorney like his father Toto, with a great knowledge of history and a passion for legal data and definitions. He felt strongly that we had no business going to Cuba. In spite of our shared experience of escaping as children, we had totally different opinions now. He was a hardliner who believed travel to the island helped support Castro and would be a betrayal of what his parents had stood for and ingrained in him.

I, on the other hand, was a former hardliner who could have respected the embargo if it were based on principle and were consistent with our treatment of other Communist nations. But the United States did business with China, Vietnam and North Korea. Why not Cuba?

Needless to say, the topic dominated our entire evening meal, but the conversation changed no one's mind. I offered to be his tour guide if he ever reconciled the suppressed hurt and anger that fueled his antagonistic viewpoint. I wondered if Julio might have a change of heart if he saw for himself how the people in Cuba lived.

Fortunately Julio's friends were not of Cuban descent, and they neutralized the heated discussion, allowing Julio and me to let go of our passionate debate. In parting, Julio and I hugged and he assured me, "If I change my mind, I will let you know, so we can go together."

The next morning before sunrise, Melba and I were already in line to board the plane. On these charter flights there were no assigned seats. I had learned that it was important to arrive early to secure seating in the forward part of the cabin. Travelers tended to haul along the special requests of family members, so the plane could be crowded and the storage space limited. It was not uncommon to see scooters, tires or a radiator as carry-on luggage on flights to Cuba. Luckily we were able to sit comfortably in the first-class section.

There was definitely something mystical about this journey. Melba and I traveling together brought back so many memories. Melba remarked how fast life goes; here we were returning after nearly forty years, half a lifetime — and it seemed like only yesterday that we were leaving *La Pecera*. She appeared both excited and apprehensive during our short flight. As we circled for landing, Melba began a curious surveillance through the window. She commented on the lush, green vegetation and the richness of the red Cuban soil below.

"I am already glad we came," she smiled with tears in her eyes.

I wrapped my arm around her shoulders and held her in comfort, knowing that the emotional ambush had only just begun. As we aligned with the runway and the wheels touched ground, she peered into the nearby fields and said nostalgically, "I remember the day we left, going down this very runway, building speed for take-off, looking out at the royal palms and wondering if I would ever see them again. And here they are, just as beautiful as ever, waving in the breeze, welcoming our return!"

Marquesa Melba

My friend Luis picked us up at the airport, and drove us the long way so that Melba would see a more picturesque, less industrial part of Havana where the extent of the architectural decay was not quite as pervasive. We were on our way to the *Hostal Valencia*, where Ana Mildred had reserved the suites that had been our great-grandparents' bedrooms and where Abuela Amélia had been born.

"*¡Bienvenidos a su casa!* Welcome to your home!" Ana Mildred greeted us. "If there is anything that I can do, please let me know." Before handing us her business card, she added her home phone number, and we thanked her for her gracious hospitality.

As I settled in the room and emptied my suitcase, I lost myself in a trance, imagining Abuela Amélia as a child, running through the hallways of this grand old building. It was eerie knowing that her voice had once reverberated off these very walls.

Melba and I met in the lobby and started exploring the narrow streets of Old Havana on our way to have lunch at *La Bodeguita del Medio*, where I was happy to see René and Marianita. I introduced them to Melba, and they immediately asked for her requests. Marianita told Melba the name of each composer and revealed the poetry and circumstances behind every song.

With every melody, Melba began to reminisce about the love ballads Mami had sung and the glorious stories of Havana Papi had told. She complimented Marianita's talent and then added, "Lyrics in Spanish are so passionate and romantic. These songs will now have a completely different meaning for the rest of my life!" I could see Melba transform before my very eyes as her hand gestures grew more animated and her Spanish more fluid.

For the next two days we explored Old Havana, visiting art museums and as many tourist attractions as we could squeeze in. Melba was a very energetic person and she wanted to see as much of the capital as possible, so we did a lot of walking. After a great dinner at *El Aljibe*, we returned to the hotel close to midnight and I asked Melba if she wanted to go out again.

"You mean now?" she responded incredulously.

"Of course! The night is young in Havana!" I exclaimed.

"Not for me!" she replied. "I just want to go to my room to journal the events and my feelings about today—and then get some rest." It was the only time in my life I had ever seen Melba worn out.

"Sleep well, for tomorrow is a big day," I reminded her. We were going to meet Father Elpidio López the next morning. As promised, Ana Mildred had given me his phone number, and we had spoken several times before our visit. Even with his busy schedule as the pastor of two churches, he offered to give us a guided historical tour of the Sotolongos in Havana.

"*Buenos días, Padre,* we finally meet face-to-face! Please pray for my sister, for she has offended a man of the cloth."

Even though I had shared with Melba all the information I had been given regarding our ancestors, she had teased me, "I think you've paid the *padre* to concoct this riveting story, or else he has been drinking too much *vino* at Mass!"

He laughed, "You are forgiven, *Marquesa,*" as he kissed her hand.

As we left the hotel, he reiterated the importance of the *Hostal Valéncia* in Sotolongo history. He then pointed out various properties throughout Old Havana where succeeding generations had lived. He also showed us several former Sotolongo *solares,* city blocks of once-grand multi-family residential buildings.

As we walked toward the harbor, Elpidio pointed to the hillside across the channel. He explained how the Sotolongos had donated this large tract of land to guard the entrance to the Havana harbor after the English had temporarily taken control of Cuba in 1762. The Spanish were then able to build *La Cabaña* barracks on the donated land adjacent to *El Morro* fortress, increasing the coastal protection against another invasion.

The Sotolongos had also donated *La Loma De Soto,* the hill of Soto, on the outskirts of Old Havana. The *Atarés* fortress had been built at this strategic location due to its elevated and advantageous view of the old city.

We stopped by Elpidio's church, *La Merced,* where he showed us a book titled *El Curioso Americano,* published in the early 1900s. This anthology chronicled the activities of the founding Cuban families dating back to the 1500s. It contained extensive information about the many government posts the Sotolongos had held.

Elpidio was in awe of the role the Sotolongos played in Cuban history. He addressed Melba and me with a level of respect bordering on reverence that was disconcerting and told us that it was a genuine honor for him to be in the presence of Sotolongo descendants. I found it quite intriguing and wondered what had triggered the young priest's fascination with our particular lineage. But one thing was for sure: Ana Mildred was right—he was an expert on the Sotolongo family.

At one point I asked Elpidio if he could help us research the Neyra family, but he did not show much interest. He did know that the Neyras were also descendants of Spanish nobility and had been successful Cuban merchants and politicians, but they were nothing compared to the Sotolongos. The Neyras also had been involved in the building of the railroad so he took us to the train station where the first locomotive in Cuba was on display. Elpidio offered to take us to meet a friend of his aunt who was nearly one hundred years old and had personally known slaves owned by the Neyra family. Of course I wanted to go right away, but he said it was too far, and he would have to make arrangements for another time.

He added that he had ancestors who had been slaves of the Sotolongo family. Anyone named Sotolongo who is black, he explained, is a descendant of a Sotolongo slave. "There is not a drop of black blood in the Sotolongo lineage," he said. Elpidio, a black man himself, expressed this with an unusual sense of pride that I found rather strange. I then stressed my strong feelings about slavery—that the selling of human beings was the greatest evil ever committed by mankind. He was remarkably philosophical about it, something that I greatly admired.

Elpidio had mentioned several times that I had a relative in Madrid—Federico Martínez de Sola, also a Sotolongo descendant who had recently been in Cuba doing similar research. Federico's documents had shown that we shared the same ancestor, but our lineages had split ten generations ago in the city of Trinidad, near the southern coast of Cuba. Elpidio gave me his telephone number and suggested that I call him. He also mentioned that Federico had copies of the Sotolongos' noble titles, *El Marquesado de la Real Campiña* and *El Marquesado de la Real Proclamación*, as well as an original rendering of the family crest.

I asked Elpidio, "Where did you meet Federico?"

Elpidio laughed. "On the street!" Federico, a devout Catholic, was wandering Havana with his wife, Carmen, looking for a church to attend Mass. He had asked a policeman for directions just as Father Elpidio was passing by, so he let them know that his church, *La Merced*, was just down the street. They struck up a conversation on their way to the service, and Federico told Elpidio that he was in Cuba researching his ancestors, the Sotolongos. Stunned, Elpidio told him that he already had extensive information about his family.

"What an amazing coincidence!" I exclaimed, promising Elpidio that I would get in touch with Federico in Madrid.

Melba had one last request. She wondered if she could view the one document I had forgotten to give her a copy of, the birth certificate for our great-grandmother, Amélia Sotolongo Limendoux, who had married her cousin, Alejandro Abascal Sotolongo. So Elpidio agreed to take us to *Ángel Custodio*, the church where these historical records were stored.

We arrived at the large, neo-Gothic church near the former presidential palace. Elpidio, known by everyone there, was able to directly enter the archives. Hundreds of ancient, leather-bound volumes that dated back to the 1500s were neatly stored in tall bookcases. I was surprised they were exposed to the bright light and the humidity, since there was no air conditioning. Each thick book contained thousands of names handwritten so long ago that in some places the ink had eaten through the pages. It took us a couple of hours to find what we were looking for, but finally Melba's persistence paid off. She cried, *"¡Aquí está!* Here it is!" We made a copy and took a photo of the book, then hustled to catch a taxi to get Elpidio back to *La Merced* to celebrate his afternoon Mass.

"Make sure you contact Federico!" were his last words as we thanked him profusely and hugged good-bye.

The next morning, we headed to Varadero. I was especially touched by Ana Mildred's parting gift, a ceramic tile inscribed with the lyrics to my favorite song, *"Contigo en la Distancia."*

"I know the composer, César Portillo de la Luz, very well. We hosted his seventy-fifth birthday party here at the *Hostal Valéncia* a few years ago. Would you like to meet him?" she offered.

"Of course!" I replied enthusiastically. "I was briefly introduced to him at a jazz club after a performance and would love to see him again."

Ana Mildred smiled, "I will set it up. Call me when you get back to Havana."

Homeward Bound

As we arrived in Varadero and drove down Primera Avenida, *Melba sadly* observed that the coconut palms that had once neatly lined both sides of the boulevard had been uprooted and never replaced. No longer did manicured landscaping and perfectly pruned oleander accent the neglected, yet stately homes.

The first thing Melba wanted to do was look at the beach where we had played as children. She stood staring at the ocean and commented with a wistful look on her face, "I'd forgotten how much the water looks like emeralds." As Melba turned to survey the beach, she noticed how much everything else had changed. Tropical storms had eroded our sandy playground, and many of our childhood haunts, like the bowling alley and Mr. Williams' hot dog stand, were long gone. This stretch of shoreline definitely had lost some of its luster.

After lunch we decided to go to Cárdenas to visit Alfredito's grave. We stopped to buy flowers across the street from the cemetery and proceeded to the entrance gate. But no one looked familiar. I asked the new administrator if Sabanilla was around, and he emphatically declared there was no one by that name who worked there. I was confused. How could he not know the man who had looked after the graveyard for so many years?

A well-dressed gentleman had driven up to the entrance and stood at the doorway, waiting for a pause in our conversation. The new administrator told him that I was looking for someone who had worked there.

"What's the name?" he inquired.

"Sabanilla," I responded.

"How do you know him?" he wondered.

I explained that I had met him on a previous trip. "He was a friend who helped me find my brother's grave, and I just wanted to say hello."

The man was quiet for a moment, seeming to gather his thoughts. Then he said, "I am sorry, but Sabanilla died last year." He explained to the new administrator, "Sabanilla had looked after the cemetery for longer than you have been alive!" He then added that the old man's real name was not Sabanilla but Agustín Moisés Benítez Sánchez. Sabanilla was his nickname in honor of his nearby hometown. After noticing my disappointment, he offered to take me to Sabanilla's grave.

Dr. José Arego Muro introduced himself to Melba and me, and as we followed him out the door he explained, "I am a physician, but I have a great interest in local history. I have been working for years at the daunting challenge of refurbishing the cemetery." He added, "Since I have so little time and limited resources, you can see it is a never-ending project."

I complimented him, "Thank you for pursuing such a noble cause. Our brother is buried here."

He escorted us to Sabanilla's grave, where I stood for a few moments in respect and appreciation, mourning the death of a man I barely knew. His sense of gratitude toward my father had opened my eyes to another dimension of Papi's character. I pulled a few flowers from Alfredito's bundle and left them on his grave.

Dr. Muro recalled where he had heard the name Neyra. "There were several Neyras in Cárdenas, and many were involved in politics since the city's beginning. In fact, there is a Neyra grave nearby, Gerardo Neyra. I can take you there next."

At the tomb he explained that Gerardo owned the Cárdenas Jucarro Railroad during Cuba's colonial days and had hanged himself in 1895 when the sugarcane mills were burned and his business collapsed during the War of Independence. Months later, I verified Dr. Muro's story about the failure of the railroad in the book, *Sugar and Railroads: A Cuban History, 1837-1959*.

He asked if we had been to the *Museo de Bellas Ideas*, the Museum of Beautiful Ideas, also known as the Elián Gonzáles Museum—named after the little boy who lost his mother at sea while fleeing to the United States. He survived the ordeal, only to endure a long political struggle to send him back to Cuba. "You really should visit Sr. Ernesto Álvarez Blanco, the director there." Dr. Muro excused himself and said it was getting late. We thanked him and then headed toward Alfredito's grave.

I had taken Kiko's advice and had read *The Celestine Prophecy*. Suddenly,

Insight No. 7 sprang into my mind: Stay alert to every coincidence, every answer the universe provides for you.

"Melba, this is the third time that I have been told by someone that I need to go to the Elián Gonzáles Museum. I think we should go after we are finished here."

We placed flowers in the rusted tin can used as a vase at Alfredito's grave and said a prayer. We then walked over to Tío Ramón's grave, where I left the remaining flowers. I thanked him for all he had done for us and thought of the wonderful days he had made possible at the beach. How I wished he could have rejoined us in the United States. Without his love and support, the family was never quite the same. Melba and I decided to make a rubbing of Tío Ramón's stone to bring back to Lalita as a gift, along with the photo of his grave she had requested.

On the way back to the car, we saw the doctor once again, thanked him and told him we were on our way to the museum. "You'd better hurry!" he warned, "They close at five."

We dashed through the city to get there just in time. The museum was an impressive structure that had been recently restored, and it brought back many fond memories. In my childhood it had been a firehouse, and Abuelo Matanzero had taken me there many times to climb the fire trucks and to talk to the firemen about their harrowing adventures.

A courteous woman at the front door asked if she could help us. "Yes, we are here to see Sr. Ernesto Álvarez Blanco," we breathlessly inquired.

"Where are you from?" she asked.

"We grew up here but have been gone for many years," I explained.

In spite of her skeptical expression, she asked us to please wait while she called him. But there was no answer. "Why don't you follow me, and we will see if he is still here," she offered.

We used a side door to bypass the exhibits and caught him just as he was locking the door to his office. The assistant introduced us and as we shook hands, I explained, "Dr. José Arego Muro suggested that we visit you. I am sorry it is so late—we can come back tomorrow."

"No, no," he insisted. "I always have time for a Neyra," as he led us back into his office. "Your family has been a big part of the history of Cárdenas. I have a lot of files on the Neyras—magazine articles, pictures and speeches from the Senate, but I will need some time to gather the information."

He gave us his home phone number and good-naturedly asked me to give him some notice next time. We thanked him for staying late, and I assured him that he would be seeing me again.

"It will be an honor," he replied.

Melba and I got back into our car and headed for Varadero. I told Melba, "We just hit the jackpot, because Sr. Ernesto Álvarez Blanco is a certified city historian with access to all records. He can also help us in other parts of the country via his colleagues, which is essential because we know that our family was spread across the island."

Later that evening, we took Kiko to dinner. When I introduced him, Melba thanked him for all the information he had given me. "I am so glad to finally meet you. I have now caught the same genealogical bug!" she confessed.

Kiko proceeded to impress Melba with his extensive knowledge and capacity to remember dates and details. He spoke of arranged marriages, which preserved both families' wealth and power, and quarrels over naming rights for newly acquired properties. We both sat back and enjoyed his fascinating historical monologue.

On the way home, Melba commented on Kiko's mental sharpness and wondered about his age. I told her I had once asked Kiko how old he was, but he was secretive and curiously caught up in the vanity of not revealing it. I never understood why he was so elusive.

The following morning after breakfast Melba and I took a walk along the beach. There was something very special about sharing the shores of Varadero with my sister again. With every step, we romanticized a lifetime of childhood memories compressed into one continuous dialogue.

"I wonder where all those friends are now?" Melba mused.

"I know that Betty and Mary live in northern Ohio, near Akron." The sisters had been from the city of Matanzas and had lived across the street at their grandparents' beach house during the summer months.

We also talked about Tony Caravia, who used to help me terrorize the neighborhood. Tony was from *Ciego de Ávila*, a town right in the center of the island. He and his family used to summer in Varadero at the Imperial, while his father made the long commute on the weekends. Unfortunately, Sr. Caravia drowned one August afternoon, right in the same stretch of surf where we all played.

Both Melba and I thought how wonderful it would be if there could be some sort of reunion, but it would not be easy to organize. The group had lost contact and was spread all over the United States—including Montana, where the Torres brothers—Oscar, Raúl and Jorge—had gone to live. The only one who had not left the island was *El Chino*.

It was so much fun to recollect the details of those good times with someone who had shared them. "Doesn't it seem as if it were yesterday?" Melba asked, as she sadly noted the absence of the *pirulí* vendors. We would buy the bright, cone-shaped, translucent lollipops from the beach vendors who walked the shores with their rustic, wooden pegboard holders slung over their shoulders, ringing hand bells and calling, "*¡Pirulí! ¡Pirulí!*" Then we would all form a big circle under the tropical sun while standing up to our waists in the warm aquamarine water, eating our sweet treats and telling stories for hours.

Melba sentimentally wondered, "Ed, where have the forty years gone?"

Emotional Embargo

I had let Elvirita know that Melba and I would be visiting, but I gave her no precise time. I had learned to be vague about our arrival in order to prevent the family from preparing a big feast that I knew they could not afford.

When we returned to Cárdenas the next day, Melba said, "I can't believe we were born here." Our hometown could easily have been a poster image for the failures of the Revolution. We weaved through the pothole-scarred streets, dodging hundreds of bicycles and pedestrians, searching for old landmarks that could barely be identified. Many buildings were in near ruins, most in desperate need of repairs. As we drove down *La Calle Real*, Royal Street, the dilapidated structures were only remnants of the regal homes that had once decorated both sides of the main boulevard.

"I thought you were exaggerating in trying to prepare me, but now I see what sad shape the town is in. What a shame part of our family is stuck living here," Melba lamented as we drove towards Tía Elvira's home.

The remains of El Europa, *the hotel which Tío Ramón had once owned*

In spite of the terrible living conditions, our greetings were always exuberant, and Tía Elvira was overjoyed to see Melba after four decades of forced separation. Elvirita, her husband, Omar, and their children soon joined us. Our cousin Jorge and his wife, Sonia, also brought their family. After sharing what was going on in our lives, it did not take long before Tía Elvira brought up Melba's legendary scholastic achievements. Her medals and awards had been stored, but as different family members left the country and passed them on for safekeeping to those left behind, they were somehow lost. In jest, I asked to see mine.

"Those never existed!" laughed Elvirita, who, like Melba, had studied engineering.

Elvirita and Melba sat next to each other and busily chatted about the past forty years of their lives. But Jorge was very quiet. He appeared distressed and admitted how much he missed his brother Guillermo, who had recently left the island with his wife and two sons to live in Miami. Every year, the United States allowed up to twenty thousand Cubans to legally enter the country. Because of the great demand, the visa applicants' names are drawn from a lottery and Guillermo's family had been lucky winners.

I thought of my father's separation from his brother, Jorge's father, decades earlier and was saddened to see the same sorrowful cycle repeat itself. Jorge masked his depression by continually offering us something to eat or drink in an effort to make us feel welcome. It was a compulsive Neyra trait that I had also observed in my father.

Tía Elvira, however, was beaming with joy from our visit and having her family together once again. She was so sweet and peaceful, always with such pleasant regard for everyone. It was then that I realized how much she reminded me of Mami. I found it interesting, for they both had married brothers who were also very alike. It seemed that the Neyra men had established a tradition of marrying kind and understanding spouses that accommodated their own willful personalities. That was certainly true for my father, my uncle, my cousins and me.

I had already shared with Elvirita my genealogy research and had brought along copies of my findings. She was impressed with the amount of data I had accumulated and had started some research of her own. We compared notes. I knew her work would be very helpful, since she lived in Cárdenas with access to local records. I told her about our visit to the Elián Gonzáles Museum the day before and that I was going to return to meet with the director, Sr. Ernesto Álvarez Blanco, for additional information.

"I know him," Elvirita said. "Let me know if I can help."

I thought Tía Elvira would also be a terrific resource since she had lived in Cárdenas all her life and still had a sharp mind. However, she was apprehensive to talk about the Neyras—in particular her father-in-law, Abuelo Neyra. "I don't recall" was the repeated response to questions she was far too alert not to remember.

I mentioned that I knew Abuela Amélia's parents had strongly disapproved of her marriage to Abuelo, because his mother, my great-grandmother Josefa, had been a *mulata*, a stigma within their social class. My great-grandfather José de Jesus had been infatuated with the beautiful servant, but the Neyras had tried to sweep the love affair under the rug, and my grandfather's official story had been that his mother died at birth.

Abuelo later abandoned Abuela Amélia after she was diagnosed with Parkinson's disease while she was in her forties. I was also aware he had squandered the family wealth, but in the end that did not really matter. Once the Communist government implemented its version of social and economic equality, everyone lost their money. However, I perceived that there was far more to my grandfather's circumstances than met the eye.

Abuelo Neyra had been an impeccable dresser. I never saw him without a tailored suit, a heavily starched white shirt and his neatly knotted trademark black bow tie. He always sported a fedora and when he was not wearing it, would rotate the hat round and round in his hands in a circular motion.

I was intrigued by the fact that I never saw Abuelo Neyra outside in the daytime. When he visited Papi, it was very early in the morning, always before sunrise, while we were still in bed. Abuelo never stayed long, but occasionally Papi would invite me to join them. My grandfather would be perched on the edge of my father's bed, twirling his hat and making a soft sound while compulsively smacking his lips. I never understood much of their coded conversations, and I always thought his predawn visits were peculiar, but no one ever talked about it. In fact, there seemed to be a certain aura of secrecy in regard to his entire life.

Tía Elvira was surprised at the details I remembered, but she still was not interested in airing any of the family's sordid past. I respected and admired her loyalty, but this was information I was longing to know and understand. She became particularly elusive when I started asking questions about something that had puzzled me for years. Abuelo Neyra had supposedly attended medical school, like his father, grandfather, uncle and cousins—but it was a career that he abandoned. I had heard rumors that he may have been appointed to a city government post in the health department but I was never able to confirm whether it was a real job or a political favor due to the fact his father, José de Jesus, had been the Municipal Doctor of Cárdenas.

Elvirita had remained silent but I could tell by her expression that she had more information to divulge. She asked me to follow her into the kitchen to help with carrying out the refreshments. I picked up on her subterfuge and as soon as we were away from the others, she confirmed, "There is a lot that I want to tell you, but I can't do it in front of my mother. She is very loyal to the Neyra family. She will never speak ill of anyone, and besides, her generation is known for keeping secrets. Let's talk some other time when we're alone." I dropped the subject, and we went back into the living room carrying the drinks.

With each visit, I noticed various home improvements had taken place. In spite of a proud reservation about accepting our financial help, Elvirita expressed her gratitude by telling us the front door and the masonry walls were now repaired and painted, and their roof did not leak anymore. I was happy to offer assistance—it lessened the guilt from both my affluent lifestyle and my previous support of the embargo, which had been so easy for me to ignore while living in the comfort of the United States. I thought about my dinner conversation with Julio just a few nights earlier in Miami and wished he could be here with us now.

Of course, during family visits my cousins and I never talked about politics. It was not in their best interest to reopen old wounds or complain to us about a regime that completely controlled their lives. Mostly we recalled memories of days gone by, for now we lived in two different worlds. But once the repertoire of family stories had run dry, and our emotions had drained all our energy, it was time to hug and kiss good-bye, not knowing when or even if there would be another reunion.

As Melba and I began to say our good-byes, Elvirita produced a box containing some news clippings and Abuela Amélia's letter seal as a parting gift. "I've been saving these for you," she said. I felt as if I had been handed some secret treasure and thanked her for the present as we said our last good-bye.

"I had no idea how emotional this visit would be," Melba confessed as we drove back to Varadero. "I am exhausted!"

"Yes, I know just how you feel," I somberly empathized.

Melba continued, "Just think, Ed. This is where we came from. We have been so fortunate, and for them life is so hard. It's wrenching but therapeutic to return to one's roots. Somehow it puts life into perspective." She hesitated for a moment, then finally added, "I now understand why you have become so adamant against the embargo."

Family Pride

It was our last night in Varadero, and we had a delightful dinner overlooking the ocean, admiring the sunset at our summer place from my special table on the second-floor balcony. Melba commented on how fast the time had gone by—yet it seemed that in just a few short days we had reconstructed and reconciled our past. Then she added, "I have never seen you as happy as I have seen you here."

"Yes, even my therapist Jerry has told me Cuba seems to heal the holes in my soul," I cheerfully acknowledged.

The following morning we took one last walk on the beach and then got on the road back to Havana. Once we arrived in the capital, I called Ana Mildred to check on the possibility of having dinner with the composer César Portillo de la Luz. She confirmed that we should meet her in the lobby of the *Hostal Valencia* that evening.

The conversation at dinner was interesting and rather intellectual. As the group discussed the philosophical ideas in the books they had recently read, I tried to change the subject by asking the composer about the woman who inspired the lyrics of my favorite song.

He smiled enigmatically, "No one knows that but me."

His current wife, whose name was America, joined in trying to get him to tell, but she already knew he would not.

"You can't imagine how many times during interviews people have tried to trick him into revealing his muse," she said, "but they have never succeeded."

After our meal he graciously invited us to his home. On the way there, I thought I would take one last shot at discovering the mystery woman. But America jumped in and pronounced, "Even I don't know!" America was quite a bit younger than César and a very colorful character. She then concluded with certainty, "I really don't need to know who she is. He has been married so many times, but at his age, I am sure I will be his last—and besides, look who is driving his car. Me!"

Once at their home, he was kind enough to sing that famous song. Then he laughed, "Do you know how many people have told me that they were conceived in a moment of passion while their parents were listening to *Contigo en la Distancia!*" We all laughed and talked late into the night until Melba and I finally took a taxi back to the hotel in the wee hours of the morning.

On our last day we leisurely hung out in Old Havana. That afternoon we spent hours in deep discussion at *El Mirador*, The Lookout, an outdoor rooftop restaurant right in the heart of the old city with a panoramic view of the harbor. It was such a pleasant, sunny day to just sit and reminisce.

Melba said, "All that we have learned helps me to better understand Papi's family pride and realize how different he was from Mami. I can now see his point of view and also feel his passion for Havana."

"I'd give anything to be able to talk to Papi again for just one hour, and discuss what I have learned about our family." I ruefully confessed, "I realize there were things he may have tried to allude to when I was younger, but I ignored them, and now I am seeking them out like a determined detective!"

In the warmth of our love and friendship I expressed feelings that I had concealed for years. I admitted to Melba my regrets about not offering a toast to her and Brian during their wedding reception at our home on that gorgeous October day over a decade before.

At that dinner I kept reviewing in my mind exactly what I was going to say. It was to be short and simple: "This day is as beautiful as you deserve. May you and Brian live happily; I love you." But my emotions were so raw, I could not speak at all. I had been on edge since early that morning, and by the time I went to bed I was very upset. Lynn asked me what was wrong, but I could not reply. I was sobbing. Even though it was past midnight, I went outside to be alone and had the hardest and longest cry of my life.

For years I had been in some fog of denial, but Melba's marriage to Brian finally had forced me to confront the death of Barry, her first husband and my best friend. With teary eyes, I raised my *mojito* and finally delivered my toast to her eleven years late. After wiping our tears, Melba and I talked about Barry for the first time since he had passed away fourteen years ago.

"Barry always spoke of writing a book about us leaving Cuba. He was fascinated by our story and dreamed of visiting Cuba. When he died, I found some of the notes he had already made in his wallet. They meant a lot to him," Melba confided.

"I would love to see what he wrote. Maybe he's got some ideas I can use—I am thinking about writing one myself!" I told Melba.

This trip with Melba was the most meaningful time I had ever spent with my sister, and it allowed us to reconnect many missing pieces of our fragmented lives. Melba enthusiastically exclaimed, "I am so thrilled that my daughter Tina has made me a grandmother! Maybe someday my grandchildren can swim in the warm and calm waters of Varadero, too."

Our memorable tour had come to an end, and Melba and I were on our way to the airport the next morning. As always, leaving Cuba brought back apprehension about going through Immigration. I suggested Melba proceed first, in case there were any hitches and she needed my assistance in going through her travel documents. She was processed quickly and sent on to the departing gate. Ironically, I was the one held up. The agent said that I could not leave, that my paperwork was not complete. A supervisor was called over to assist, but by now my experience had taught me to relax and just allow the dysfunctional bureaucracy to spin its wheels. As he approached me, I smiled and said, "Don't worry about it. Take your time. If it takes a couple of weeks to resolve it, I'll just go back to the beach!"

He laughed, "Don't worry, Señor Neyra, you are getting out of here today." We both chuckled, and I was finally allowed to pass through the guarded door. Melba was waiting for me on the other side in a near panic, concerned I was being detained and would miss the flight.

During takeoff, Melba commented from her first-class seat, "This is a lot more comfortable than our *Pedro Pan* flight in 1962!" Once we landed in Miami she had only moments to catch her connecting flight home to Virginia, so our good-bye was rather hurried but very loving. As Melba hugged and kissed me, she exclaimed, "Thank you! This trip has been the greatest gift you could have ever given me."

Reconstruction

"*What's happening, Ed?*"

After returning from Cuba with Melba, I confirmed to Jerry that he was right about the island's therapeutic effect on my soul. "My sister noticed how happy I was while we were visiting there. I told her I have you to thank for that."

"I have also learned from you that whenever there is a strong sensory reaction, underneath lies a discovery, a lesson, a hurt to be healed. As Melba and I walked along Varadero Beach, we reminisced about our childhood friends, and those memories awakened a desire to see them again. I long for that idyllic time of my life and keep thinking about reuniting the group once again, as impossible as that may be."

Jerry explained, "We have discussed your separation from your mother during the two most crucial periods in your psychological development—the first few months of life and preadolescence. In addition to creating difficulties establishing intimacy, another common consequence of separation is the desire to pursue the past as an attempt to create connections and develop a feeling of belonging. The loss of innocence so early in your life inevitably results in later attempts to recreate it. Often gatherings and reunions are fulfilling a human desire to connect to the comfort zone of the past, before this separation occurred. Your fascination with genealogy is also a manifestation of this insatiable quest."

Jerry continued to usher back memories and feelings that had been buried so deep I had not known they existed. He taught me techniques that were beyond anything I had ever considered, and reviewed using meditation as an exercise to go outside of time and space to reach the inner self, the subconscious.

The first time I tried this new approach, I had an incredible revelation. I found my safe place, just as Jerry had instructed me, where the mind can go to feel secure. It was the seawall facing the ocean at Varadero where I used to watch the sunsets. But what was really interesting is when I reached out to my inner child, he responded in Spanish!

Jerry prodded me, "Think about it, did that little boy know how to speak English?"

"Of course not! I skipped English class to play on the beach."

"Then how could the conversation be in anything but Spanish!" Jerry deduced. "What did your inner child reveal?"

"He is really angry!" During this meditation, I had revisited our departure day. But as I scanned through the mental images from *La Pecera*, I realized that Papi was not in the crowd. That was impossible. How could he not be there to say good-bye to his children, whom he might never see again? I was confused.

Jerry intervened. "Do you think the image was accurate, that your father really was not there?"

I was not sure, so after I had this revelation, I had called Melba to share my experience and asked her if she remembered Papi being at the airport. She confirmed that he had not been there.

Jerry interjected, "The subconscious mind will not regurgitate a past trauma until the conscious mind is ready to deal with it. It contains a safety mechanism, unwilling to process what the emotions can not yet bear."

That is where I had been stuck for years.

I had asked Melba if she knew why Papi was not there. She was unsure but did have some ideas of her own.

"Papi was very much against our leaving and was very resentful that Mami had been influenced by Tía Gladys." Melba added, "Maybe he just could not stand to have his wishes disregarded."

Melba's explanation made sense. He was not in charge, not in any sense, so he took a stand against Mami's and Tía Gladys' decision. The strongest way to demonstrate his opposition was to be absent. Why be present in a situation where he felt totally helpless? Also, Papi had been a politician, extremely vested in the belief that Castro's regime would not last—so in his mind there was no valid reason to send his children to a foreign country.

Remembering how I had felt when each of my own two sons had turned eleven, I tried to imagine sending them all alone to a strange land with no real assurance of when or even if I would see them again. A wave of desperation and grief had engulfed me—and that was just from thinking about it. I still could not conceive why Papi had not said good-bye to us.

So what had truly kept him away?

I realized he had given me the answer all along. *Los Neyras no lloran.* He could not bear to risk my last memory of him as a man weeping. Pride yet again stood in his way. This credo had contaminated not only our farewell but much of his life as well as my own.

As I let go of the anger, I no longer felt the pain of his abandonment. The more I understood my father, the more I recognized the roots of my own behavior, and the easier it was to forgive him.

Jerry explained, "Everyone has some degree of spiritual wounding, their soul shattered by some trauma. It is during our spiritual journey that we attempt to repair the damage. Forgiveness is essential for reconstruction."

Beach Bums

"*Wouldn't it be fun for all of us to get together again?*" Melba had said wistfully during our stroll along Varadero's beach. The seed that she had planted in my mind about a reunion began to take root and I kept replaying the many fond memories of freedom and fun, especially that last summer of 1961. It was an innocent time in such a memorable place—our own Caribbean version of *Beach Blanket Bingo*. I understood from Jerry's lessons my desire to recreate the past, but I still longed to see those fellow beach bums with whom we had romped in the sand and surf.

I dreamed of transforming the banks of my pond into Varadero Beach. A truckload of fine sand, a few fake palm trees and assorted beach props would complete the effect. I could already picture the gang drinking *mojitos* under the umbrellas behind a sign that read, "Varadero, USA."

A few months later, the phone awakened me early on the Saturday morning after Thanksgiving. It was my friend Pat, inviting me to join his cousin Mike and wife, Betty, for breakfast. They had been in town for the holiday and were now heading back to their home in northern Ohio.

I was really looking forward to seeing Betty. She had always been my favorite of all of the girls in the group—beautiful, but also caring and friendly, always smiling and speaking kind words. I was trying to think of the last time I had seen her and realized it had been decades!

Betty and her sister Mary had actually found refuge in Cincinnati because of Melba. The niece of the Mother Superior at St. Ursula Academy had heard our story and asked if we knew of any children left in Cuba who might be looking for refuge in the United States. Melba told them about our friends, visa waivers in hand but still waiting for their *telegramas* to be cleared for departure.

The generous niece pursued the necessary arrangements, and later that year in August 1962, Betty and Mary arrived in Cincinnati. It was so much fun to see them, especially nice for the girls, for each was reuniting with a close childhood friend. They all attended high school together and graduated from the Academy.

Their parents, like ours, followed them to Cincinnati years later and even lived near us for a while but eventually moved down to Miami seeking a warmer climate and the familiar culture they had left behind. The girls got married and moved to different cities, so over time we had lost contact.

As Betty walked into the restaurant, the cascade of memories from Varadero was uncontrollable. It seemed as though forty years had sped by as swiftly as a single night's sleep. Betty looked great, as beautiful as ever. I could see the joy in her eyes and felt our bond from the past ignite as I greeted her with a warm, lasting embrace. Of course, it did not take long before we were swept into reviewing old friends and good times.

Betty had a fairly good grip on the whereabouts of several old friends. Her mother was still living in Miami, the mecca for Cuban immigrants. With so many connections, there was always somebody telling somebody something—Lynn called it "The Cuban Hotline." Betty was aware that I had gone back to Cuba and was curious about what was going on there.

I filled her in, "*El Chino* still lives in Varadero; he was the only one of our group who did not flee. I also met his wife and son."

"How is he? What is he doing?" Betty wondered.

"He's doing well. He still rides a motorcycle and is a photographer."

Betty laughed, "That doesn't surprise me, since that's what his father did too."

Mike and Pat politely stayed in the background of our conversation while Betty and I invariably circled back to our childhood. As we reminisced about our last summer together in Varadero, along with the sadness in preparing to separate from our family and friends, Betty revealed, "You know, I have pictures from the day of your departure."

I was puzzled. Then she reminded me that her family had driven to Havana to bid us farewell. Stunned, I had no recollection of her being there. I must have blocked it out, subconsciously superimposing my father over my friends in that final mental farewell portrait. I had been completely unaware that any photos existed, and this information touched a raw nerve. No one in our family had snapped a single shot. It was a grim day we all wanted to forget.

Betty described the photos. There were some of the group, one of Melba actually climbing the steps to board the plane, and one of the aircraft as it went airborne. She noticed my flabbergasted expression and continued, "As a matter of fact, I also have an album containing many additional pictures. It is titled, 'Varadero, Our Last Summer, 1961.'"

I could barely sit still. "Could I please have copies?" I begged. I even offered to travel to her home to make the duplicates.

"Of course, but you don't need to make a four-hour trip. I'll send them to you," she volunteered.

By then we had long since finished breakfast. There was still so much more to talk about, but Mike and Betty had a long drive ahead. We all hugged good-bye and in parting made a vow that we would not wait so long to meet again.

"I should hope not—that would put us into our nineties!" Mike joked.

A few weeks later, I received a package from Betty with the photographs she had promised. I immediately made copies for Melba and Lalita. When I called Betty to thank her, we shared a huge laugh about one particular shot of the four girls on the beach. It was priceless, because it so clearly revealed each of their personalities. Lalita looked a little disgruntled, even on this bright, sunny day. Betty looked joyful just to be with her friends. Mary seemed totally oblivious to what was going on. And Melba was posing as if she were a movie star promoting a film.

I kept reviewing these pictures—and the thought of trying to get the group together continued to haunt me. Of course Melba and Lalita were

The bathing beauties of Varadero Beach from that last summer of 1961

both excited about a beach bums' reunion. I had also discussed it with Lynn, and she thought it was terrific idea.

The following January, on a cold, dreary winter day, I went to my usual lunch spot near my office. From behind me, two tables away, I heard a familiar voice. I listened carefully to make sure, but I knew it had to be Martha. Martha Muñoz had been born in Cárdenas and had come to Cincinnati with her parents in September 1962. She had also gone to St. Ursula and graduated with Lalita and Betty. Energetic and fun, she had occasionally hung out with us in Varadero and had certainly been part of our group in Cincinnati. In high school she had even given my friends and me dancing lessons. Grinning, I approached her table to say hello.

"Oh, my God, Eduardo, I can't believe it! I have not seen you since before you were married. How are you?"

We chatted for a little while about our families. I told her that I was thinking about organizing a reunion with the group from Varadero and wanted to talk to her about it. Martha was ecstatic.

My next call was to Betty. "We'll be there!" she said without hesitation. I asked about Mary—Betty was sure she would be interested in coming too. I then asked Betty if she knew how to get in touch with anyone else. She offered to contact her mother in Miami; maybe she could help. As we went down the list of names, we realized that some would be almost impossible to find. The Torres brothers—Oscar, Raúl and Jorge—had moved to Montana, and no one had heard from them since. But she did think that her mother might be able to help us track down Tony Caravia, since the two mothers still kept in contact.

One night, Betty called to say she had learned Tony was living in a suburb of Detroit. After several conversations with Detroit's directory assistance, I found a Tony Caravia in West Bloomfield, Michigan—but his number was unlisted. Finally, Betty's mother came through with his correct phone number.

When Tony answered the phone, I instantly recognized his voice.

"How in the world did you find me?" he wanted to know. "I have not talked to you in forever! How are you?"

We had reminisced for nearly an hour before I realized I had not yet told him about our plan for a beach bums' reunion at my home in Cincinnati. Tony exclaimed, "I would not miss it for the world!"

The Beach Bums at my home, forty years later

Castaways

We finally set a date for that June of 2002—forty years after our last crackling bonfire on Varadero Beach. We worked hard to get our home and grounds ready to welcome the Beach Bums and their spouses. Lynn was so helpful and supportive that you would have thought it was her own reunion. She wondered what would be best to serve and I suggested, "You can never go wrong with your delicious pork tenderloin when there are a few Cubans in the crowd."

Everyone arrived on time that afternoon, eager to start the long-awaited reunion. I could feel the intense energy as the girls greeted each other joyously after so many years. The emotion of the Beach Bums being together once again was overwhelming, and it took me a while before I allowed all these feelings to sink in.

I was able to talk to each of the women for a little while, but otherwise I stayed out of their huddle. I did make one reference, though, to their photo taken on the beach. I held it up, mimicking each girl's posture and what she might have been thinking. They all laughed. "You haven't changed a bit," said Lalita. "You were a pest then, and you're a pest now."

Tony went outside for a walk in the yard. I spotted him alone by the lake, and I went down to join him. As I approached, he was wiping tears from his eyes. "You know how my father died?" he asked.

"Didn't he drown at Varadero Beach in front of the Imperial?" I confirmed softly.

"Yes, an undercurrent swept him and six others under," Tony lamented. "My father was the only one rescued alive but died while waiting for medical assistance. On the way there, the ambulance was involved in a fatal accident, killing the driver and seriously injuring the medics. That's destiny for you. At least he died at his favorite place." I had known this reunion would resurrect many memories, and with them, buried emotions.

The girls had taken over the family room, where Martha was, as always, the life of the party. She showed us a picture of her daughter, and Lynn and I commented on how beautiful she was. "As you can tell," Martha declared, "she does not get her beauty from me—but she does have my personality!" After critiquing her appearance for a moment, she added, "But I have always had beautiful legs!" To our astonishment, she pulled up her skirt to show us.

"I just love her spirit!" Lynn laughed.

I handed out a few Cuban cigars, so Mike, Pat, Tony and I had a boys' smoking photo taken at the pool-house, where our group had just finished a candlelight dinner. Mary's and Martha's husbands sat in the living room, isolated somewhat from the eye of the storm, talking about real estate, while Pat, as always, was in the middle of it all.

The hours passed too quickly. Nearly midnight, some of the group started to say good-bye, but I knew too many important issues still had been avoided. There was no way to gather a group of Cuban refugees and not talk about Cuba.

Betty asked me to share with the other girls the story about our friend *El Chino*. After I related it, they all wanted to know more about how things really were in Cuba. I had surprised them with current pictures of the beach for them to keep. I gave Tony an old photo of both of us at the Varadero Yacht Club taken by Mr. Bell on his last trip to Cuba the summer of 1959. We passed around the photo albums that I had encouraged everyone to bring to the gathering. I also had a surprise for Betty and Mary. Lynn and I had gone to their former home in the city of Matanzas and taken pictures.

I told the group how much I enjoyed going to Cuba and that I found it had been crucial in helping me to heal the wounds incurred at *La Pecera*. But I also confessed that I was not even beginning to convey the scope of what had really happened to me. That would take hours. I knew that all the laughter we had shared that night just as easily could have been tears. As I dropped this bombshell topic, the party took a more serious turn, and I was not surprised to witness the strong reactions.

"I don't want to go back to Cuba," Mary declared.

"Why not?" I questioned.

"I just don't want to give the government any money," she replied emphatically.

I told her that those high in power were not the ones doing without, and that we were only hurting the common people. I wanted to know why she still supported the embargo.

"I really don't know. That's just how my parents felt. To tell you the truth, I never really thought much about it. As a matter of fact, I haven't thought about Cuba since the day we left in 1962," Mary staunchly insisted.

"How is that possible?" I asked.

"I don't know. I just don't think about it!" she exclaimed.

Actually, I understood all too well.

The room had become quiet and tense. Lynn chimed in with how much she enjoyed visiting Cuba—how much she loved the music and the people and how badly she felt about their situation. The entire group listened intently. Somehow there seemed greater wisdom in my wife's unbiased assessments.

If you are Cuban, the issues are always depicted in black and white. So as our conversation continued, the discussion became more intense and animated. I had come to learn that choosing a side was not easy, since we had been carrying our parents' anger and pain as well as our own for decades.

Our parents went through terrible times. They lost their homes, their businesses and their way of life. There is no denying that what happened to us as children was also unjust. We were all separated from our families and friends, uprooted from our country and our culture. But that was over forty years ago, and though we could never forget, it was certainly time to accept the past and move on. Harboring rancor was corrosive and destructive—and no one was more damaged than those holding on to this hurt. If we did not resolve our bitterness, we risked passing on a legacy of resentment and fear to our children and our children's children.

Martha responded passionately, "I am not afraid to go to Cuba," she said, shaking her head. "I am not afraid of anything. I just don't want to go!"

"Do you ever miss it?" I asked her.

"Of course I miss it. But I am not afraid. What is there to be afraid of?"

I explained that I had been afraid of many things. I was terrified of going through Immigration, of not being allowed back out, of being for some unforeseen reason held hostage. The idea of a police state was still intimidating. But my greatest fears were in dealing with my own emotions that I had deeply buried. It was devastating to finally allow myself to feel the torment of having been separated from my mother as a child. Although the room had once more become intensely quiet, the tension had diminished.

"I have gone through painstaking counseling to resolve my hurt, anger and separation anxiety." I concluded by saying, "I love all of you, and I just wanted to share with you what I have learned."

The room remained silent until Betty finally spoke up. "I want to be objective about Cuba and I would really like to see it again. But many of us are following the paths of our parents. There still seems to be an unspoken promise never to reconcile out of loyalty and respect to them."

"You're right, Betty," I confirmed. "It's called an emotional contract. We've all made them and they are difficult to break without feeling guilty.

But what you need to ask yourself is, 'What price am I paying? What is the benefit, the payoff?'"

Mike then wondered, "Why don't the people just revolt?" He had military experience in the Navy and was familiar with both the catastrophic failure of the Bay of Pigs invasion and with the Cuban Missile Crisis that had brought the world to the brink of a nuclear confrontation.

"It's not quite so easy," I replied. "Fidel Castro has ruled the island with an iron fist for almost fifty years, which makes an uprising nearly impossible. He tightly controls every layer of society, from the highest reaches of government to the average citizen walking down the street. He asserts his dominance through a powerful military, a pervasive police force and local party loyalists who run the neighborhood watchdog committees. For example, whenever I go to see my family, a neighbor who normally never visits my aunt's house, always stops by to say hello and see what is going on."

"Even if Cuba were a democracy, I believe that this skillful and manipulative dictator could probably wage a successful campaign to be elected president. Remember, the campesinos, the peasants that supported him, were uneducated and had no participation in ownership. Castro bought their allegiance by freeing them from the wealthy landowners and providing universal health care and education at no cost. Most importantly, he gave them something they never had before—dignity, a sense of pride and belonging. And besides, Castro has been in power for so long that the majority of the population has never known any other leader."

"Castro is complicated," I continued. "Latin Americans and many

Europeans have a love-hate relationship with this enigmatic ruler. They may disagree with his political views and despise where he has taken the island economically, but they admire his audacity in standing up to the United States. They seem to enjoy that he has defied the greatest power in the world and survived."

"Our government made the grave mistake early on of relying on the advice of men who had fled Cuba. The exiles' justifiable bitterness left little room for objectivity. Strategic decisions and foreign policy were based on erroneous advice characterizing Castro as an incapable madman, someone who could not keep an organization together, and who would be falling from power soon, with minimal resistance. That was why we all left. We believed that his regime was fragile and temporary—that we would be returning shortly. But here we are, forty years later."

"There have been great miscalculations," Jorge Carro once said to me before his death. Jorge had been a dear friend and a brilliant attorney who once served as the dean of the University of Cincinnati College of Law. As a young man, he had attended law school with Fidel Castro. In Cuba, Jorge had been a successful trial lawyer before the Revolution, and afterward he bravely defended many accused of capital crimes by the Castro regime. He finally fled Cuba in 1967. "The disappointing reality is that Castro is a charismatic leader who can arouse the people and is compulsive about total control at any price." Jorge was very anti-Castro, yet he still described him as "a very intelligent, calculating and obsessive man with a great instinct for survival."

I further explained, "Complicating matters, there is also a restraining agreement that in order to settle the Missile Crisis, President Kennedy agreed not to interfere with Cuba. The United States cannot finance or support any military training to overthrow Castro's regime."

I related a conversation I had had with a fellow Cuban-American who once had posed the same question: "Why don't they just revolt, stop acting like cowards and do something about the situation?"

"And what did you do?" I asked her.

She seemed confused by my responding with a question. "What do you mean?"

I pressed her, "What did we all do? We fled the country. Are we cowards? You know, it is easy to criticize from the comfort and safety we enjoy in this great nation, the United States of America. The truth of the matter is that we abandoned our homeland. We are carrying concealed guilt and shame and need someone to blame."

"How did she take it?" Mike wondered.

"Not very well. She became angry and even had the audacity to call me a Communist. Like I said, Mike, it is difficult to stay rational when it comes to the subject of Cuba."

Tony confessed that he wanted to go back but had always been apprehensive. His older daughter had gone twice and absolutely loved it. His wife, Nora, who was born in Colombia, said she really wanted to go, but Tony was still dragging his feet. At one point he looked at me and said, "After hearing you talk, I think I am going to make plans to go."

Melba told stories about our wonderful experience and how she was planning to return with her husband, Brian. She even added that she would love for her daughter Tina to see Cuba, too. Lalita interjected that she still wanted to go and thought perhaps she was finally ready—but her husband, Rich, was not so sure.

By then we were exhausted and drained. It was three in the morning, hours after our first attempt to say goodnight. Even though I was tired, I was pleased by the success of the reunion and looked forward to establishing a new tradition for this to be an annual event.

Our gathering had provided the ultimate vindication. Not even a revolution or years of separation could ever break the bonds of the Beach Bums. We were castaways who had survived and thrived in spite of all the political and personal storms that had swirled around us.

NATURAL SON

*A*lthough my visits to Cuba and the Beach Bums reunion had put me in touch with my childhood, there was one trip much further back in time that still fascinated me. I wanted to go all the way back to the Old World to research my family's ancient roots. Through Father Elpidio López, I had gotten in touch with my long-lost relative Federico Martínez de Sola after Melba and I returned from Cuba. We had originally set a date to visit during the fall of 2001, but the tragic events at the World Trade Center forced us to postpone the trip.

In the meantime, I was determined to find *El Conde de San Juan de Jaruco*, the Cuban families' genealogy reference bible that both Kiko and Señor Leal had recommended. I called the owner of a specialty bookstore in Miami who told me the volume I was searching for was last published in Cuba in 1945 and would be very difficult to find anywhere. He occasionally had encountered a Cuban refugee who, in need of cash, would sell the copy he had smuggled out. But he had not seen one for several years.

My cousin Julio encouraged me to come to Miami so he could help me hunt for a copy. He knew of several antique bookstores where we could sift through the extensive inventories in person to track down the elusive volume. After several failed attempts, it was now lunchtime at our next stop. The warehouse manager happened to be tending the store, and we asked him if they had Volume 5 of *El Conde de San Juan de Jaruco*. He thought about it for a moment, and said, "If you watch the store, I will look in our warehouse across the street. I think I know where we might have one."

It was definitely my lucky day. The manager returned with a copy that had never even been opened. It was still bound in folded sheets, so I had to slice each individual page.

Looking through the treasured reference book, I could trace the Sotolongo lineage from my great-grandfather and great-grandmother back to Diego de Sotolongo y Rojas, who established the family in Cuba in the 1500s. But I still could not find the relationship to the "Juan" that Kiko had been talking about. I

The Sotolongo family crest

initially had overlooked the footnotes on the very first page of the Sotolongo Section, which explained "Juan" was Juan II, King of Spain, the father of

Duke Alfonso de Aragón, Diego de Sotolongo y Rojas' great-grandfather. Once I read the small print, the mystery of "Juan" was solved. But only for a moment since that genealogical link triggered an avalanche of royal connections throughout Europe.

I now had a better understanding of the Spanish monarchy and its direct link to us. Of course Federico had known all of this and more, but to me it was new, intriguing and confusing. I still had questions concerning relationships that just did not add up. How could we be the direct descendants of a king but not be considered royalty? It was a question I was saving to ask Federico once we met in Spain.

After working through our schedules, we were finally able to make arrangements to meet in Madrid the first week in October 2002, more than a year after we had first spoken.

"My birthday is October 7—what a great gift!" Federico exclaimed.

"That is also my father's birthday," I remarked. "What a coincidence!"

I could feel his warm personality in his aged but still energetic voice as he asked me about my father. I told him that Papi had passed away in 1997.

"I am eighty-two years old. How old are you?" Federico wanted to know.

"I am fifty-two," I told him.

"You are so young—my children are almost your age. I will call you nephew, not cousin!" he kidded.

"Okay, Tío," I agreed. "I will see you on your birthday."

I had put together a book with all the Sotolongo documents I had amassed, including copies of family trees and our crest. I was looking forward to giving it to Federico as a birthday gift. He had mentioned that he also had quite a bit of family information he wanted to share with me.

As we unloaded our luggage from the taxi in a narrow Madrid alley, a well-dressed, elderly gentleman approached me.

"¡*Bienvenido, Sobrino* Eduardo!"

"*Tío* Federico!" We hugged and proceeded into the lobby, where I introduced him to Lynn.

"She is a lot better-looking than you," he teased me. "You must be tired after your long flight and should get some rest," he acknowledged, "but I just wanted to be here to welcome you." We talked for only a short time, for he was on his way to work at Macrocina, the frozen foods enterprise he had founded years ago.

Federico had the physique and the energy of a much younger man, and I complimented him on his fit appearance and quick wit. "It's important to keep working and make sure one's mind stays active. I still exercise every day and watch what I eat, and most importantly, have never smoked."

That evening we met at Federico's home for appetizers. His wife, Carmen, a tall, thin, attractive woman with a friendly smile, answered the door. She gave us a welcoming embrace and graciously escorted us through the foyer into the large and ornate living room. Their expansive, beautiful European flat had been in the family for generations. Federico shared with us their financial struggle to retain ownership during tough economic periods throughout Spain's history. He gave us a tour and proudly showed us heirlooms that had been passed down through several generations—oil paintings and china, along with framed displays of *abanicos*, hand-crafted personal fans.

Federico suggested that we spend the following day in the country visiting Philip II's royal monastery, *El Escorial*, which was about an hour northwest of Madrid near his summer home. The next morning as we traveled through the city en route to the monastery, Federico pointed out every building he knew, along with its history. There was great energy, excitement and pride in his voice as he recounted stories about the many roles our family had played in Spanish history.

Federico expertly weaved through the heavy traffic, shifting gears as he continued his monologue on our journey. He had been a fan of the Fascist dictator Francisco Franco and believed that Spain had fallen away from the discipline that this iron-fisted regime had brought about. Federico thought that young people were too lazy, and society had become too promiscuous. He remarked, "At some gas stations and restaurants you can now even buy condoms from a coin machine! You know what those are?" It took all I had not to roar with laughter.

King Philip II had built *El Escorial* in the foothills of Mount Abantos in the Sierra de Guadarrama as a contemplative retreat to house the St. Jerome monks, who were ordered to pray incessantly for the salvation of the royal family. We toured the extensive compound, including the church and the king's living quarters at the center of the complex. My favorite part of the tour was the lower level, where they showed the tools and techniques used during construction. Detailed drawings and scaled models were on display throughout the exhibit hall, illustrating these innovative Renaissance building methods. It was interesting to learn that the mahogany and cedar used in construction had been imported from my very own town of Cárdenas, sent by the Sotolongos to their royal Spanish relatives.

El Escorial was austere compared to other palaces I had visited, and the royal apartment was quite humble, but the marble mausoleum was a notable exception. Its excessive opulence exuded ornamental reverence and a mystical ambience. The "Pantheons of the Kings" housed funerary urns gilded in gold for all the Spanish monarchs buried there—direct descendants from the same time-diluted gene pool as my own. What a weird feeling.

Once we ended our tour, Federico invited us to lunch at the Herrería Country Club, where he was a founding member. His vacation home was directly across the street from the club and just down the road from the monastery. As we enjoyed our lunch on the brisk and sunny day, we had a

My Sotolongo relative, Federico Martínez de Sola, with El Escorial *behind us*

postcard view of the immense monastery nestled in the foreground of the majestic mountains.

Federico reminisced about his life and told Lynn and me about how he and Carmen had met and their subsequent long courtship. He was also a fountain of information regarding the history of our mutual ancestors. By now I felt comfortable enough to ask him the question regarding a detail that had me puzzled for many months, "If we are direct descendants of Juan II," I wondered, "why don't we have a key to the castle?"

He jokingly replied, "Since I am a lot older than you, I should be king first." Then he added, "Or you could do what Enrique II did twenty generations ago."

"What is that?" I wondered.

"He killed his half-brother, known as Peter the Cruel, to become king in 1333."

I persisted with my question for something was still missing. I asked Federico to please speak slowly, because sometimes with his Castilian accent and soft voice I missed a few details.

Finally Federico began to explain. "We are direct descendants of Alfonso de Aragón, Duke of Villahermosa, the natural son of King Juan II."

I knew all that. I still did not understand. "Aren't we all natural children?" I objected.

He smiled and said, "*Ilegítimo.*" I must have still looked puzzled so he reiterated in a louder voice, "¡*Bastardo*! But don't let that bother you," he added. "It happened all the time."

I pulled a folded genealogy chart from my coat pocket and asked him to explain. He immediately found the error. The Duke's mother was not Juan II's wife, Juana Enriquez, but his mistress, Leonor de Escobar. Now I understood. And so did Lynn. "Just think of yourself as a love child!" she laughed. I translated for Federico what Lynn had said and he joined in the laughter. It was ironic that Federico was so accepting of kings having illegitimate children but objected to the common man buying condoms from a vending machine.

As we continued our conversation, I shared with Federico about how dangerous and unjust I thought the absolute power of a monarchy was. He agreed with me but replied with a philosophical, peaceful wisdom, as if he were a tribal elder, "You know, times were different then. You cannot apply twenty-first century thinking to fifteenth-century tradition. In those days, the monarchs were the executive, judiciary and legislative powers all in one—the ideal conditions to breed corruption and abuse of power."

"Does that remind you of Cuba today?" I asked rhetorically.

Later that evening, after dinner, Federico invited me into his old but distinguished library and removed a rare historical reference book from his extensive collection. He gently opened *Historia General de España* by Don Modesto Lafuente, Volume VI, to page 131. He brightened the lights in the dim room and carefully put on his glasses to read the paragraph that solved the mystery. "Juan II of Aragón fathered several natural children with Doña Leonor de Escobar outside his marriage, including Alfonso de Aragón, Duke of Villahermosa." I was thrilled to have the proof of the missing link in my hands and asked to borrow the book to copy the page.

The next morning, we visited Federico and Carmen to say good-bye and return the book. It was a heartfelt parting, one filled with warmth but also with sadness. Federico and I felt as close as if we had known each other all of our lives; he was my connection to the previous Sotolongos. Our final hug was especially long, and I felt as if I was also saying good-bye to the many generations before him.

On our last day in Madrid, I wanted to visit the *Palacio de Villahermosa*, now known as the Thyssen-Bornemisza Art Museum. Kiko had recommended I visit this palace, which Federico confirmed had been the home of the infamous Duke, Alfonso de Aragón, whom I now knew as the natural son of King Juan II and my illegitimate forefather sixteen generations ago.

I was hoping to find information on its origin and add to my collection of Sotolongo memorabilia, but any reference regarding the Duke was general and brief. Lynn and I spent that afternoon strolling through *Parque del Buen Retiro*, and in its wide, formal garden paths we found successive statues of the Catholic kings. I had my picture taken with each, now knowing that we were distant relatives.

I had embarked on this genealogical journey without knowing where it would lead. After learning so much about my royal ancestors, I was proud of their historical impact. But ironically, their public personas prevented the personal connection I was longing for, and in the end I felt more disconnected than ever.

Spanish Treasure

Jerry had explained that my genealogical pursuits were fueled by a desire to recreate connections and develop a feeling of belonging. The Spanish monarchs from the Sotolongo side of my family had left me cold, but I was still interested in researching the Neyra lineage while in Spain. Back in Cárdenas, Elvirita had found out that Santiago Neyra had been a lieutenant colonel in the Armada and had sailed to Cuba in the late 1700s from Santander, Spain. So even though that was all I had to go on, Lynn and I had decided to include this northern coastal town on our itinerary.

We instantly fell in love with Santander. Impressed with its cleanliness and natural beauty, this harbor town was the perfect blend of a modern cosmopolitan city with classic European architecture, surrounded by gentle mountains overlooking the Atlantic Ocean. I said to Lynn, "Just think, if it weren't for my great-great-great grandfather, we never would have visited this beautiful town."

Lynn replied, "Those Neyras sure knew how to pick the spots! Now I know why you have such a love for the sea. It's in the genes."

We stayed at the *Hotel Real*, which King Alfonso XIII had built to house his friends during their summer visits to his castle. The hotel was situated on a hilltop with a magnificent view of the shoreline and the king's summer palace, *El Palacio de la Magdalena*, in the foreground.

I immediately went down to the front desk to purchase a city map and get directions to the cathedral and the archives at City Hall. The helpful receptionist was curious about my requests.

"My ancestors were from Santander and I want to check the records in the city," I said.

"When did they live here?" she wanted to know.

When I told her it was back in the eighteenth century, she smiled in bewilderment. Being a rather young person, she was taken aback by my intense interest in so long ago. While we were talking, the porter kept moving closer, waiting to politely intervene in the conversation.

José Luis, a tall young man, already had carried our luggage to our room, and we had spoken briefly while he gave us the customary welcoming tour. "I overheard that you are looking for information on your family. My father has researched our family five hundred years back. It's his hobby. He knows the people at the archives and may be able to help you," José Luis volunteered.

Overjoyed, I responded, "I sure would like to meet him!"

"He is retired and spends his weekends in the country, where he is refurbishing a 250-year-old home and usually returns to the city late Sunday afternoon. I will ask him to contact you," José Luis offered.

Since it was the weekend, I knew my genealogical research was on hold until Monday. But Lynn and I were looking forward to exploring our newly found Spanish treasure. We walked along the boardwalk that overlooked Magdalena Beach and the harbor on our way to the many shops in the business district. The manicured flower beds highlighted the stone walls along the main boulevard. Although it was relaxing to have a glass of wine at a sidewalk café and watch the world go by, I was elated at the possibility of someone local helping me through the maze of archived records.

Our dinner that evening at a nearby restaurant offered a panoramic view of the ocean. On our walk back to the hotel, we saw a home for sale and romanticized about living there part of the year. We wandered through an elegant casino and then trekked up the steep incline to our hilltop sanctuary.

The next morning we were awakened by a breathtaking sunrise. The bright sunlight pierced through a cluster of clouds creating a spectacular display of fiery colors in the early morning sky.

We spent the rest of the day in *Santillana del Mar*, a nearby town with ancient architecture that had been meticulously restored. "They could use these people to rehab Cuba," I remarked to Lynn. As we strolled around visiting the shops, a local farmer herded his cattle right through the center of the village. Even though cars were prohibited on these narrow cobblestone streets, all the pedestrian traffic had to yield to the passing herd, stepping carefully over the trail of cow *caca* left behind.

When we arrived back at the hotel I had a message from Rafael Quijano, José Luis' father. I returned his call right away.

"*Señor Quijano, es Eduardo Neyra. ¿Cómo estás?*"

"*Muy bien, gracias.* My son told me that you are looking for information about your family. How long are you going to be in town?" he asked.

"Until Tuesday morning."

He laughed. "That is not a whole lot of time to dig into centuries of history!" But Rafael was very friendly, and he immediately offered to help. "I live just two blocks away. Why don't I walk over right now, and we can talk about your research?"

I was thrilled. Lynn and I waited for Rafael in the hotel lobby. He was a tall, husky, young-looking man in his early seventies—jovial, with a great zest for life. I offered to buy him a drink, but he wanted only water. He told me that he did not consume alcohol, and he was careful about what he ate, so we snacked on olives, Spain's most ubiquitous snack.

Rafael shared with us his own genealogical journey. He initially had concentrated on his father's side; however, he later realized it was his mother who bore the pain of his birth, so he began the search for hers. It took him eight years to trace back five centuries.

In addition to genealogy, Rafael had many other hobbies. He had composed music for his church choir, had even recorded selections that won national awards, and was very knowledgeable about operas. He had worked in commercial graphics and had a passion for art, particularly oil paintings. As fellow artists, Rafael and Lynn laughingly debated when to consider a piece finished. "You can always improve it!" he declared. "But in the end, it's a fine balance between perfection and pragmatism."

I could see the excitement in his eyes as he told us about his weekend project, going on its third year and nowhere near completion. He showed us his arms full of cuts and scrapes from his labor. "It is a modest country home with high ceilings and huge walnut beams, but the bathrooms need to be finished before my wife is willing to stay there!" he added with a laugh.

As we sat and talked for nearly three hours, I found myself enthralled by his enthusiasm. "How great just to take the time for something you love," I said.

"You have to take the time to enjoy the flowers. If not, what is life for?" he responded.

We began to talk about my interest in finding my great-great-great-grandfather Santiago Neyra's birth certificate. Rafael already knew a little bit about the origin of my family name. "The Neyras are from Lugo, but I will bring you more information when we meet tomorrow morning."

He mentioned that there had been a major fire in 1941 that nearly had destroyed the entire Santander business district. A windstorm had caused the fire to spread out of control. "Many records were lost," he lamented. But he was still willing to help me search. I told him that a fire also had destroyed family records in Cuba. That was why I was hoping to find them in Santander.

The next morning, after Lynn and I enjoyed another beautiful sunrise, I took a taxi downtown to meet Rafael in front of City Hall. When he arrived, Rafael handed me a large manila envelope with the information he had promised.

"We will go over it later," he said.

Rafael walked us right through security and up the rear stairway, using the shortcuts he knew so well. I was eager to read the packet of materials he had just given me, and it took an extreme effort to not rip it open then and there. But I knew that would be rude and more importantly, our time was precious—every minute counted.

When we walked into the archives the attendants greeted Rafael by name. He requested several birth record books from the targeted years of our search, but they were authorized to bring us only one at a time. As we spread the large book open between us, he read the names on the right-hand pages, while I read the names on the left. I picked up on his technique of following each line with the eraser end of a pencil, and we quickly developed a system and a rhythm of nodding to let each other know when we were ready to turn a page.

Occasionally he would softly whisper a family story when he came across one of his ancestors. There were quite a few. I found myself wanting to turn the pages faster, for I was on a mission, but Rafael was enjoying the process. I thought, what a nice man, happy to help a total stranger sitting here scanning through hundreds of years of birth records.

After a couple hours of paging through many books Rafael suggested, "This process is too slow and I know you have limited time. Let's walk over to the cathedral; it's just a few blocks away. If we are lucky, we may find an empty microfiche research table in their library. Although there are only four viewing stations, and they have to be reserved in advance, sometimes people either find their information quickly or get frustrated and leave before their time is up," he explained.

There was no doubt that Rafael had done this for years, for everywhere we went, not only did he personally know the staff, but he also knew the back way in. We approached the rear of the church, and he said, "If this door is open, we can save a lot of walking."

I could tell by the friendly greetings and helpful assistance that Rafael was well liked. At the church office he asked if any research tables were available. The young attendant told him she was sorry, but no. He was not surprised.

"We can make an appointment, Mr. Quijano," she suggested.

"I will take the next available," he said, "but please call me if there is a cancellation."

But Rafael was not ready to stop searching. Knowing that Santiago Neyra had been a lieutenant colonel in Spain, he suggested we look for military records. "There is a military base with the national records in Santander," he said. "I have a friend who works there, but he warned me that they operate a limited schedule with very restricted access. Let me call." Unfortunately, they were closed for the day. So our search for the time being was over, but Rafael promised to continue to help me with my quest.

He insisted that we take the bus back to the hotel, since he thought the taxis were too expensive. I went along thinking I could read the Neyra packet he had given me while waiting for our ride. The information made reference to the two different spellings of the same family name: "Neyra" and "Neira," which originated in Lugo, Spain, a province in the northwestern part of the country in the autonomous region of Galicia. The Neyras originally had settled in the village of Sarria but eventually migrated northward to Lugo,

The Neyra family crest

the capital city of the province bearing the same name. "*Eres Gallego*," Rafael said. A friendly, generic name given to those from Galicia.

The Neyras later extended through the other provinces of Galicia, like León and Cantabria, and later southward to other autonomous regions, including Las dos Castillas, Extremadura and Andalucía. He gave me a copy of the various Neyra family crests, modified by area.

Rafael's information included an anecdote about Sancho de Neira, a captain in the Spanish army. After Sancho engineered a victory in a territorial battle, the river Arce was renamed the river Neira in his honor. Rafael also had found evidence that the name Neyra is so old, it was known in Spain long before the invasion of the Moors in the 700s.

By now we were so deep into our conversation that we had let our bus sail right by. "The next one will be along in thirty minutes," Rafael informed me.

"Why don't we take a taxi?" I suggested. Once inside the cab, he continued to impress me with his knowledge.

Ruy de Neira had helped Don Fernando III, "*El Santo*," conquer Sevilla and was registered as one of its *conquistadores*. Rafael went on to tell me what he had read about the ancient history of the Neyra family—that they were descendants of Darius III, the king of Persia who had tried to conquer Egypt and was defeated by Alexander the Great at the Battle of Gaugamela.

As the cab driver let him off in front of his home, I thanked Rafael profusely, and he assured me he would continue researching on my behalf. It will take a while, he warned, and wanted to know where I would be going next.

"Barcelona," I answered.

"*Adiós, buen viaje!* Have a good trip!" Rafael wished me as he waved good-bye.

Lynn and I met at the hotel for lunch. We discussed how much we both liked Rafael and what a treat our initial conversation with him had been. I showed her what he had given me, including the Neyra family crests. I was very grateful for Rafael's assistance and for sharing his resources, but the extent of the search was beginning to wear on me. It had become a much bigger project than I ever had imagined. So much information, so many people, so many centuries. Originally I had wanted just to put together a family history for my children, but I found myself once again on a much longer trail. "Where is the end?" I wondered aloud.

We spent the rest of the afternoon savoring our last day in Santander, while shopping for a gift for Rafael. Lynn found a book about opera for him, an extensive volume about the stories and music of the major masterpieces.

At dawn, we were awakened one last time by the colorful morning sky, and we unwillingly prepared to depart. There was a knock on the door from José Luis to deliver a gift from his father—a gorgeous coffee-table book with breathtaking photos of our new favorite city.

"Tell him thank you," I said, "and please, this is for him." In it I had written, "*Para Rafael, un amigo en el camino de la vida, para toda la vida. Gracias.* To Rafael, a friend in the journey of life, for life. Thank you."

It was a short flight to Barcelona, which turned out to be unimpressive—but after Santander I am not so sure that any place in Spain could compare. The weather had grown cooler, with rain showers moving in. We visited the usual tourist attractions, the Olympic Park for the 1988 competition and several museums. We stayed at *Le Meridien*, which was near *Las Ramblas*, the historic promenade full of cafés and every kind of vendor. Both tourists and locals crowded this former canal that was always hopping with aspiring musicians, gypsies doing card tricks and panhandlers asking if you could spare a dime.

During a taxi ride to the hotel late one evening Lynn exclaimed, "Look! Neyra's Restaurant." We already had eaten dinner so we drove on. But by the time we had arrived at the hotel, my curiosity had gotten the better of me. I considered going back but it was past midnight. I called and found out that Antonio Neyra, the owner, was not in but was expected the following evening. I was looking forward to meeting him.

When we arrived at Neyra's Restaurant, the well-dressed waiter greeted us at our table with a friendly smile. There was no doubt by the way he had interacted with other clients that he was the owner. When he returned with our drinks, I introduced Lynn and myself. "We are Neyras," I said, and he insisted on buying our drinks.

We started sharing information. He originally came from Lugo and joked, "All Neyras come from Lugo!"

I had brought him copies of the papers that Rafael had given me. He was very appreciative, so we toasted our ancestors. He confirmed some of the data and said that he actually had been to the Neira River, which was about thirty kilometers southeast of Lugo. He offered to help in my research.

"I visit Lugo regularly," he said, adding that he still had family there and friends who could also assist.

"How many children do you have?" I asked.

"A boy and a girl," he proudly answered.

I reached in my pocket and gave him two watches from our business. My newfound relative looked at the Neyra logo on the faces and said, "Thank you! My children will have fun showing these to their friends and will wear them with pride!"

Lynn took our picture, highlighting his Neyra menu, but not until Antonio darted off to find his tuxedo-style bolero jacket. The restaurant grew crowded and busy, so I hugged him good-bye and wished him good luck.

The long flight from Spain gave me time to reflect on how the complex landscape of my family history was now illustrated with additional layers of colorful details. But there was still one element missing: I wanted to return to Cuba with my youngest son, Justin, to put him in touch with his heritage.

¡Vamos!

Justin had never shown any interest in going to Cuba. Every time I had brought up the subject, he simply ignored me. For a young man with so many strong opinions and bold answers, his silence was puzzling. Only one thing was clear: strolling down Memory Lane with Dad was out of the question.

I respected his stance, although I was disappointed. I wanted so much to take him, just as I had taken Nathan. But I knew better than to try to convince him to embark on anything against his will. Even though he was now twenty years old, Justin could still be a stubborn, surly critter, especially once his mind was made up, so I thought it was best to just let it go.

However, he soon began dropping little hints. "I really would like to go someplace warm," he would interject, right in the middle of a conversation about something completely different.

Not certain whether he was serious or just baiting me, I ignored him.

Then one day, he finally got right to the point, "Dad, I would like to go to Cuba. Will you take me with you?"

"*Vamos*, let's go!" I answered without hesitation. I suggested celebrating *Año Nuevo* with our relatives since I had such fond memories of New Year's Eve parties. It was a Cuban tradition to party all day while roasting a pig, to eat a big meal, drink and dance until midnight—then toast with your glass of *cidra*, a Spanish version of champagne, but sweeter and with less alcohol. It was also a tradition to eat twelve grapes just as the clock struck midnight—in hopes for prosperity and good luck throughout the coming year. Even as a small child I was allowed to stay up late to take part in the joyful festivities to welcome the New Year.

Just as I was getting carried away with the romance of the past, Justin brought me back to earth with a thud. "Dad, I am sure *cidra* and grapes are rationed in Cuba, just like everything else. Besides, no offense, I want to celebrate New Year's Eve with my friends, so let's go before Christmas."

I immediately began to make arrangements, excited to be taking my youngest son to see my homeland. I felt that it would somehow complete this forty-year odyssey. By the time we circled Havana's José Martí International Airport for landing, Justin was positively buoyant, already pointing out the window as we surveyed the island's shoreline.

"Everything looks so green and bright!" he remarked.

"Yes," I responded. "I think it's about eighteen degrees back in Cincinnati."

Landing on Cuban soil had always been so emotional for me. But something was very different this time. Although excited about being with my son, I felt an inner peace that I had never experienced on any other trip before. Even my usual anxiety about going through Immigration and Customs was absent.

Awaiting us was my faithful friend Luis. As we drove into Havana, I was very laid-back, not spewing my usual travelogue description of every building we passed, so Luis assumed the role of tour guide. Justin did not seem surprised by the desperate condition of the buildings or the cars. After all, he already had seen many photos and had heard my endless stories. But he was filled with questions regarding how life worked, how much people earned and how they were able to make ends meet. Luis explained that to survive everyone had some sort of side gig.

I wanted to take Justin to *El Aljibe* for our first dinner in Havana. The portions were enormous—but not for Justin. I described the chicken as "*el mejor del mundo*. The best in the world."

Justin delightedly mimicked me, "You Cubans don't just say something is great, one of the best or even the best in town. It's always *el mejor del mundo!*"

After dinner, Justin was ready to move on and celebrate our arrival in Cuba at a nightclub, but I reminded him that we had a long, exhausting week ahead of us. "Yeah, you old guys should probably get some rest," he laughed.

Early the next day Justin and I began our tour of Old Havana. By now I had learned much about the area and its history and could proudly sprinkle into the conversation the roles that his ancestors had played. We stopped by the *Palacio de los Capitanes Generales,* since I had been in contact with the archivist, Señorita Magaly Torres, to whom Señor Eusebio Leal had referred me.

Magaly Torres had obtained a photo of a huge scroll of the Sotolongo family tree for me. The five-by-ten-foot illustration transcribed with hundreds of names had to be fetched from storage. It was so large that a maintenance man had to supply a ladder to provide a vantage point high enough to get a shot of the whole chart laid out on the floor. I was very grateful for all the trouble she had gone through.

After Justin and I left the museum, we hailed a coco taxi to take us to the *Hotel Nacional*. The bright yellow, three-wheeled scooter with a fiberglass shell was shaped like a coconut and seated a driver and two passengers. As we drove down *El Malecón*, Justin seemed to take great interest in everything he saw. It was a busy week in Cuba. Havana was hosting its annual film and jazz festivals. We bought drinks and toured the grounds while the movie stars hung out at the patio bar and garden. As we were leaving, a replica of an antique car was unloading passengers at the main entrance of the *Hotel Nacional*. It was a new type of taxi in Havana. I asked the driver if she was free.

"No, but I am definitely looking for business," the young lady answered with a smile, as she introduced herself as María.

"*Bueno!*" I laughed. "Give us a complete tour of the city—I want my son to see it all, María. The good, the bad and the ugly."

She was surprised to hear that I was born in Cuba and was delighted that I was now introducing it to my son. So off we went, touring in a convertible. What a great way to see Havana! Having no roof made for an ideal view of the stunning architecture and numerous historical monuments.

As we drove, I became even more aware of how insatiably curious Justin was. We were having animated conversations about the economy, politics and the difficulties of everyday life in Cuba. Justin also had great interest in how government policies affected the people. I found his political views and cultural interests energizing. Here we were, with the car's top down, cruising through the capital, engaged in a philosophical discussion.

"This Communist crap just does not work!" Justin exclaimed in frustration, gesturing toward the crumbling streets and buildings.

I explained that Communism was good in theory since it advocated helping the poor and sharing resources with those in need—a commendable humanitarian concept. But people were too complex with different values, priorities, skills and work ethics to voluntarily embrace such utopian ideals. With limited incentives and no opportunities to pursue your own business ideas, the lowest common denominator prevailed and a mediocre standard of living was the result.

Communism eliminated poverty but generalized misery and has never worked successfully anywhere in the world. In every case, a dominant dictator and his chosen cronies imposed this "equality." An acquaintance of mine once defined Communism as socialism enforced by terrorism. However, I admitted, capitalism had its own set of problems. Nothing was ever simple when people were involved.

Justin then asked María where these "new" antique cars were made. "*Aquí*, here," she answered. "The antique fiberglass bodies are built in Cuba, and the Volkswagen frame and motor come from Mexico."

I was impressed with the workmanship, but Justin assured me it was pretty basic. He was a logical thinker with an appreciation for the inner workings of all things mechanical. This was something he knew a lot about since he had customized cars as a hobby. A perfectionist with a great eye for detail, he quietly pointed out a few of the taxi's flaws. María further explained this car was part of a pilot program to see how well the tourists liked them. We thought it was great, traveling in the tropical sun with an unrestricted view of Havana.

We stopped for lunch at Palco Gardens, a wonderful restaurant that had just reopened in an elegant residential area near the convention center, where many old mansions were now offices for foreign companies. Unaware of its hours, we arrived thirty minutes early, but in the tradition of Cuban hospitality, they took our order and cranked up the kitchen without any mention of inconvenience. We asked María to join us, but she declined.

"I love to spend time alone with my father," she explained. "I would not want to deprive you of an intimate lunch with your son." I appreciated her response; I had invited her out of courtesy, but I really wanted to be alone with Justin.

We had made arrangements with María to pick us up afterward, but she returned very late. When she finally arrived she apologized profusely and explained she had been delayed by a flat tire. In Cuba many cars did not carry a spare, since they were often stolen; Maria had to drive across town in order to get it repaired. Although Justin and I were normally very impatient, we were now both surprisingly calm. "Go with the Cuban flow" seemed to be our new motto.

María was still rattled by the incident so we put her at ease, hopped into the buggy and headed for the Partagás Cigar Factory in central Havana. The guide wanted to wait to gather a larger group before walking us through, but he obliged us after I let him know that I would tip him well for a quick private tour. As we were shown every facet of cigar production, some workers tried to sell us samples on the sly.

After our sightseeing tour, we had one last stop—I wanted to buy tickets at the *Hotel Nacional* for the Tropicana floor show that evening. While waiting for our tickets to be confirmed, I offered to buy María a drink. By now our driver was feeling comfortable with us and willing to reveal her thoughts about living in Cuba. She told me that she had gone to visit friends in the Bahamas, but she missed Cuba so much that she often cried, and by the end of the trip she was more than ready to return home. "In spite of all its shortcomings, I love Cuba," she professed.

María philosophized about the living conditions and defended the Communist regime with a certain objectivity in her respectful criticism of the things that did not seem to work. She repeated a saying from her father, a retired military man, "Cuba is like a beautiful woman; easy to enjoy, but hard to understand."

I admitted to her that I, too, missed Cuba even after all these years. That's why I wanted my sons to see it while I was still alive, so that I could share in their experience. To me that was far more important than the bitter political dispute between the two countries that had gone on for almost a half century. I put María at ease by revealing that I was very much against the embargo, and that I had personally witnessed how difficult it had made life for my family in Cárdenas.

"We know that not all exiled Cubans support the embargo, but we are afraid of the violent retaliation of the hardliners in Miami who want to return, wreak revenge and reclaim the island," María lamented.

I knew that Maria, like the majority of the current Cuban population, had been born long after the Revolution and had never known anything except Castro's rhetoric. "Maria, I can tell you that I lived through the Revolution and it was ugly. I can understand the anger of the hardliners—I once felt that rancor myself. But I know now that those of us who left, as well as those of you here, we are all victims. We have all been damaged by one man's obsession for power and will pay the price for generations to come."

After we finished our drinks and my tickets were confirmed, she drove us back to the hotel. In parting she posed a riddle, "Do you know the similarities between Cuba and Mister Rogers' neighborhood?"

I was clueless and shrugged my shoulders.

She replied with a smile, "The Cubans make believe they work, and the state makes believe they get paid."

I laughed, settled my debt and we hugged good-bye.

Justin and I returned to the hotel room for a little afternoon *siesta*. When we both awakened, Justin jokingly accused me of giving him the finger. I responded by telling him, "*¡Tú estas loco!*"

"I'll show you *loco!*" he exclaimed. Our single beds were about two feet apart, so Justin reached over and landed a tight-fisted blow to my arm. I saw his huge grin and thought, I will take care of that smile. So I retaliated with a punch back. Neither of us would stop the slugfest, and eventually the laughing got so intense that the blows had little effect. Finally Justin grabbed the frame of my bed to pull his target into closer range—but by then our uncontrollable laughter had left us with no punch at all.

That evening, while enjoying a delicious meal at *Las Fontanas*, we encountered our first blackout in Cuba. I had heard that they happened often, but somehow I had always lucked out and missed them—possibly because I mostly stayed in tourist areas, where they lost electricity less frequently. But most establishments were well prepared; within minutes we were eating dinner by candlelight, and the courtyard was safely illuminated with oil lanterns.

After dinner Luis drove us to the Tropicana to see the world-renowned show that had been in production since 1939. I had been there before, but it was part of my "Cuba tour," and I thought Justin should see it. We had front-row seats to watch the island's most infamous nightlife entertainment. It was fun to see Justin's reaction and to hear his response afterward.

"Awesome!" he exclaimed. He was impressed with the costumes, the immense size of the multilevel outdoor stage—but the gymnastic act was by far his favorite. The strength, athleticism and agility of the performers was dramatic.

As we left the show and waited for the valet to bring our car, I told Justin, "Let's get some rest since tomorrow is a big day. We are driving to Cárdenas."

Luis began to make fun of my hometown. He called me Eduardo Cárdenas, so I called him Luis Sagua. Our friendly rivalry had developed into a proud but jovial town-bashing. In the car I boasted, "Wait until my son sees my hometown. He will be impressed!"

Luis directed a droll remark to Justin, "Remember your comment about *el mejor del mundo?*"

"*Sí*," answered Justin with a grin.

Luis smirked sarcastically, "You may want to keep that in mind tomorrow when you see Cárdenas!"

Legacy

*The following morning the weather looked a bit threatening. The cold winds signaled *un norte* was moving in. As we drove from Havana to Varadero, the sky grew darker.

"I thought it was always sunny in Cuba," Justin kidded.

"It will blow over; it always does," I replied confidently.

As we sped along the Central Highway, I told Justin that sections of the road had been built by my mentor, Marty Byrnes, Sr., back in the 1950s. Marty had befriended President Batista and had told me many stories about frequenting the island during its boom years. Long after Marty's death in 1976, his daughter had given me newspaper articles documenting the highway project, as well as Marty's unique Christmas gift to Batista—a pair of Newfoundland dogs.

"How did he get the contract to build it?" Justin wanted to know.

"Well, Marty was quite the promoter, and I imagine there was some kind of financial reward for the former president. That's the way things always got done in Cuba. Bribery."

Justin was intrigued. His long-term plan was to become involved in our paving company. "Do you think we could build roads here?"

"Maybe someday, but not right now. It's not legal. The U.S. embargo prohibits American companies from doing business on the island," I explained.

"I don't get that. What's this embargo really about?" he demanded.

"It's complicated, but anger and revenge are certainly involved. Do you remember how upset and animated Papi would become whenever he talked about Fidel Castro? His face would turn bright red, and the veins in his neck would throb during our discussions. My parents' generation had their lives wrenched apart, and that resentment still simmers today. Since Castro personifies the horrors of the Revolution, the Cuban exile community has promoted and supported the embargo to hasten his demise."

I further explained, "It's been in place for over forty years and the embargo has never fulfilled its objective—to strangle the Cuban economy, fomenting a revolt and ultimately causing a regime change. Ironically, this policy has had the opposite effect. In Cuba, the embargo is often referred to as *el bloqueo*, which literally means 'blockade.' Castro leverages the subtle connotation and uses this perceived military aggression to unify the Cuban people by conveniently blaming the United States for the failures of his revolution."

"If it hasn't worked, why is the embargo still in place?" Justin wanted to know.

"That involves money and politics. For example, Papi was a regular contributor to a Cuban exile organization that raises money for a variety of Cuban-American causes. This organization donates money to the campaigns of politicians supportive of the embargo. One of these representatives from Florida might then trade votes with his Midwestern colleague: 'If you support the embargo, I will support your dairy farm subsidy.' Each gets what he wants at no political cost. It is this practice of trading votes that manages to place special interest groups above doing what the majority of the public may really want. This is all perfectly legal. As I mentioned, democracy, too, has its flaws."

"If the embargo were based solely on principle, we would not do business with China, North Korea or Vietnam—or any other oppressive government, including Saudi Arabia. Unfortunately, the embargo carries a steep price that is only borne by the common people in Cuba, like Tía Elvira and her family."

By the time we stopped at the Valley of Yumurí, the sky was clearing. I was so glad Justin was able to enjoy the panoramic view through the large binoculars mounted at the overlook. Yumurí's spectacular beauty had never been desecrated by Cuba's political turmoil. My hometown was dilapidated, the beach at my summer place had eroded and many historical landmarks were in ruins, but the Valley of Yumurí remained magically unchanged since that fateful trip to Havana back in 1962.

When we reached my summer place, the weather continued to cooperate, but there were still a few dark clouds hovering on the horizon. The surf, always my measure of what was to come, was unusually restless for the normally calm waters of Varadero.

Justin wanted a complete tour, and I could not wait to show him the rooms, the courtyards and the beachfront, all filled with childhood memories. It had become a tradition for me to take a picture of each family member at the waterfront terrace wall from where I had once viewed the ocean for countless hours. Justin even wanted to see the exact window where I used to sneak out at night. I then suggested tomorrow might be a better day to hang out at the beach, so we should go and visit the family today.

On the way into the city of Cárdenas, our first stop was my brother's grave. I wanted Justin to see where his uncle was buried and to drop off some flowers—but the flower vendor was not open. It was near the cemetery's closing time, and even the gatekeeper was nowhere to be found. I was concerned that if the attendant did not see us arrive, he might just lock us in.

"What if we were trapped inside overnight?" I teased Justin.

"No need to yell for help—the only people close enough to hear us are dead!" he joked back. Just to be safe, we parked the car at the entrance and walked right through the unattended front gates.

It was jolting to see Alfredito's grave in such terrible condition. The head of the chamber was not a dome at all, but rectangular—nothing like what I thought I saw and described previously. I was rattled by the disparity and questioned the nature of reality itself. Are we so influenced by our emotions that perception is our reality?

As we strolled back to our car, we never saw a single person. Justin noticed the back of one tomb chamber was so deteriorated that we could actually see the human remains inside. Luckily, the cemetery gates were still open, and we did not have to jump the fence. Justin took my photo while I stood on the sidewalk Papi had lobbied to build, and then we moved on.

Justin saw where I was born, where I was baptized and the schools I had attended. As we drove through the rundown city, he became fascinated with a rainbow he had spotted. "Dad, let's drive to where we can get an unobstructed view!"

So I headed to the bay side of town. Justin suddenly exclaimed, "Look, now there are two! I have never seen perfect twin rainbows before! Have you? Let's get a picture." What an incredible shot—in the foreground was a monument honoring the first Cuban flag.

I told Justin what I knew about its history. Narciso López, a Venezuelan general who volunteered to fight for Cuba's independence from Spanish rule, was in New York soliciting American support and contemplated the difficulties that would lay ahead in Cuba. He decided that a flag was needed to boost patriotism and improve the morale of the Cuban nationalists. As the story goes, he was inspired upon awakening from a nap in a local park; he saw white clouds floating in a blue sky, highlighted by the red glare of the sunset with an oscillating star at its center.

Excited and moved, Narciso shared his vision with his friend, the poet Miguel Teurbe Tolón. Miguel designed the flag with three blue stripes, representing Cuba's three territorial divisions at the time—Western, Central and Eastern—and two white stripes between them, standing for the purity and justice of its liberators. A lone white star within a red triangle represented the unity of the Cuban people amidst the blood spilled by its heroes in the struggle for independence.

The twin vibrant rainbows now crowned the Bay of Cárdenas, showcasing the flag proudly waving in the embrace of a gentle breeze. It was totally silent; no one else was in sight. It felt as if God had stopped the whole world to provide this spiritual and serene moment just for the two of us. What a lasting impression to end our tour of my hometown as we headed toward my aunt's house.

Tía Elvira was delighted to see us and especially to embrace the one Neyra family member she had never met. "*¡Hay, Dios,* this young man is so tall!" Tía Elvira exclaimed as she hugged Justin. It was such a joy as well as a comical contrast to see this embrace between my elderly, petite aunt and my six-foot-three young son. Of course it did not take long for the word to get around, and within less than twenty minutes, we were having a family reunion with my cousins, their spouses and their children all gathered to celebrate our arrival.

Soon Elvirita and I got into a side conversation sharing newly found family information. I told her about my trip to Spain and meeting our long-lost Sotolongo relative, Federico Martínez de Sola. I told her how helpful Rafael Quijones had been and that he had since found Santiago Neyra's birth certificate, not in Santander, but in Santiago de Compostela, and gave her copies of all his findings.

Elvirita had been very involved in researching records in Cárdenas. In fact, she and Sr. Ernesto Álvarez Blanco had become good friends. Elvirita was the ideal research partner—she had analytical and research skills from her engineering education. Although she also had limited access to local records, more importantly, she had heard stories from the past about our family from her mother and neighbors.

I was hoping to spend some time alone with Elvirita on this trip. I asked her to escort Justin and me to visit Yeya, an old family friend who had picked up gossip like a sponge from the streets of Cárdenas for nearly a century. We drove to her place, hoping to find out more about Abuelo Neyra.

On the way, Elvirita began to reveal what she knew about our family's past. Abuelo had been an alcoholic and a neglectful husband; Abuela, who was a few years older, was a very educated, sophisticated and socially connected woman who greatly disappointed her parents by marrying him. After they had four children and she developed Parkinson's disease, he abandoned them and then sunk into a downward spiral, squandering the family's wealth while indulging in booze and women. One night while driving drunk, he struck and killed a pedestrian. The punishment for his behavior was ten years in jail.

However, after he had been incarcerated for only a short time, his family leveraged their political clout to reduce his sentence to house arrest. I suddenly realized why Abuelo had visited Papi only very early in the morning while it was still dark—to avoid being detected violating the terms of his sentence. I began to understand what the secrecy and his mysterious lifestyle had been all about.

Elvirita told me that he died while living with an *africana* named Natividad with whom he had cohabited for many years. The family had speculated that perhaps he had been seduced by the spell of *Santería*, a West African religion of rituals, prayer, divination and offerings that included animal sacrifices. *Santería* came from the word "*santo*," meaning "saint," and used Catholic saints as code names to secretly worship their many gods.

I asked if they had any children together. Elvirita said no, Natividad was a much older woman caring for two grandchildren who called Abuelo "*Padrino*, Godfather." We discussed some possible reasons. Had he perhaps been present at their baptism? Was it just a term of endearment? Or had he actually been their sponsor into *Santería*, which required a godfather for formal initiation?

"Do you know these grandchildren?" I inquired.

"Not really, but I've run into them occasionally, and I've heard they are very nice," she responded.

Elvirita continued, "My father was the only one to visit Abuelo as he grew older and more frail. One day he received an urgent message to go immediately to see Abuelo, who had been very ill and believed that he was near death. Weak and barely able to speak, with tears flowing down his face, Abuelo asked my father to please forgive him for the terrible life he had led, the bad example he had set as a father and the pain he had caused his family—and to please forgive the way he had treated Abuela Amélia. He was hoping that somehow my father could convey his repentance to your father, who was already living in Cincinnati," Elvirita explained.

I asked her, "Do you know if your father was able to reach Papi?"

"I don't know, but I doubt it. By then the phone lines had been cut off, and communication was rather difficult, especially trying to discuss such emotional issues in a family that attempted to hide their shame for so long."

Elvirita resumed, "But ironically, it was my father who died unexpectedly shortly afterward when he was only forty-seven. He was extremely depressed over seeing Abuelo in such poor physical and mental health, as well as distraught after your father's flight out of the country."

I acknowledged, "Your father's death was a devastating blow to Papi, just after he had arrived in the United States. And then Abuelo died eight months later. These tragedies triggered Papi's own battle with depression, and his occasional bouts of drinking back then were a futile attempt to medicate his loss."

I suddenly realized there was a deeper dimension to these tragedies but the political implications prevented me from discussing it aloud with Elvirita. The Neyras had been exceedingly loyal Cuban patriots dating back to the War of Independence. In spite of losing their political power after the Revolution, there was no way Tío José would have left Cuba; Papi would have remained right by his brother's side had Melba and I not been sent to the United States. The reasons for my father's resentful and sullen attitude, as well as his refusal to assimilate during my tumultuous teenage years were much clearer to me now. Castro's Revolution had done more than change career paths for the close-knit brothers; it had torn them apart and wracked my father with regret for the rest of his life.

Elvirita interrupted my epiphany with her own Pandora's box of paternal revelations. She divulged that after Abuelo's death her brother Jorge discovered a lifelong secret of her father, Tío José. Jorge had received a message from Natividad to come over and go through Abuelo's things, where he found dozens of letters addressed to his father, safeguarded near

Abuelo's bedside. They exposed a lifelong love affair with a woman named Caruca that had begun years before Jorge had even been born. Among the papers, he also found the title to a car Tío José had given her as a gift.

But there was more. She told me that years later her mother had visited Papi in Miami at his request. Though they had not seen each other for over fifteen years, they had always been very close. It was then that Papi beseeched Tía Elvira on behalf of his deceased brother.

"My dear sister," he had addressed his sister-in-law, "I hope you have found the strength and love to forgive my brother, José. May he rest in peace."

"*Sí*, Neyra, I have," Elvira lovingly had responded.

I then asked Elvirita if she knew anything about Papi's affair. She immediately denied it, but I quickly countered, "I don't believe you."

She looked at me and smiled, "You have done a lot of digging."

I tried to pry further, but Elvirita would not budge. So I continued to question her about Abuelo and Natividad. "Do you know where they lived?"

"Yes, it's just a few blocks away. It's a *cuartería*." A *cuartería* was a large, rundown home subdivided into small rooms for rental to the impoverished. "Are you sure you want to go there?" Elvirita wondered.

"Yes, I want to see it all," I confirmed, "from palaces in Spain to *cuarterías* in Cuba." As we drove, I tried to provide Justin the highlights of our conversation, but Elvirita had thrown so much at me that I found myself needing to recover emotionally before I could translate it all. Besides, this was such a different world that it would take some explaining—explaining things that I did not completely understand myself, and perhaps was not fully ready to reconcile, including the shame that had been hidden for so long.

As we approached the decrepit living quarters, and I stood at the entrance, I wondered how a man from such a privileged past could disintegrate into accepting such appalling living conditions. Knowing what I had already learned through my travels and research, I tried to imagine how an educated man from an affluent family with political power, married to an intellectual woman, a descendant of Spanish nobility, could fall into such an abyss.

Elvirita noticed my dismayed reaction. "Maybe it would have been better not to come," she ventured.

"Absolutely not. I needed and wanted to know all of it," I emphatically replied.

We finally pulled up in front of Yeya's house, and Elvirita spotted her sitting in the living room watching television. Elvirita called to her in a loud voice, and tried to explain we were seeking information about our grandfather, José Neyra. But Yeya was not only old and could not hear, she showed strong signs of dementia. I quickly sensed we were getting nowhere, so we said good-bye and headed back to Tía Elvira's home.

On the way, I asked Elvirita if she knew anything about Abuela Amélia's extensive jewelry collection. Once again she grew quiet. I told her I heard that Tía Nina had left the pieces behind in Cuba. Elvirita explained that my cousin Conchita, Tía Nina's only child, had adopted a daughter, Marisa. It was her belief that Marisa had been given the jewelry. I was inquiring particularly about two rings Papi owned that had been in the

Sotolongo family for generations. I knew they were valuable, but my real interest was sentimental. Elvirita knew exactly which rings I meant.

We stopped by Marisa's home, which Tía Nina had given her and which had originally belonged to my grandparents. But no one answered the door. Elvirita then suggested we visit Marisa's souvenir store in a park close to the center of town. As we approached her, Elvirita introduced us. Marisa greeted me with a kiss and wanted to know how Melba was. She was apparently far more informed about us than I was about her. After our polite greeting, Elvirita then brought up the subject of my father's rings. Marisa's demeanor changed instantly and she became cold and brusque.

I tried to pacify Marisa. "I don't expect that the rings should be given back—I am willing to pay for them. Since my parents are dead, I would love to have some memento from their past."

"I am so sorry that your parents passed away, but I know nothing about the jewelry. Tía Nina probably sold the rings before she emigrated to the United States," Marisa replied defensively, in spite of her sincere condolences.

I knew Tía Nina was too proud to sell the family jewels, but I was also aware Marisa was not going to volunteer any additional information. So we all said good-bye, and as we walked away Elvirita told me that Marisa's alcoholic biological mother, Corolia, had been rumored to sell some jewelry. Elvirita suggested we visit her next, but I convinced her that doing so would be fruitless. The rings probably had been bartered long ago for a bottle of rum.

White Sand, Black Market

*b*y *the time we returned, my aunt had cold drinks ready, and Elvirita steered* the group into the kitchen, where she stood like a spokesmodel alongside her brand-new refrigerator. She gracefully extended her arms towards the shiny appliance and said, "¡*Mira!* Look!" Then she smiled and thanked me.

"It's my privilege," I quietly responded.

Just then Omarito walked in. Justin met his cousin, and off they went into a conversation in Spanglish while the rest of us sat down to continue our chat. Elvirita told me she had also invited Sr. Ernesto Álvarez Blanco, who recently had been promoted to historian for the city of Cárdenas.

After he arrived, the new city historian proceeded to show us books, documents, city records and newspaper articles regarding the Neyras in years past. He said there was not a single government post in the city or even in the province that a Neyra had not held. In fact, Dr. Alejandro Neyra, the grandson of Santiago, the first Neyra that set foot in Cuba, was instrumental in the fight for Cuban independence from Spain. In 1894, Alejandro had founded *Sala de Armas*, Hall of Arms, a local underground revolutionary organization. Clandestine meetings rumored to include José Martí were held in Alejandro's home, and his large living room was used as their arms repository.

Sr. Ernesto Álvarez Blanco also gave me copies of handwritten transcripts from City Hall meetings where the dialogues included several Neyras. Another document he had found was a very special surprise—the actual program from a speech presented in 1941, by Dr. Santiago Verdeja Neyra, then president of the Senate. Both he and Abuelo were great-grandsons of the original Santiago Neyra. It must have been the senator's power and influence that had gotten Abuelo his reduced sentence.

Sr. Ernesto Álvarez Blanco had found records of Papi's many municipal projects, including the construction of the long sidewalk to the cemetery. I was surprised to learn that both Papi and Tío José had initiated building the highway that directly connected Cárdenas and Varadero, which I had traveled countless times. There were also articles with photos of other structures funded by donations from the Neyra family: *El Progreso* business school, social clubs like *El Coliseo* where I had once dreaded dance lessons, and *Santa Elvira,* the church in Varadero. Oddly enough, I had attended that church all of my young life and had never known my relatives were instrumental in building it.

Justin and Omarito rejoined the party, and Justin excitedly related his first black market shopping adventure. He and Omarito had driven somewhere in Cárdenas and knocked on the front door of a private home. A woman opened it with caution and only wide enough to view her customer. She saw Justin first and peered at him suspiciously. Omarito jockeyed into position to be seen, and then told the woman, "It's okay. It's my cousin from America."

"Yes, I see the Neyra resemblance. But I can tell that this one has eaten well." She was referring, of course, to Justin's size.

"*¿Cuántas quieres?* How many do you want?" she inquired, still shielding herself behind the door.

"*Dos*, Two," Omarito answered.

"*Un momento*," she cryptically responded.

Justin and Omarito waited outside on the sidewalk and within a few minutes the woman returned. She handed over the disguised merchandise, two bottles of ginger ale filled with whiskey. Justin and Omarito argued for a moment about who was going to pay. Ultimately Omarito convinced Justin that since he was the host, it should be his honor as he handed the woman his two dollars.

On the way back Omarito explained to Justin that workers stole the liquor from an all-inclusive resort in Varadero. No one kept track of who consumed the liquor so it was easy for an employee to smuggle alcohol out in soda bottles and then sell it on the black market.

Justin was intrigued by the whole process. They huddled in the kitchen, Omarito squatting on a small stool and Justin on an upside-down bucket with his knees hitting his chest, swapping life experiences while sipping their contraband. Once in a while, Justin would call to me, wanting to know how to say a certain word in Spanish. The big laugh came when I told Justin to lift his shirt and they saw his tattoo. Much to my chagrin, he had branded a Cuban flag on his chest right after he turned eighteen and could do so without parental permission.

I could not believe we had been visiting for more than seven hours. The sun had set long ago. It was very late and, sadly, time to say good-bye. We were ready to return to Varadero.

The next morning, Justin asked me upon awakening, "Did you know that I got into your bed during the night? The mosquitoes were eating me alive by the window."

I had known, but it was a king-sized bed in a large room, and we had plenty of space. "The good news is that we did not keep each other up with our snoring," I responded.

Sharing my bed with my twenty-year-old son at my summer place had brought back fond memories of the games that I would play at bedtime when he and Nathan had been little boys. We would shout, "Roly poly, waka moly," and then I would hug each one into a ball and we would fall out of bed together. They would both giggle like fools and say, "Let's do it again!" And again and again until I was completely exhausted.

Another one of Justin's favorites was called "Fight Over Me." Often in the morning when we awakened, the boys would climb into our bed. Justin would wedge himself between Lynn and me. We would both tug on him, saying, "He's my boy!" "No, he's mine!" As soon as we stopped the tussle he would say, "Fight over me again!" I could not believe how fast time had slipped away; it seemed like only yesterday my grown son had been just a little boy.

Justin snapped me out of my reverie, wanting to discuss our plans for the day. I suggested, "I would like to show you the rest of Varadero, but that will only take a couple hours. Afterwards, we can head back to Havana for the *criollo* pig roast Ernesto and Marielmy are hosting this afternoon."

After breakfast as we walked out of the restaurant, we stopped to look at the water from the terrace in front of the ocean wall. Although it was a warm and sunny day, the surf was still fairly rough, and the beach winter-season deserted. "Let's jump off this wall together," I challenged Justin. "The sand is soft. I used to do it all the time as a young boy."

"Are you crazy?" he laughed. "You're not jumping off that wall—it's almost ten feet down. You'll blow out your knee and ruin the rest of our trip by making me carry you around!" So I obeyed Justin's joking reprimand and never took the leap.

We rented scooters to take our tour of Varadero, exploring the twelve-mile beach resort from the entrance at the drawbridge to the very tip of the peninsula, known as *La Punta De Icacos*. As we whisked past my favorite landmarks, I would yell out a little of their history.

We took a short detour to stop at Kiko's house. I wanted Justin to meet him, and I also needed to return his antique gold pocket watch that I had taken to the United States for repairs since the parts were not available in Cuba. I knew Kiko was disappointed at our brief visit, but I wanted to complete the rest of our tour before we had to return our scooters and get on the road to Havana.

Along the way I took Justin's picture next to a concrete sculpture shaped like a vintage mobster car in the front yard of Al Capone's former home, now a restaurant known as *La Casa de Al*.

At the other end of the peninsula, we visited the grounds of the Du Pont mansion, which had been converted into an exquisite small hotel and golf club, and whose natural caves had been converted into a roadside bar.

We then raced past many new hotels, and Justin was impressed with both their size and opulence. He wondered aloud, "What embargo? The rest of the world is certainly doing business here!"

CUBA LIBRE, FUERTE

*d*uring our drive back to the capital, Justin expressed how much he had enjoyed meeting the family and getting to know his cousin. "I had so much fun! I wish someday everyone in the family could get together. Everybody in one place at one time," he suggested. "Wouldn't that be great? We should be able to do that, don't you think?" He was eager to hear a positive response.

What I loved about Justin was that in his mind anything was possible, and I was touched by his sentiment, but I understood the difficulties of coordinating such a romantic request. Organizing a family reunion, with our relatives now spread all over the globe, would not be easy. "Look how difficult it can be just for our family of four to plan a trip together. There are tremendous logistical issues and insurmountable political obstacles," I explained.

As we entered Havana, we followed Ernesto's directions to the pig roast. Or rather, we thought we did. He had warned me it might be hard to find, so we took the next exit to call him for help.

"How did you wind up there?" he snickered. "You did not follow my directions. You went out of the way."

When he was finished giving me a hard time, I retorted sarcastically, "Yes, I know. It doesn't take long to go far out of the way when you are traveling seventy miles an hour on a highway without a single road sign or exit number."

I returned to the car where Justin had waited patiently for me. So once again we started down the highway, counting exits. I thought Justin should be pretty good at this since as a little boy he had counted everything in sight. We used to call him "The Count" after the Sesame Street character.

I feared we were still lost until Justin finally spotted a key landmark from Ernesto's instructions—a bright green barn on the left. We then drove down an unpaved, narrow country lane. Our car kept bottoming out as we maneuvered to avoid the craters. Finally we heard music and saw the smoke from the fire pit. By now all of the guests had eaten, and some had already left. But Marielmy dished up a generous portion of the abundant feast for us, and Ernesto offered a welcoming drink.

"*Un Cuba libre, fuerte,*" Justin requested. A *Cuba libre* was a rum and Coke with lime, and *fuerte* meant "strong."

Ernesto responded, "*¡Ah, quieres una mentirita!*" Justin looked at me, confused. I explained that *mentirita* meant "little lie." The joke was in reference to the fact that Cuba was not "*libre,*" free.

Justin replied, "*¡Una mentirita fuerte, por favor!*" Ernesto just laughed and brought the bottle.

During the long trip from Varadero to the party, Justin had asked me if there were any retirement provisions for Cuban workers. I did not know and suggested he ask Ernesto. Ernesto explained that women could request to retire at age fifty-five, men at sixty. However, retirement was not mandatory, and you could work without age limit as long as you were physically and mentally capable. Justin also wanted to know how much they collected and how the benefit was set. Ernesto replied it was determined by a government board, and it ranged anywhere from five to ten dollars a month, depending on what their income had been during their working years.

"How do you even find a job in the first place?" wondered Justin.

"It's all about who you know in the military or where you have a friend," replied Ernesto.

Justin and Ernesto continued their conversation about how things worked, or did not work, in Cuba. Justin commented on the contradictions. "You know, Cuba seems to exist in a hundred-year time warp. What a great contrast, to see at a traffic light one man in a horse and buggy with a *machete* at his waist, while the guy in the next lane is sitting behind the wheel of a new Mercedes-Benz talking on a cell phone."

We had a wonderful evening talking to the other guests outside in the country breeze. For me it brought back childhood memories of *Noche Buena*, Christmas Eve, Cuba's most celebrated holiday. It was customary to have an all-day party, dig a big pit and roast a whole pig. Family, friends and neighbors would stop by to drink a toast to the holiday and the New Year. It was always a lot of fun, with the preparations and festivities seeming to last all week. Some streets were barricaded so people could dance in the middle of the road—just like a big block party.

Ernesto's party triggered many recollections, and I told him how much I appreciated sharing this Cuban tradition with my son. After taking a few photos of the event and the charred pig, Justin and I were ready for a good night's rest. As we left the party, Ernesto invited us to dinner the following night.

On the ride home Justin boasted that he thought his Spanish was beginning to come back and added with a cunning tone, "Dad, if I could stay here for a month or two, I could learn the language and speak fluently."

"Maybe since you have such an interest, I will buy you a book when we get home," I offered.

He shook his head. "It just wouldn't be the same."

"I'll have to sleep on that idea," I laughed. "And better yet, get yourself a good night's rest—tomorrow is our last day."

"I know, stop reminding me," he groaned.

On our final day in Cuba, Justin and I went to see a few of the landmarks he had not yet visited. We visited the modern art museum, *El Salón de Arte Cubano Contemporáneo* and went though the capitol building. Our last stop was Ernesto's gallery, since Justin was looking for a painting to take home. I wanted him, like his brother Nathan, to have a memento of our trip to Cuba together.

We arrived at the gallery, and Ernesto escorted Justin around, explaining the meaning of the abstraction on each canvas. I went upstairs with Marielmy to their office while Justin stayed with Ernesto to choose a painting. Justin had an eye for art; he knew right away which one he liked best. They soon came upstairs, and Justin said, "I found one."

"Great. Let's take it." I responded.

"Don't you want to see it?" Justin asked.

"Of course, but it's for you. If you like it, that's all that matters," I explained.

That evening, Ernesto picked us up and drove us to *La Guarida*. This renowned *paladar* was located on the third floor of a rundown, subdivided mansion. To get to the restaurant, you had to climb a grandiose but dilapidated marble staircase, skirting the tenants' laundry drying on hallway clotheslines. You then walked down a long corridor underneath makeshift wooden scaffolding protecting you from the deteriorating plaster ceiling above. In spite of the inconvenient and dangerous access, Queen Sofia of Spain had dined there two nights earlier, and its eccentric ambience had been the setting for an Oscar-nominated Cuban film, *Fresa y Chocolate*.

Ernesto took us to the airport the next morning and brought with him Justin's new painting packed for travel, along with the Customs' registration required to get it out of the country. I felt very calm this time while going though Immigration. Somehow my customary anxiety and the flashbacks had faded.

We waited for nearly five hours for our scheduled flight, which gave me plenty of time to reflect on our trip. I had been concerned about whether Justin would like being in Cuba and worried that he would become annoyed with all the inconveniences. But he had repeatedly displayed a wonderful ability to adapt and enjoy himself without the slightest complaint. Justin's questions and comments throughout the trip were illuminating. His curiosity had opened my eyes to conditions and limitations that I had either ignored or denied. This visit to Cuba had been an awakening, and our time together like a dream come true.

Our flight was finally called to board. As we stood on the apron with jet engines roaring in the background, Justin put his arms around my shoulders, drawing me into a sideways hug. He leaned close to my ear, and said, "Dad, thanks for bringing me to Cuba. These have been the best days of my life."

"What did you enjoy most?" I asked, nearly choking with emotion.

"Meeting the family. And the Tropicana show was awesome. But the best part of all was spending time alone with you."

Spiritual Spiral

"*What's happening, Ed?*"

"You know, Jerry, my trip to Cuba with Justin seemed to expand my consciousness to a new level. His astute observations helped clarify my own perceptions. I realized I had been romanticizing, viewing the island through my own poetic and nostalgic lens."

"I also noticed that Cubans who still live on the island, as well as many of us who fled to the United States, speak of history and our own lives in terms of either before or after the Revolution. It seems as if we are cursed to be forever frozen in 1959. Some are still feeding a fury that is as choking as the exhaust of those junkers they drive in Havana."

Jerry explained, "People who have not dealt with their pain tend to get stuck in the past—and are therefore unable to move forward, sometimes for days, sometimes for decades. They're immobilized by fear and indecision. And in this particular case, you're also speaking of guilt and shame, about having fled your country and culture and having left others behind—or having been left behind."

Jerry defined guilt as self-inflicted punishment, the result of doing something you thought was wrong. Shame was much more searing; a deeper wound. Shame resulted not from what we had done, but from thinking, "Something is wrong with me." It was also passed down from generation to generation, until someone was finally willing to do the hard work of breaking the chain.

"I know, 'The sins of the father are visited onto his children and his children's children,'" I quoted from the Bible.

Jerry continued, "It's an encumbering legacy, but we have the choice to unload the burden or perpetuate it. We can free ourselves from the shackles of guilt and shame by accepting responsibility for what we made happen or allowed to happen, and through confession and genuine remorse to those whom we have wronged. Also, as a mature adult, you must not forget the vital step of self-forgiveness."

"What is a mature adult?" I asked.

"Someone who owns his responsibilities. All of us grow up physically, but becoming a mature adult is a conscious choice. A mature person has inwardly nurtured and healed the wounds incurred in all the stages of growth, from infancy through adolescence and on to adulthood. He has grown in his own spiritual journey to become the person he has inspired himself to be, not the person he thinks his parents wanted him to be or one who still blames others for his own shortcomings."

Jerry went on to explain that our spiritual journey was an upward spiral. Although you might circle back to the same place, it was never on the same plane. This continuous circular rising movement was built on layers of insights and the ultimate goal was for us to develop into emotionally healthy, loving, mature adults.

"As an example," he noted, "You have gone to Cuba and come back to Cincinnati, and then repeated that cycle. Every time you learn something different. This experience raises you to a higher level in your own spiritual journey, which is uniquely your own and never ends."

"These paths are blessed with obstacles which are meant to be overcome, the means by which we learn lessons and grow. God has also given us the freedom of choice between good and evil. We are all capable of immense kindnesses and horrific cruelties. Within us lies the battlefield between these two combatants."

"Who wins?" I asked.

Jerry responded philosophically, "Whichever one you choose to feed."

Going Home

*O*n *my next visit to Cuba, I hoped to fulfill a lifelong dream of taking a* cross-country tour of the island. I had made arrangements to fly into the eastern city of Holguín with my friend Jeff, and then head west to meet Elvirita in Cárdenas. However, when we landed at Holguín's Frank País International Airport, it was hardly a warm welcome, and the young *compañera* at Immigration probed into every detail of my trip.

"Why are you visiting Cuba?" she coldly questioned.

"I am here to visit family," I explained.

"Where does your family live?" she demanded.

"In Cárdenas," I curtly replied.

"Why are you landing here when your family lives on the other side of the island?" she retorted with a tone of revolutionary rancor.

"I didn't know there would be a problem with wanting to see our beautiful island," I responded, feeling like a reviled *gusano* all over again.

She pulled me into the Customs area as her questioning turned into a group interrogation, with her supervisor and several other agents joining in. They barraged me with a series of questions: Where are you staying? Who is traveling with you? Where did you rent your car? Who is the driver? They checked every garment in my suitcase and reviewed every page of printed material in my briefcase. They even opened a personal sealed note that Lynn had slipped into my luggage as a surprise—the ultimate invasion of privacy. It was hard for me to keep my composure as I watched them read my wife's card before I could.

While I was being harrassed, at the station behind me there was a loud commotion. An extremely angry Cuban-American was in a shouting match with another cluster of agents who had confiscated an iron he had brought for his family. He was enraged that the agents were seizing the appliance, probably for themselves—just because they could.

After an hour and a half of this fruitless intimidation, I was finally cleared for entry, where Luis was waiting for us. This threatening confrontation had stirred up all those old fears, and I was beginning to wonder whether this adventure would be worth the anxiety.

I thought it was fitting to begin our tour of Cuba near where Christopher Columbus had allegedly first set foot in 1492, describing it as, "The most beautiful land that human eyes ever beheld." As we headed east to Baracoa, we got to enjoy the panoramic view far longer than we wished. Our sleek BMW sedan, which sat low to the ground, was no match for the neglected, rough roads and before long we found ourselves broken down on the shoulder. The fuel filter had been ripped off by a large rock, and gasoline was hemorrhaging from the severed fuel line.

Within a few minutes, locals pulled over to help. Without even greeting the *campesinos* getting out of their 1955 Chevy truck, Luis ran up to them asking, "Do you have a piece of rubber hose?" gesturing with his hands the length and holding up his pinkie as a measurement of its diameter. The driver was silent for a moment, then rummaged through his rusty assortment of spare parts strewn on the floor of the cab beneath his seat. Miraculously, he reached into the motley collection and pulled out the perfect hose.

While our Good Samaritan helped Luis jerry-rig a fix for the fuel line, I talked to his companions who were lamenting forgetting a bottle of rum at their previous stop. I told them, "I have a full one in the trunk," and went to fetch it.

As I retrieved the bottle, one of the men peered under the hood of our sedan. He immediately proclaimed his alternative assessment of our situation. "Do you know what the problem is? These fancy new cars have too many things under the hood. Look! You can't even see the engine! How do people work on these things?" We laughed heartily at the irony of his wisdom. Their old jalopies had fared far better than our modern machine.

On the road once more, we headed west. In the village of El Cobre, just outside the city of Santiago, we visited the most famous church in Cuba, *La Basilica del Cobre*, built in 1926 in memory of the patron saint of Cuba. We stopped in Camagüey for a brief lunch and continued along to Santa Clara, visiting the many small towns along the way. As we went past Che Guevara's memorial in Santa Clara, Jeff remarked, "All these towns, with their revolutionary monuments and crumbling colonial architecture, are beginning to look alike to me."

"Yes," I confessed. "This worn-out scenery is running together like a single postcard in my mind, too."

Every night along the way I had to deal with the frustration, and overcome the anger, of Luis being subjected to the unfair hotel restrictions. As a Cuban citizen, it was illegal for him to stay in the tourist hotels with us, so he had to find a *casa particular*, a private home with rental rooms, for the night. At a few small hotels we were able to finagle his way in—but a bribe was essential.

Communist bureaucracy continued to interfere with our trip. Cayo Coco was a pristine resort area on the north coast of central Cuba well known for its natural reserve for marine birds. However, we could not even cross over the *Pedraplen*, the long, scenic causeway that connected the key to the mainland. Since Luis was not a tourist, he needed a pass, which we had earlier applied for and had been assured would be waiting for us at the guardhouse. But the permit had never arrived at Cayo Coco. I was furious and refused to proceed without Luis. So the gatekeeper, who had tried to help us resolve our dilemma, had no choice but to finally turn us away.

"How ironic," Jeff mused. "The Cuban who fled his country has more privileges than the one who lives here."

My dream adventure had become more like a nightmare. I had been confronted by the ugly face of Cuba, with constant inconveniences and police state harrassment over trivial travel details. But I still wanted to see my family, so I cast aside my optimistic intention of a leisurely sightseeing trip across the entire island. Instead, we sped westward to Cárdenas, dropping Jeff at the hotel in Varadero on the way.

Present Tense

I have never been so happy to arrive in my dilapidated hometown and hug Elvirita and Tía Elvira hello. It was especially bittersweet, given what had happened so far on this trip. Also, the laws in the United States recently had been made harsher regarding family visits to Cuba. So these annual gatherings would sadly be coming to an end, since permission to travel to the island now would be restricted to once every three years.

But we did not stay at their house very long, for Elvirita had arranged a meeting with Mimi and her sister Mercedes, the adopted granddaughters of Natividad, Abuelo's mistress. I was eager to hear their perspective of what kind of man he had been.

Mimi and Mercedes were overjoyed to see me. They opened their arms as if I were their long-lost brother and ushered me into their crumbling home. They conveyed their great love and respect for Abuelo, warmly attributing their survival and well-being to his caring and affection, something that I had not experienced and could only imagine.

"He was my godfather, you know," Mimi proudly boasted. "He arranged my baptism." I realized she was a Christian after seeing the crucifix on the decayed wall of her living room and was relieved to know that Abuelo had not been under the spell of *Santería.*

"He and Natividad adopted us so we would not be sent to an orphanage." The eyes of this sixty-year-old woman lit up as she told us their childhood story. "Your grandfather always made sure we had enough to eat. He had credit everywhere."

Elvirita turned her face subtly toward mine and whispered with a grin, "Our fathers' credit, she really means," and I nodded in acknowledgement, knowing that Tío José and Papi had covered Abuelo's debts for most of his life after he had burned through the family's wealth.

The two women then shared memories about Abuelo. He once had been arrested for creating a scene to incite a demonstration at a local grocery store, by complaining loudly about the lack of food. He was hauled off to jail, and Tío José had to bail him out, pleading, "He's just an old man."

"He drank a lot, you know," Mimi admitted. "And when intoxicated, he just wanted to be left alone." I could tell she had come to terms with his heavy drinking.

"What did he drink?" I asked.

"Oh, he loved rum!" she answered me with a grin.

"How did he treat you?" I wondered.

"He was always a strict disciplinarian and would throw whatever he had within his reach to get our attention, but he was always sure to miss," she smiled. "He would command sharply, 'Natividad, look after the girls.' "

"Did he ever spank you?" I asked.

"No. Never. He was very respectful, and he never walked around in his underwear. He was a sharp dresser, you know," she added. I nodded, recalling his tailored suits, heavily starched white shirts and signature bow tie.

I brought up my memory of the strange noise Abuelo made with his mouth, overlapping his upper lip with his lower one and making a suctioning sound. As I mimicked it, they both laughed and confirmed that they remembered it, too.

Mimi became mournful as she directed our attention to the very bed where he had died. I gently put my arm around her shoulders. "I took care of him during his final years," she sorrowfully told me, "for Natividad was too old. I prepared his meals and bathed him. One day I brought him the glass of milk he had requested, but after holding it for only a moment, he fell over and died right before my very eyes."

How ironic—this woman had a stronger connection and had received greater care from having known my grandfather than anyone in his own family. As she hugged me good-bye, she said, "Please know you always have a home here." I was touched by her generosity, especially since they had so little.

On the way back, I told Elvirita that I had learned from our cousin Conchita, Tía Nina's daughter, that my father's affair had been with a woman named Raquel. She was a well-educated, flamboyant blonde from an affluent family who had been a major contributor to Papi's political campaign. According to rumor, she even had donated an Oldsmobile convertible.

When we arrived, Elvirita confronted her mother, who gave the story only a fleeting validation. I asked Elvirita to try to find out how I could contact Raquel. I had heard that she once lived in Houston, Texas, but if some of her family members still lived in Cárdenas, they might know more.

"She would be nearly ninety," Elvirita objected.

"Yes, I know. You'd better find her fast. I don't have much time left," I half-joked.

Conchita also told me that my father had given Raquel my grandmother's rings before he had fled the country. Since he could not leave Cuba with any valuables, he had entrusted them to her for safekeeping.

Elvirita responded with surprise. "Do you think that is true?"

"Conchita told me that Papi admitted it long before he died," I relayed.

"I don't believe that," she sneered. "I think Conchita was merely protecting Marisa by using Raquel as a scapegoat. Is that why you want to find Raquel?"

"No." I explained, "I just want to know more about Papi from others who knew him well. Also I want to tell her he passed away, and that I have forgiven him for their illicit romance, in spite of how much heartache it caused Mami."

I then shared with Elvirita information I had received from Rafael Quijano in Santander. He had continued to excavate Neyra family data and had sent me military records from the General Military Archives of Segovia for fifty-seven Neyras registered as nobles, ranking officers or infantrymen, from 1774 to 1918. Included with the packet was an apologetic handwritten letter that began, "Sr. Neyra, I am sorry to send to you what I have found regarding Santiago Neyra."

When reviewing the military registrations, Rafael had discovered that Santiago's formal surname was actually Jacobo, and he had filled his life with transatlantic travels and conquered territories in Spain, Colombia, Peru and Cuba. But he was then discharged from military service for *no cumplir*, not fulfilling his duties. In the package were copies of his letters dating from 1868, including one to Queen Isabella II, requesting reinstatement. They cited medical reasons for non-performance and for having been AWOL for months at a time.

Because of the prominence of the family name, and his string of accomplishments, the military response was not a direct refusal, which encouraged Jacobo to continue to pursue his appeal. He repeatedly used his father's name, affluence and impressive military record to try to convince them, but after eighteen excuse-filled letters, they were forced to send their regrets. Rafael had reassured me that he meant no disrespect in uncovering such an unflattering portrait of my ancestor. I had told him it did not matter—I only wanted to know the truth. Besides, I had heard rumors that would never be found in any military documents. Once Santiago had reached Cuba, he was hypnotized by its beauty. He fell in love with a woman and decided never to return to Spain.

Even though Rafael continued to send me more information, I still had longed to go back to Spain to the family cradle. So I had visited the northwest provinces and saw for myself towns that bore the Neyra name and homes displaying the Neyra crest in stone. Elvirita was eager to hear about my recent trip.

"Did you see Federico?" She spoke of him now with genuine affection; after all, she, too, was a Sotolongo.

"Yes, Lynn and I went to dinner with Federico and Carmen. I brought him a crystal vase engraved with the Sotolongo coat of arms. He was very touched. You should have seen his face!" I proceeded to review with Elvirita the highlights of my second trip to Spain, where I focused on finding out more about our Neyra lineage.

After one night's stay in Madrid at the Hotel Adler, we were on our way to Galicia. We flew into Santiago de Compostela, the site of one of the world's most renowned religious shrines. On our ride from the airport we passed many devoted pilgrims on foot, staff in hand, displaying the signature scallop shells on their way to the majestic cathedral that soared over *Plaza del Obradoiro* honoring St. James the Apostle. I also learned that Diego de Neira, a knight of Galicia, had founded the cathedral's chapel of *Santa Maria del Camino* and both he and his son, Juan Otero de Neira, were buried there.

We stayed right next door at the world's oldest hotel, the remarkable *Hostal de los Reyes Católicos*, constructed in 1499 by Ferdinand and Isabella as an inn and a hospital for the weary and the ill who came to pay homage at St. James' shrine.

We took a day trip to rural Estrada, about twelve miles southeast of Santiago de Compostela. I was curious to find out more about the *Pazo de Oca*, a remote Galician summer palace that had been built centuries ago over the ruins of an ancient fortress and had been purchased by María de Neira in 1586 from King Philip II. I found out from the groundskeeper that *Pazo de Oca* was currently owned by the Duquesa de Medinaceli, who inherited it from her uncle, the last male Neyra to own it. Since he was a priest and had no children of his own, he passed it on to her in 1948.

We left Santiago de Compostela and went on to the ancient city of Lugo, which had been founded before the birth of Christ and still retained the Roman wall that encircled the original boundaries of the old city.

Elvirita was amused by one of my surprising sidelights from Lugo. While having drinks in the Grand Hotel lounge, we were offered some of the local wine. It was quite good, so I asked the bartender if I could buy a bottle. You can imagine my surprised response when he returned, showing me the label branded "Viña de Neira." Of course I then had to visit the vineyard seventy miles away and left Spain with several cases!

As our driver took us through the narrow, winding roads of Spain's northwestern countryside, I traced his route on my Galician map. There were many *aldeas*, villages, named Neira embedded in the hills and valleys of this lush region. Along the way I had my picture taken on the banks of River Neira and then walked across the Roman bridge bearing our name.

"Elvirita, our name is plastered all over Galicia. From the northern coastal town of La Coruña on southeast to Lugo and Sarria, from east to west, no matter which direction we traveled, there was a Neira *aldea*— Neira de Arriba, Neira de Abajo, Neira de Palmas, Neira de Rey, Neira de Jusá, Neira de Cabaleiros."

One of the *aldeas*, Pazo de Neira, included a dilapidated six-hundred-year-old country estate. "Wouldn't this be a great rehab project?" I had teased Lynn. "We could live in the Spanish countryside part of the year, with chickens, pigs and goats in a town that bears our name! In fact, the home's facade already has our crest. What a deal!"

Elvirita's groaning laugh was just as incredulous as Lynn's had been.

Lynn and I on the banks of River Neira under the Neira Bridge

Undeterred, I finished up with the most ironic part of my travelogue. As we continued on through Neira del Rio, I gasped as I saw the road sign for the next town, "Castro de Neira." Evidently we were all descendants of Gallegos from neighboring *aldeas* in Galicia!

Elvirita and I both chuckled. "Castro de Neira!" she repeated. "Can you imagine what our fathers would think if they knew we might be even distantly related to Fidel Castro?"

After we had a good laugh, I tried to summarize the remaining information I had gleaned about the Neyra history during this trip. The Neira family was renowned throughout Galicia, and they had received many land grants. They were awarded numerous military honors, occupied various political posts and held titles such as *caballero*, *conquistador*, *general* and even *marques*.

"We come from a very aggressive bloodline," Elvirita remarked.

"You might say that," I confirmed. "Their territorial pursuits, political ambitions and military accomplishments went well beyond Spain and Cuba. It would take me the rest of my life to visit these places—they are spread all over the globe!"

In South America, there was the town of Neyra in the province of Boyacá in Colombia, conquered in 1793 by General Juan José Neira. And in Argentina, Neyra Lake was in the province of Corrientes. In the vast Pacific Ocean, there was Neira Island, in the Banda Sea in Indonesia. In 1567, Álvaro de Mendaña de Neira claimed to have discovered the Solomon Islands, which he named in expectation of finding gold mines like those of the ancient king.

"Are we all related?" Elvirita wondered.

"Yes, and amazingly we are all originally from the province of Lugo. The names Neira and Neyra are one and the same, because people recorded early civil records according to sound. However, as they traveled beyond Lugo, the spelling with a 'y' became more prevalent, especially outside Spain," I explained.

"Elvirita, it seems that there is no end to a search like this," I reluctantly admitted. Even though I had left Spain, I had consulted with several experts who were still helping me. A genealogist, Miguel Carbajo in Madrid, was locating old documents, as was a research specialist at the Archives of the Indies in Sevilla. Fernando Hidalgo of Grupo Almagacén, a Sevilla research team, informed me at a dinner meeting that the Neiras married the Quiñones centuries ago—and the Quiñones were documented to have witnessed the birth of Christ.

"Imagine, Elvirita, one billionth of a drop of our blood may well have been present at our Savior's birth. How exciting is that?" I exclaimed rhetorically.

Elvirita then proceeded to ask, "Have you been able to find out anything further about our Sotolongo heritage?"

I laughed. "It all depends on how far back you want to go!" I had been able to trace our direct Sotolongo lineage beyond King Juan II all the way back to Girard Count de Paris, who had married Charlemagne's daughter, Rotrou. Rotrou connects us to Clovis, the Merovingian kings and Joseph of Arimathea and the Holy Grail—and even further backward to 11 B. C. with King Francisco of the Sicambrian Franks.

However, the connecting dots that far back began to fade, as did my own interest. Despite my family's fascinating history, it was time to stop digging; excavating the past could easily consume the present.

Which One Are You?

After returning back to Varadero to meet Jeff at Los Delfines, *I went down* to sit at the wall, gazing into the horizon to reflect upon how revealing this particular trip had become. Although I had enjoyed bringing Elvirita the treasure trove of genealogical information from Spain, I was ready to go home. From my seawall perch, Cincinnati once again seemed so far away. But now the vast distance provoked homesickness instead of apprehension.

That evening Jeff and I had dinner at my favorite spot on the balcony, overlooking the surf and the setting sun. As we talked over drinks, we both abruptly fell silent. He looked at me almost sorrowfully and said, "Ed, my buddy, I hate to disappoint you, but I would really like to head back to the States tomorrow." This was three days earlier than our original plans. I was grateful for my friend's straightforward honesty.

"Me too, Jeff," I admitted. "Me too."

The next morning, we awakened early and headed straight to the Havana airport. On the way there, I thought about how much I missed my family and longed to go home. When we arrived at José Martí International, we quickly reviewed our options and found there was a flight leaving shortly. But we had very little time to purchase new tickets, get through Immigration and catch the flight, which already had begun boarding.

As the Immigration officer scrutinized my travel documents, he detected an inconsistency in my paperwork. Being Cuban-born, my visa had required my name to match my birth certificate, Julio Eduardo Neyra. On the other hand, my passport showed my Americanized name, Edward Julius Neyra. He seemed confused and alarmed by this discrepancy.

"These names don't match," he declared with authority.

I patiently explained, "One is the Cuban version, and one is American."

He stared at me as if I had two heads. "Are you trying to tell me they are the same?"

"*Sí, señor!*" as I stole a glance at my watch.

"Well, which one are you?" he commanded.

For a split second I was stunned. How ironic that a by-the-book Communist clerk should confront me with the very issue I had been grappling with for forty years. But now the answer came swift and sure. I had reconciled the impact of having been ripped away as a child from my family and my homeland. My voice was calm, reasonable and almost casual as I replied, "They are both me."

The agent grudgingly nodded his approval and stamped my visa for final clearance. I thought I was home free, but I had one last hurdle. As I went through Security, and my carry-on luggage was scanned, another alert guard spotted an antique stamp collection that had been in our family for decades, which had been given to me as a parting gift. She abruptly stopped the conveyor belt.

"What is that?" she demanded.

"A stamp collection," I politely answered, trying to hide my impatience.

She continued her interrogation, "Where did you get it?"

"A family member gave it to me," I explained.

"You cannot take that out of the country without a certificate of authorization!" she pronounced.

In the meantime, since I had set off the alarm, a third guard was wanding me with a metal detector. As I emptied my pockets, a Listerine PocketPak fell to the floor. The guard who was about to examine the stamp collection was distracted and wistfully exclaimed, "I love those!"

"You can have them," I offered.

"Oh, no, we're not allowed to accept anything."

So I conveniently laid the breath fresheners on the conveyor belt within her reach. With a knowing glance, she closed my briefcase and cheerfully wished me a safe flight home.

"... Home," I blissfully murmured to myself. "Home ..."

THE ULTIMATE JOURNEY

In this quest to share my heritage and culture with my wife and sons, to preserve the ties between the old world and the new, I rediscovered my own passion for Cuba and sparks of its magic everywhere I went. And now that I have reconciled and embraced these two disparate cultures woven within my soul, I feel a genuine love, respect and admiration for both.

The therapeutic value of undergoing psychological counseling and putting my life experiences in writing has given rise to insights I would have never reached otherwise—insights with which the reader might identify, regardless of ethnicity. You do not have to be an immigrant, much less sent away from your home as a child, to feel disconnected and abandoned. As flawed beings, our difficulties reveal that human weakness is universal but plays out differently in each and every one of us. However, within every obstacle lies a pearl of wisdom, a choice, a lesson—if we allow it.

To most of us, these lessons do not come easily. The security, happiness and freedom that we all seek come from within, from accepting who we really are and from acknowledging and embracing our fears. Yet most of us spend a lifetime searching for fulfillment externally, only to be consistently disappointed.

My frenetic pursuit of the American Dream was a diversion. Instead of confronting the effects of the traumatic separation from my parents as a young boy, I spent most of my life as a grown man trying to find something or someone to mend me. It was only once I stopped placing that blame on others and accepted it as my own responsibility that I finally found the path to inner peace.

Researching my family's history revealed that the toxic stain of pride had branded generations with an angry birthmark, and I certainly was no exception. Pride is the refusal to acknowledge our own hurt, the unwillingness to let someone know how we feel and that we need them. This corrosive behavior enables grief, guilt and shame to fester and scar; inflaming a debilitating hostility that swells within us, paralyzing the spirit and preventing us from giving or accepting love.

To overcome these destructive and divisive emotions, we must be willing to release our harbored hurt and learn to forgive others. But even a more daunting task is to also learn how to forgive ourselves. Forgiveness is the fountain of love. This nourishing wellspring heals and transforms a hardened heart into one full of compassion, endlessly enriching our relationships with others and opening our hearts to happiness.

Lynn, Nathan and Justin, I took you to Cuba to see my childhood home, to experience the tropical paradise I had left behind. I wanted you to stand next to a royal palm and behold its majesty; to walk along the shores of Varadero and feel the warm surf caress your feet; to sit upon my seawall and marvel at a magnificent sunset melting into the Caribbean Sea; and to hear the rhythmic sound of the gentle waves that once had lulled me to sleep. I wanted you to see and feel the Cuba I had lost.

Ironically, in this arduous but illuminating journey of self-discovery, it was you who helped me find what I thought I had lost. Your insights and impressions of my beloved homeland brought clarity to my romanticized memories. I learned that home is not a place; it is the feeling of belonging, of being with the ones you love. Thank you for bringing me home!

Los quiero. I love you.

ACKNOWLEDGMENTS

This journey would have never taken place without the encouragement of my dear wife, Lynn, and good friend Jeff. I will be forever grateful for their persistence in convincing me to return to Cuba and accompanying me on my maiden voyage back to my homeland. Once I overcame the fear of going to Cuba and returned with each of my two sons, I was amazed at how their candid observations and intriguing questions helped develop my own objectivity about the island. As a parent, I was proud of their maturity and thankful that their unique perspective helped me tackle many of my own unresolved issues. I am also grateful to Dr. Jerome Kleinman, who helped me realize this journey to my roots extended far beyond the ninety-mile stretch of warm water across the Florida Straits.

Thank you to "Kiko" Garcia, an avid amateur genealogist in Varadero Beach, who piqued my interest in learning more about my family's history with his cryptic comment: "I know who you are." Little did I know that this odyssey would take me back several hundred years and cover many countries around the globe.

As I delved deeper into my family's past, I have many relatives to thank for helping me uncover myriad details, including my cousin Julio Pastoriza; Uncle Beni Pérez; Aunt Elvira Neyra, and my cousins Elvirita, Guillermo and Jorge Neyra; my Grandfather Neyra's adopted granddaughters, Mercedes and Mimi; and my cousin Lalita and sister Melba.

I also appreciate the assistance I received in Cuba from Cárdenas city historian Ernesto Álvarez Blanco; Sotolongo expert Father Elpidio López; Havana historian Eusebio Leal; museum archivist Magaly Torres; and the *Hostal Valencia* manager Ana Mildred Vidal. They willingly made time for me, even when I showed up for a visit unexpectedly.

In Spain, I am indebted to Rafael Quijano, who generously shared his expertise and volunteered many hours of selfless research; and of course, my long-lost Sotolongo relative, Federico Martínez de Sola, who savored and shared with me the fascinating details of our illustrious family history.

I appreciate the efforts of the professional editors who helped shape this manuscript throughout its nine-year gestation. Coleen Armstrong was essential in editing the first draft of my story. Later, Howard Wells cast his own editorial impressions that tightened the voluminous manuscript. Karen Bells, a Cincinnati *Business Courier* reporter, provided a unique reader perspective and suggested many ideas on how to improve the story. I would also like to give special thanks to my assistant, Sue Van Pietersom, who diligently verified facts, clarified ideas, and helped me express my thoughts creatively yet succinctly.

Many thanks to family and friends who volunteered to read the manuscript, and whose corrections and suggestions also improved this book, including Christopher Baker, Beatriz Miyar, Edy Carro, Michele Laumer, Mary and Ron Beshear, Julio Pastoriza, Lalita Bollinger and Melba Campbell.

I would like to commend Richard Hunt, my editor at Clerisy Press, who committed to publish my story early on, knowing I was just a novice writer whose manuscript was still quite rough. With his vision, he greatly improved the dramatic structure of the narrative. Richard and his staff of Jack Heffron, Donna Poehner and Terri Lewis spent hours reviewing and preparing *Cuba Lost and Found* for publication.

Finally, no book that includes the saga of *Operación Pedro Pan* could ever be complete without a huge thank you to my dear friend Elly Chovel. Elly worked tirelessly to find and document the *Pedro Pans* scattered throughout the United States. Her sudden and tragic death in 2007 was a great loss. I am forever indebted to Elly for her encouragement in writing this book, and more importantly, her lifelong dedication to helping all kinds of children without parents through the charity she helped found in Miami, Operation Pedro Pan Group, Inc. It is in Elly's honor that the proceeds of this book shall be shared with this organization she so dearly loved.